Living in Christ

The New Testament

The Good News of Jesus Christ

Margaret Nutting Ralph

saint mary's press

The Subcommittee on the Catechism, United States Conference of Catholic Bishops, has found this catechetical text, copyright 2012, to be in conformity with the *Catechism of the Catholic Church.*

Nihil Obstat: Rev. William M. Becker, STD
                 Censor Librorum
                 December 20, 2011

Imprimatur: † Most Rev. John M. Quinn, DD
                 Bishop of Winona
                 December 20, 2011

The nihil obstat and imprimatur are official declarations that a book or pamphlet is free of doctrinal or moral error. No implication is contained therein that those who have granted the nihil obstat or imprimatur agree with the contents, opinions, or statements expressed, nor do they assume any legal responsibility associated with publication.

The publishing team included Gloria Shahin, editorial director; Joanna Dailey, development editor; Maura Thompson Hagarty, PhD, contributing editor and theological reviewer; Woodeene Koenig-Bricker, contributing writer. Prepress and manufacturing coordinated by the production departments of Saint Mary's Press.

Cover Image: © The Crosiers / Gene Plaisted, OSC

The publisher also wishes to thank the following individuals who advised the publishing team or reviewed the work in progress:
Msgr. David Hubba, MA
Timothy Milinovich, PhD

Printed in the United States of America

1152 (PO5941)

ISBN 978-1-59982-075-0, paper
ISBN 978-1-59982-120-7, e-book

Contents

Section 3: The Johannine Writings

Section 4: The Letters of Paul

Introduction

On the wall in my office is a picture of Jesus and two disciples on the road to Emmaus (see Luke 24:13–35). As I was writing this book, I frequently glanced at that picture. It epitomizes for me what I hope this book will accomplish—that you, your teachers, and I will meet on life's journey and, while discussing the New Testament, will encounter, in the Holy Spirit, the Living Word, Jesus Christ. We will discuss what God our Father has chosen to reveal to us about himself and about his only begotten Son. In listening to the Word of God and to one another, we will be strengthened and encouraged to live our lives in cooperation with the coming of his Kingdom. And as we read, discuss, absorb, and pray with the New Testament, the Risen Christ will be present with us.

The spirituality of many Catholics is rooted in the awareness that Christ is present with us in a unique way in the Eucharist. Too many of us seem less aware that Christ is also with us, although in a different way, in the proclamation of Scripture in the liturgy. How is this so? The Word of God is a saving Word that brings us salvation: "The word of God constantly proclaimed in the Liturgy is always, then, a living and effective word through the power of the Holy Spirit. It expresses the Father's love that never fails in its effectiveness toward us" (*Lectionary for Mass,* page 14).

In Luke's account of the disciples on the road to Emmaus, he tells us that the disciples did not recognize the presence of the Risen Christ when he "interpreted to them what referred to him in all the scriptures" (Luke 24:27). My prayer for you and your teachers is that as you study Scripture together, you, like the disciples on the road, will find yourselves asking in wonder, "Were not our hearts burning [within us] while he spoke to us on the way and opened the scriptures to us?" (24:32). In addition, I pray that you are able to recognize the presence of the Risen Christ in your midst, now and always.

Margaret Nutting Ralph

The Word of God

Part 1

A Matter of Perspective

Have you ever looked for your own house or your own apartment in satellite photos on the Internet? By zooming in and out, you can adjust your perspective. You can change your point of view from the very widest possible angle to the very narrowest. You can see your city or town as it appears from space, and then you can zoom down to your own block and even to your own front door.

Imagine viewing the various forms of the New Testament writings through a wide-angle lens. What do you see—scrolls curling at their top and bottom edges; leather-bound books, carefully copied in Greek and Latin characters? Perhaps you see your family Bible, or the paperback New Testament you may have used in a class or two. What do these writings mean? What are their origins? What do they mean to us today?

In this student book, we consider these questions by beginning with a wide-angle view of the New Testament. In this first part, we begin by discussing the meaning of God's Revelation and key concepts related to Scripture, including biblical inspiration, biblical inerrancy, and the canon. We will also discuss the relationship between Scripture and Tradition and the role of the Magisterium in the interpretation of Scripture. Then we consider the New Testament as part of the larger whole of Sacred Scripture. Finally, we begin to narrow our focus to the twenty-seven books of the New Testament and review them in their various literary categories.

The articles in this part address the following topics:

- Article 1: "Revelation and Inspiration" (page 10)
- Article 2: "Covenants Old and New" (page 14)
- Article 3: "An Overview of the New Testament Books" (page 18)

Article 1 Revelation and Inspiration

We know about God because he reveals himself through love. We are made by God and for God, out of love, and in this is our meaning and purpose. As human beings we are oriented toward God by our very nature and by an interior call placed deep within us. Saint Augustine wrote, "We were made for thee, O God, and our hearts are restless until they rest in thee." Only in God, and in union with him, will we find true happiness. Similarly, the psalmist wrote:

> My soul rests in God alone,
> from whom comes my salvation.
> God alone is my rock and salvation,
> my secure fortress; I shall never fall.
>
> (Psalm 62:1–3)

© Ron and Patty Thomas Photography/iStockphoto.com

God gradually, in both words and actions, communicated himself to us, his beloved children, first through Creation itself, then through that inner voice we call "conscience." Through the wonders of Creation, from the smallest cells to the most majestic mountain ranges, we learn something of God. From the voice within, if we listen to it, we learn something of what God expects of us as human beings. From both the created world and our own understanding, we can come to realize that God exists, that he is the cause of everything and the goal of everything. We can learn about him from the evidence of his works and from our own God-given gift of human reason.

Catholic Wisdom

God's Revelation of Love

God has revealed himself to us out of love. In the Book of Genesis, we learn that he revealed himself to our first parents, promised them salvation, and offered them his promise of a Redeemer. God made a lasting covenant with Noah and with the entire human race (see Genesis, chapter 9). When God chose Abraham, he made a covenant with him and all his descendants. Through Moses, God revealed his Law, and through the prophets, prepared his people "to accept the salvation destined for all humanity" (*Catechism of the Catholic Church* [CCC], 72).

But God wanted to communicate more than his existence. He wanted to communicate his very self and his love for us. He did this gradually, through the centuries of human history, in his words and actions. He also revealed himself through his covenants with his Chosen People. Finally, as the writer to the Letter to the Hebrews wrote: "In times past, God spoke in partial and various ways to our ancestors through the prophets; in these last days, he spoke to us through a son" (1:1–2). That son, the Son of God, is Jesus Christ. In Jesus Christ is God's final and full Revelation; he is God's Final Answer to every question of the human heart. (We discuss salvation history more fully in the next article, when we discuss the intimate relationship between the Old and New Testaments.)

In this student book, we study God's Revelation transmitted through the written word of the New Testament. But first, let us think about Scripture as a whole, both the Old and New Testaments. You may have wondered why Scripture has been so treasured by every generation and passed on so carefully through the centuries, or why it has been translated into almost every language on earth. Have you ever wondered why we proclaim Scripture in every celebration of the Mass, or why we quote Scripture when we want to make a special point on an issue? This is because Scripture transmits the **Divine Revelation** of God to us. It records his plan for us, his love for us, and the gift of the Son of God, Jesus Christ, to us. As a record of God's Revelation, as truly God's Word, we revere Scripture as sacred and holy. We realize that Sacred Scripture comes from God and that he is the author.

Does this mean that God dictated Scripture, word for word? No. God is the author because he inspired the human authors of Scripture. Through **biblical inspiration**, under the guidance of the Holy Spirit, God used the natural gifts of specially chosen human beings to communicate the truths, without error, that we need to know for our salvation. The phrase "without error" is sometimes misunderstood to mean that every fact presented in the Bible is historically or scientifically accurate. However, when we speak of **biblical inerrancy**, we refer to only those truths that relate to our salvation, to our faith or to our morals, how we are to live as God would have us live. We discuss this concept further in later articles in this student book.

Divine Revelation
God's self-communication through which he makes known the mystery of his divine plan. Divine Revelation is a gift accomplished by the Father, Son, and Holy Spirit through the words and deeds of salvation history. It is most fully realized in the Passion, death, Resurrection, and Ascension of Jesus Christ.

biblical inspiration
The gift of the Holy Spirit, which assisted human beings to write biblical books, so they have God as their author and teach faithfully and without error the saving truth that God willed to give us.

biblical inerrancy
The doctrine that the books of Scripture are free from error regarding the truth God wishes to reveal through Scripture for the sake of our salvation.

Bible
The collection of Christian sacred writings, or Scripture, accepted by the Church as inspired by God and composed of the Old and New Testaments.

Tradition
From the Latin *tradere,* meaning "to hand on." Refers to the process of passing on the Gospel message. It began with the oral communication of the Gospel by the Apostles, was written down in Scripture, and is interpreted by the Magisterium under the guidance of the Holy Spirit.

Church
The term *Church* has three insepa-rable meanings: (1) the entire People of God throughout the world; (2) the diocese, which is also known as the local Church; (3) the assembly of believers gathered for the celebration of the liturgy, especially the Eucharist. In the Nicene Creed, the Church is recognized as One, Holy, Catholic, and Apostolic—traits that together are referred to as "marks of the Church."

Yet the human authors of Scripture were not robots. The inspired biblical authors did not go into a trance and wake up to find that they had written Scripture while in some altered state. Rather, God revealed himself through events, events that the authors, under the inspiration of the Holy Spirit, understood as significant communications from God. The authors, understanding the spiritual ramifications of these events, and seeing God present and powerful in them, preserved their spiritual meaning for future generations. These written accounts were treasured, preserved, organized, and passed down to us. In that way, under the inspiration of the Holy Spirit, the Revelation of God was made accessible to human beings through the written word.

The Bible As We Know It

The process of forming what we know as the **Bible** (from the Latin word *biblia,* meaning "books" or "library of books") took many hundreds of years. The Bible began as many separate pieces of oral tradition and writing, announced and written by separate evangelists and authors at various times in various places. Gradually, through what we call Sacred **Tradition**, the Church authenticated the writings as the truth revealed by God. The writings of the Old Testament were first organized by God's Chosen People, the people of Israel, and then gradually the New Testament writings were collected and organized. Through reliance on Tradition, the **Church** discerned which books are sacred. The New Testament was authorized with twenty-seven books, and the Old Testament with forty-six. Together this list of books authenticated by Tradition and accepted as God's Revelation by the Church is called the canon of Scripture. The word *canon* comes from the Greek word *kanon,* meaning "measure" or "standard," which evolved into the word *canon,* meaning "rule."

Sacred Scripture together with Sacred Tradition "make up a single sacred deposit of the Word of God" (*Dei Verbum,* 10) (*CCC,* 97). This deposit of the Word of God enables the Church to contemplate God who is "the source of all her riches" (97). Both Scripture and Tradition together make up the **Deposit of Faith** from which the Church transmits to every age all that she is and believes. Depending on Scripture alone for the truths of salvation (as many of our Protestant broth-ers and sisters do) deprives us of the living transmission of authentic Church practice and teaching through the ages; and looking to Sacred Tradition without Sacred Scripture, without the Word of God at its core, would be an exercise in futility, empty of meaning. We need both Scripture and Tradition to live the full and meaningful life God intends for

Who Interprets Scripture?

"The Church, in her doctrine, life, and worship, perpetuates and transmits to every generation all that she herself is, all that she believes" (*Dei Verbum*, 8, § 1) (*CCC*, 98). Through her mandate from Christ, the Church alone, through her teaching authority (the Magisterium, from the Latin word *magister*, meaning "teacher"), has the right and task to interpret the authentic meaning of Scripture and Tradition. This right was given to the Church by Christ, who entrusted all his teachings to the Apostles. What Christ entrusted to the Apostles, they, in turn, through their preaching and writing, under the inspiration of the Holy Spirit, handed on to the entire Church, through the Pope and bishops, from one generation to the next, until Christ returns in glory.

The Church's teaching authority is not limited to Scripture but extends to the doctrine, life, and worship of the entire Church. Although the Church is entrusted with the task of interpreting Scripture, this does not mean we cannot study or discuss Scripture among ourselves, or read and pray with Scripture on our own. Because we are baptized Christians, the Holy Spirit is with us, and the Church encourages our prayerful reading of Scripture (see *CCC*, 2653).

But we must always be mindful that Sacred Scripture, Sacred Tradition, and the Magisterium form the three-footed foundation of scriptural interpretation and all the teachings of the Church. All three work together to help us to understand the meaning of God's Revelation in the past and in the present. Even those who interpret Scripture as serious scholars (called exegetes) are subject to the teaching authority of the Church in their writing and teaching about Sacred Scripture.

Deposit of Faith

The heritage of faith contained in Sacred Scripture and Sacred Tradition. It has been passed on from the time of the Apostles. The Magisterium takes from it all that it teaches as revealed truth.

Magisterium

The Church's living teaching office, which consists of all bishops, in communion with the Pope, the bishop of Rome.

covenant

A solemn agreement between human beings or between God and a human being in which mutual commitments are made.

us. Indeed we need a third element, which is the teaching authority (the Magisterium) of the Church. The **Magisterium** draws all that it teaches as revealed truth from the Deposit of Faith, contained in Scripture and Tradition.

Scripture, Tradition, and the Magisterium

The relationship between Scripture, Tradition, and the teaching authority of the Church is illuminated by these statements from *Divine Revelation*:

> Tradition and scripture make up a single sacred deposit of the word of God, which is entrusted to the church. . . .

> The task of giving an authentic interpretation of the word of God, whether in its written form or in the form of tradition, has been entrusted to the living teaching office of the church alone. Its authority in this matter is exercised in the name of Jesus Christ. (10)

> This magisterium is not superior to the word of God, but rather its servant. It teaches only what has been handed on to it. At the divine command and with the help of the Holy Spirit, it listens to this devoutly, guards it reverently and expounds it faithfully. All that it proposes for belief as being divinely revealed it draws from this sole deposit of faith. (10) ✝

Article 2 Covenants Old and New

We are accustomed to seeing the Bible divided into two sections: the Old Testament and the New Testament. As you read in the previous article, it has taken many hundreds of years for the Bible to be organized and collected in this way. To understand the meaning of Sacred Scripture, we must see the Old Testament and the New Testament as one book, one Word of God. The Old Testament prepares for the coming of Christ in the New Testament; the New Testament fulfills the promises of God made in the Old Testament. Thus we can say that, in reality, "All Sacred Scripture is but one book, and this one book is Christ, 'because all divine Scripture speaks of Christ, and all divine Scripture is fulfilled in Christ'" (Hugh of Saint Victor, quoted in *CCC*, 134).

When Jesus, the Word of God, walked among us, he clarified the relationship between the Scripture of the Old **Covenant** and himself as the inauguration of the New Covenant, the new Revelation of God in his only Son: "Do not think that I have come to abolish the law or the prophets. I have come not to abolish but to fulfill" (Matthew 5:17). In Jesus Christ the Old Covenant and the New Covenant were brought together. The writings of the Old Covenant were fulfilled in him, and Jesus revealed their ultimate meaning. Through him the sins of all, including sins against the Old Covenant, were redeemed. While Jesus walked among us, the writings of the New Covenant, the New Testament, remained to be written.

Jesus Christ: Pantocrator, © 1987 Br. Robert Lentz, OFM / Courtesy of Trinity Stores (www.trinitystores.com), (800.699.4482)

In this icon, Jesus is majestically portrayed as the Pantocrator (Greek for "Ruler of All"). He holds the Gospel of Matthew, and the quotation is based on Matthew 25:40 in the Parable of the Last Judgment.

Pray It!

Hear, O Israel!

In the *Shema* (pronounced sh-MA and meaning "hear" in Hebrew), Jews have, since the time of Moses, professed their faith in the one true God: "Hear, O Israel! The LORD is our God, the LORD alone!" (Deuteronomy 6:4). The passage continues: "Therefore, you shall love the LORD, your God, with your whole heart, and with your whole being, and with your whole strength. Take to heart these words which I [God] command you today" (6:5–6).

Sound familiar? Jesus himself quoted the *Shema*, adding, "You shall love your neighbor as yourself" (Mark 12:31), also from the Law (see Leviticus 19:18).

Our faith in the same God, the one and only true God, leads us to him as "our first origin and our ultimate goal" (*CCC*, 229), preferring nothing to him, and accepting no substitute for him.

Many Jews say the *Shema* every morning and evening. Try it yourself, adding Jesus' commandment to love our neighbors. It may very well strengthen your faith.

Acceptance into the New Testament Canon

Who decided whether a certain piece of writing or letter could be accepted as authentic Christian teaching and included in the canon of the New Testament? These matters were finally decided by the leaders of the early Church, called *episcopi* (Greek for "overseers") or, as we say now, bishops. The bishops confirmed what the Holy Spirit had inspired in the worshipping community through the use and acceptance of these books. They relied on apostolic Tradition, as we mentioned earlier, to decide whether a book should be included in the canon (see *CCC*, 120). Within this Tradition these four criteria were used, and a particular book had to meet all four to be included in the New Testament:

1. **apostolic** A book had to be based on the preaching and teaching of the Apostles and their closest companions and disciples.

2. **community acceptance** If the Christians of an important Christian community accepted a book as valid and consistent with their beliefs and practices, it would be accepted into the canon.

3. **liturgical** If Christians were using this book in their liturgical celebrations, especially the Eucharist, then the early bishops concluded that it was valid for growth in prayer and in faith.

4. **consistent** A book's message had to be consistent with other Christian and Hebrew writings; it could not contradict what was already accepted as the Word of God.

© Jill Fromer / iStockphoto.com

Two Covenants, One Bible

Through Apostolic Tradition, the Old Testament and the New Testament were eventually joined together as we have them now. But this in itself was a long process that began with the Greek translation of the Law, the Prophets, and the Writings, called the Septuagint. These writings, the major part of what we now know as the Old Testament, had been written on scrolls. In the second century AD, the Church put the Septuagint into **codices**, or books. (The singular is *codex*.) With the Septuagint the Church also included apostolic writings about Jesus Christ, also written in Greek, which had been accepted as part of the canon. In this way the Old Law and the New Law were literally bound together in one book.

By including the treasured apostolic writings in the codices, along with Jewish Scripture, the Church affirmed the validity of God's Revelation in the Old Covenant. In doing so it declared that the one God who created the world and established the Old Covenant with the Jews was the same God who sent his Son, Jesus Christ, to save us and to establish with us the New Covenant in his Blood. This covenant will last forever. Jesus is the fulfillment of God's promises to the Chosen People over the centuries.

The early Church recognized that in order to understand the marvels that God has accomplished through Jesus Christ, one must understand them in the light of God's self-communication to the Israelites, his Chosen People. The coming of Christ did not negate the previous covenants that God has made with his people. Christ's coming did not negate the covenant with Abraham and his descendants, through which God made a people for himself and revealed his law through Moses. The Church also recognized that, in Jesus Christ, God had joined both the Old and the New Covenants together, that they were truly one, and that they belonged together in one collection of books. ✝

codices
Book-like manuscripts that replaced scrolls.

Live It!

The Book of Our Lives

When the bishops of the early Church assembled the New Testament, they used four criteria to decide if a book was valid. In the same way, we can apply similar criteria to the "book" of our own Christian lives. Are we living an apostolic life? Are we being true to our beliefs and practices as members of our local parish community? Do we celebrate the liturgy faithfully? Are our lives consistent with the Word of God? Are our lives a book of truth that anyone can read? As Saint Paul wrote to the early Christians, "You are our letter, written on our hearts, known and read by all, shown to be a letter of Christ . . . written not in ink but by the Spirit of the living God" (2 Corinthians 3:2–3).

3 An Overview of the New Testament Books

Article

The twenty-seven books of the New Testament are divided into five categories, as follows: the Gospels, the Acts of the Apostles, the Pauline letters (including the letters attributed to Paul), the catholic epistles, and the Book of Revelation. The categories and the books they contain are listed for you in the chart on page 19.

The Gospels

The **Gospels** of Matthew, Mark, Luke, and John are central to the Sacred Scriptures because Jesus Christ is at their center. They are our primary source for all that is revealed in the life and teachings of Jesus. Because they reveal and proclaim Jesus as our incarnate God and Savior, they are called *evangelion* (meaning "good news" in Greek). The writers of the Gospels are known as the Evangelists. (We also use this word in a contemporary sense when we call a preacher of the Gospel an evangelist.) Our English word *gospel* comes from the Old English word *godspel*, which means "good tidings." In Luke's Gospel, when the angels appear to the shepherds, they say: "I proclaim to you good news of great joy that will be for all the people. For today in the city of David a savior has been born for you who is Messiah and Lord" (Luke 2:10–11).

Fundamentally, the Good News—the *evangelion*, the *godspel*, the Gospel—is Jesus himself.

The four Gospels are similar but not identical, and we will discuss their similarities and differences in detail later in this student book. Each of the Gospels was written by a separate Evangelist in a different historical situation and was originally written for a particular audience. Yet all four agree on the essential truths concerning the mystery of Christ, including his Incarnation, life, Passion, death, Resurrection, and Ascension.

Gospels

Translated from a Greek word meaning "good news," referring to the four books attributed to Matthew, Mark, Luke, and John, "the principal source for the life and teaching of the Incarnate Word" (*CCC*, 125) Jesus Christ.

This scene of the Birth of Christ is from a Latin manuscript from the Abbey of Notre-Dame des Prés, France. Decorated manuscripts are known as illuminated manuscripts. The paintings within them "light up" the text.
© DeA Picture Library / Art Resource, NY

The New Testament	
Category	**Books**
Gospels	Matthew Luke Mark John
The Early Church (Luke)	The Acts of the Apostles
The Letters of Paul	Romans Philippians First Corinthians First Thessalonians Second Corinthians Philemon Galatians
Letters Attributed to Paul	Ephesians Second Thessalonians Colossians
The Pastoral Letters (Attributed to Paul)	First Timothy Titus Second Timothy
A Sermon (anonymous author)	Hebrews
The Catholic Epistles	James Second John First Peter Third John Second Peter Jude First John
The World to Come	The Book of Revelation

The Acts of the Apostles

The Acts of the Apostles is considered a "sequel" to the
Gospel of Luke because in it Luke continues his account of
the saving work of Jesus, now extended through the Church,
under the guidance of the Holy Spirit, to the **Gentiles**. The
Acts of the Apostles recounts the spread of the early Church
from its origins in Jerusalem to the ends of the earth, to
the limits of the known world, to the center of the known
universe: the city of Rome. Again we discuss this book in
greater detail in articles to come.

Gentile

A non-Jewish person. In Scripture the Gentiles were those outside the covenant, those who did not know how to fulfill God's will. Without this knowledge, they could not be in right relationship with God, as so were considered "unholy" or "unclean." In the New Testament, Saint Paul and other evangelists reached out to the Gentiles, baptizing them into the family of God.

The Pauline Letters

The compilation of letters in the New Testament is extensive and varied. There are twenty-one in all. They are all called letters, but some are more like short treatises on Christian life and faith. Thirteen of these are attributed to the Apostle Paul, although Paul is thought to have written only seven: First and Second Corinthians, Romans, Galatians, First Thessalonians, Philippians, and Philemon.

Letters Attributed to Paul

The letters attributed to Paul but thought not to have been written by Paul are Ephesians, Colossians, First and Second Timothy, Titus, and Second Thessalonians. Among these, the three pastoral letters are so named because they were addressed to Timothy and Titus, young pastors, or shepherds, whom Paul had mentored and had put in charge of the churches at Ephesus and Crete. These letters are concerned with pastoral issues and situations that warrant Paul's advice and counsel.

The Letter to the Hebrews was once thought to be written by Paul, and, after it was accepted into the canon of the New Testament, it was placed at the end of the letters attributed to Paul. However, the consensus among modern scholars is that is it a non-Pauline letter. It has been assumed to have been written for Jewish Christians, but its author and audience are not known.

The Catholic Epistles

The other seven letters were written by other writers and are called the catholic epistles. The word *catholic* here means "universal." These letters were not addressed to one particular local church but to a wider Christian audience—to all the faithful of the universal Church.

The Book of Revelation

The New Testament collection ends with a much read, much quoted, and much misunderstood book called the Book of Revelation. When we discuss this book, we will consider its author, its intended audience, and its literary style. For now we can note that the Bible begins with a picture of the vast

The Conversion of Saint Paul

Saul (or to use his Roman name, Paul) was a fervent and observant Jew, and was totally against this new version of Judaism (as he saw it at the time) that had sprung up around a belief in Jesus as Savior, Messiah, and Risen Lord. He had held the coats of those who stoned the martyr and first deacon Stephen to death, and he joined with those who were going from town to town, capturing these believers in Jesus and putting them in prison.

Saul was on his way to Damascus to do just that when he was confronted by Jesus himself, who asked him, "Saul, Saul, why are you persecuting me?" This question was the beginning of Saul's conversion. (You may want to read accounts of this incident in the Acts of the Apostles 9:1–19, 22:3–21, and in Paul's First Letter to the Corinthians 15:8–11.) After a period of prayer and study, Paul (who used his Roman name when dealing with the Gentile world) began to preach, teach, and write the letters that bear his name. He became the man and the saint we know as the Apostle to the Gentiles—those non-Jews who had never known the one true God. Through Paul they found God in God's Son, Jesus Christ.

and empty universe, on the verge of Creation, and ends with an affirmation of hope for a New Creation, in the lives of the original audience, in our lives, and in the future: "Amen. Come, Lord Jesus!" (Revelation 22:20). All of God's Revelation, from the creation of the world to the hope for the world to come, points to Jesus Christ.

The Stages of New Testament Formation

Let us step back a moment. As we ponder these twenty-seven books bound together in the New Testament, we might well wonder about the process by which they were formed. How did they come to be?

In general, we can say that the New Testament was formed in three broad stages:

1. **The life and teaching of Jesus** Jesus lived and taught among us until his Ascension.

2. **The oral tradition** The Apostles handed on what Jesus had said and done, in that fuller understanding brought about by the Resurrection of Christ and the guidance of the Holy Spirit.

3. **The written books** The inspired authors selected certain elements from what had been handed on, either in oral or written form, often with synthesis and explanation (that is, in a process of editing), to bring us the truth about Jesus (see *CCC,* 126). These written accounts eventually became what we know today as the New Testament. We consider the formation of the New Testament in greater detail in future articles. ✝

Part Review

1. How does God communicate himself to us throughout history?

2. How did God communicate himself to us most fully and finally?

3. Why do we revere and venerate Sacred Scripture?

4. What is biblical inspiration?

5. What are the two other elements needed (besides Scripture itself) for the foundation of scriptural interpretation?

6. What is the relationship between the Old Testament and the New Testament?

7. What is the significance of binding together the Old Testament and the New Testament into one volume?

8. What are the four criteria for the acceptance of a book into the New Testament canon?

9. What are the two stages of New Testament formation that precede the written accounts?

Part 2

Understanding the New Testament

Even when speaking the same language with someone who grew up in the same country, the same culture, and perhaps even the same family, communication can be difficult. Interpretation of words often depends on not only their literal meaning but also the inflection or tone of the human voice that utters them. Even a simple affirmation can have many different meanings. A short comment like "Yeah, right!" can be enthusiastic. It also can be edged with sarcasm: "Yeah, *right!*" In this example, the difference can be suggested by printing the sarcastic remark in italic type. But to be certain of the meaning of this phrase, we would really need to know more about the *context* of the conversation. We would need to know the speakers and their particular cultural or historical situation. We might need to know the subject matter or the concerns of the speakers in this instance. Are they speaking in figurative language? Are they engaged in a serious conversation or merely joking with one another?

As you can imagine, interpreting a language that is not our own, that is written rather than spoken, and, moreover, written in an ancient language that has its own conventions and literary forms, is even more difficult. For this reason the Church encourages Scripture scholars to study life in Israel at the time of Jesus and the Greco-Roman culture in which the New Testament was written, in order to establish the context for these ancient writings. In the articles in this part, we benefit from this contextualist approach as we continue to study the New Testament.

The articles in this part address the following topics:

Article 4 Context: Literary Form

You may remember that when we discussed the role of inspiration in the writing of Scripture, we said that the human authors of Scripture were not robots and that the Holy Spirit did not dictate Scripture word for word. Rather, the scriptural writers chose both their wording and the form in which their writing was expressed, all the while remaining true to the message of God, which was their reason for writing in the first place. In interpreting their writings, we must be attentive first of all to what God wishes to reveal for our salvation. But, because of the wide variety of **literary forms** found in the Bible, it is important that we understand what they are and how they are used. Such an understanding is important to understanding the core truth that God wishes to convey through the writings of the inspired authors. As *Divine Revelation* declared:

© Julián Rovagnati / iStockphoto.com

> The interpreters of sacred scripture, if they are to ascertain what God has wished to communicate to us, should carefully search out the meaning which the sacred writers really had in mind, that meaning which God had thought well to manifest through the medium of their words.
>
> In determining the intention of the sacred writers, attention must be paid, among other things, to *literary genres.*
>
> . . . Hence the exegete must look for that meaning which the sacred writers, in given situations and granted the circumstances of their time and culture, intended to express and did in fact express, through the medium of a contemporary literary form. (12)

literary forms (genres)
Different kinds of writing determined by their literary technique, content, tone, and purpose (how the author wants the reader to be affected).

Literary Forms Today

You are probably already familiar with literary forms through your own study of literature. These forms include history, poetry, sermon, parable, biography, fable, science fiction, and so on. And it should be no surprise to you that literary form affects the meaning of a piece of writing.

You discern this meaning every time you read a newspaper or surf the Web for news and articles. For example, a news story is supposed to be objective and inform you of facts: who, what, where, and when. An editorial (usually at the back of the first section of a newspaper) is commentary. It is based on the news but is supposed to take a stand; the author tries to persuade you to his or her point of view. A sports story emphasizes a person's talent in a particular sport and usually fails to mention that person's character flaws. A comic strip can report a conversation between characters with no claim at all that such a conversation ever took place.

We might wonder if future generations will correctly interpret our varied literary forms in media today. Is a comedy show that is based on news events the "real news," or is it commentary? Is a radio talk show that discusses current events "real news," or is it an editorial, an effort at persuasion? As contemporary watchers, listeners, and readers, we can usually tell the difference. But we may wonder what these media will look like to researchers many years from now.

Literary Forms in Scripture

Understanding the literary forms found in Scripture can help to prevent misunderstanding and help us to discover what the inspired author intended to teach. It is for this

Live It!

Find the Literary Form

As you learned in this part, because the Bible contains many different literary forms, it is important to recognize the literary form of each book. Get acquainted with the New Testament. Of the literary forms listed below, how many can you find in the New Testament?

- an historical account
- a personal letter
- a teaching lecture
- a book of advice
- a set of prayers
- an exhortation
- an apocalyptic writing

Which of these is the easiest to recognize? Which is the easiest to understand?

reason that it is essential for us to learn to consider the context of literary form when reading any book in the Bible. As we discuss each New Testament book, we will include a discussion of the literary forms within that particular book.

It is important to note, however, that Sacred Scripture is not just another form of literature. It must be read and interpreted in light of the Incarnate Word, Jesus Christ, who through the Holy Spirit opens our minds and hearts to "the meaning which the sacred writers really had in mind, that meaning which God had thought well to manifest through the medium of their words" (*Divine Revelation*, 12). Even with our use of literary and historical contexts, only the Holy Spirit can help us to fully understand Scripture, for it is his work and he is its author.

Literary Conventions

Different literary forms often make use of particular literary conventions. A **literary convention** is a defining feature of a particular literary form. For instance, if a story begins, "Once upon a time . . ." you immediately conclude that the story you will hear will not be based in history but will be a fairy tale. If you receive a letter that begins "Dear . . ." you know that this is just the way people begin a letter; it is not an expression of special affection for you. Just so, when the author of a book says that he has had a vision in which he saw a lamb with seven horns and seven eyes, you need to understand the conventions of **apocalyptic literature** in order to understand just what that author is teaching. This kind of writing, using highly dramatic and symbolic language, is found in the Book of Revelation, and we will discuss it further when we consider that particular book.

Understanding Literary Forms and Conventions

A common presumption that is often made when reading the New Testament is that the inspired writers report events just as we would have witnessed them had we been present when the events occurred. However, biblical authors are not historians or reporters intending simply to recount what exactly happened. Rather, they are ministers of the Word, intending to teach the significance of Christ in the lives of

literary convention
A defining feature of a particular literary form. An example would be beginning a letter with the greeting "Dear."

apocalyptic literature
A literary form that uses events and dramatic symbolic language to offer hope to a people in crisis.

those to whom they are writing, including us. In order to understand the richness of their teachings, we will always have to consider their words in the context of the literary forms and conventions they have chosen to use. ✝

The War of the Worlds

Widespread panic followed the broadcast of a radio program called "The War of the Worlds" on October 30, 1938. The program was a radio play adapted from a novel of the same name by H. G. Wells. The writer and narrator of this play, Orson Welles, was a dramatic actor and later, filmmaker. The plot revolved around an invasion from Mars, reported in a realistic manner from Grovers Mill, New Jersey, and included realistic interviews with "astronomers" and "the Secretary of the Interior." Listeners who tuned in from the beginning understood that this was a radio play. Others, who found the show as they surfed through stations with the radio dial, thought that the narrator was a real broadcaster and that the reporting and interviews were real.

© Bettmann/CORBIS

Although the play was set in New England, panic ensued in many places throughout the nation as listeners discovered the program on their radios. When the radio play reported the evacuation of New York City, people in other cities began to evacuate as well. Others called their local police, radio stations, and newspapers. Some went to their churches to pray, thinking that this was the end of civilization as they knew it.

Gradually, as the truth became known, the panic died down. It was certainly a tribute to the compellingly realistic writing of Orson Welles. But it also points to the importance of knowing the literary form of the work you are reading (or listening to)—in this case, not news, not history, but a fictional radio play.

Article 5 Context: Historical and Cultural Situation

As you may remember, in the first article in this student book, we discussed the Revelation of God and biblical inspiration. We noted that in Scripture, God used the natural gifts of specially chosen human beings to communicate the truths, without error, that we need to know for our salvation. The Bible is "the book" we turn to when we want to understand the truth about ourselves, our lives, our world, and our future. We do not turn to the Bible for answers to all questions we may have—questions about science, for example. The inspired authors of the Bible were not scientists or historians or reporters. Their aim was to teach the truth that God wanted to convey through Scripture.

However, the inspired writers do use the events and culture of their times in their writing. They may write something by way of explanation or application that reflects a presumption (something *presumed* to be true) of the time or circumstances in which they are writing. We do this ourselves. We say, "The sun will rise tomorrow at 7 AM." Scientifically speaking, the sun does not rise. Earth revolves around its axis in relationship to the sun, and when our part of Earth reaches a certain point in revolution, the light of the sun shines on us. But when we describe the sunrise, we say nothing about revolving. Even when we know the scientific truth, we still hold to our conventional way of speaking.

In a similar way, the facts of an event or incident that the inspired writers relate may even, in our time, be seen as scientifically false. For example, scientifically speaking, the world cannot have been created in six days, as the account in Genesis relates. But the author of Genesis was not writing about science. The author's sole aim was to explain the world and human origins as created by God out of love. Thus the literary form, or genre, of the Book of Genesis is not a scientific report but rather an account created to express a truth of faith. If we insist on looking for "scientific truth" in the Bible, we will not

© Jim David / Shutterstock.com

moral truth

A truth dealing with the goodness or evil of human acts, attitudes, and values.

be respecting literary form and will be missing the truths of faith that God would have us know—about him and about ourselves. When reading the Bible, we must always ask, "What is the inspired writer trying to teach?" It will be something about God and our relationship with him.

Does the Bible Support Slavery?

When we read the Bible, we must learn to separate what is being taught from what the writer is presuming is true, due to his own historical or cultural situation. One good example is the issue of slavery.

During the Civil War, people both in favor of and opposed to slavery used Scripture to add authority to their arguments. A person who believed slavery was moral might have said: "Scripture teaches that slavery is fine. In Ephesians we read: 'Slaves, be obedient to your human masters with fear and trembling, in sincerity of heart, as to Christ, not only when being watched, as currying favor, but as slaves of Christ, doing the will of God from the heart' (6:5–6). This passage illustrates that it is the will of God that we have slaves and that our slaves should obey us." Is this a legitimate use of Scripture? Is the inspired author of Ephesians teaching that slavery is moral? Let us look more deeply into this letter to find the answer.

Finding the Moral Truth

The author of Ephesians is teaching an important **moral truth**, a truth about good and evil, but that truth is not that slavery is moral. Rather, the truth that the author is teaching appears earlier in the letter, when it is stated that the Ephesians should "be imitators of God, as beloved children, and live in love, as Christ loved us and handed himself over for us as a sacrificial offering to God" (Ephesians 5:1–2). The author then applies that truth to the social structure existing at the time. He does not ask if the social structure is just. He simply applies his spiritual insight to that structure.

Remember, Ephesians is a letter. A letter is written to a specific audience in a specific setting. What is said in a letter depends on the people to whom the letter is being sent and what they need to hear. The Ephesians had slaves. That was a fact of life and not one that the author of Ephesians questions. Rather, the author recognizes the existence of the Ephesians' social structure and applies his spiritual insight within that social context.

In teaching his spiritual insight, the author of Ephesians does not address only the behavior of slaves. He applies his core teaching about the necessity of love to husbands and wives, to children and parents, and finally to slaves and masters. Masters are told to "act in the same way toward them [i.e. their slaves], and stop bullying, knowing that both they and you have a Master in heaven and that with him there is no partiality" (6:9).

Science and the Bible

Because God is the source of all truth, there can be no contradiction between the truths of religion necessary for our salvation and the truths of science. However, this does not mean these truths are identical. It is sometimes difficult for us to clearly define these differing truths in our minds when reading the Bible. What is a presumption about a scientific or social matter in the Bible, and what is its core spiritual teaching? An example from history might help.

When a teacher in Tennessee taught Darwin's theory of evolution in a public school in the 1920s, he was brought to trial for teaching something contrary to Scripture. (The teacher, John Scopes, was found guilty and fined one hundred dollars—about one thousand dollars today—but the verdict was overturned on a technicality.) Unfortunately, this trial popularized the "science versus religion" debate, implying that if you pursued scientific learning, you could not also embrace the truths of Scripture. In this case, a scientific theory—the relationship of material forms to one another—is not an area of biblical study. It is a scientific question, not a spiritual one.

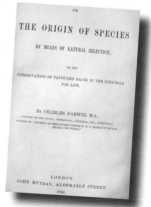

When a biblical author touches on such topics, he is expressing a presumption of his time, not a teaching. We do not turn to Scripture for answers to scientific questions. Rather, we turn to Scripture for answers related to matters of faith and morals: for example, answers about God, his purpose for us, his plans for us, and how we are to live our lives in his love.

Now, with this information in hand, we are prepared to respond to whether it is a legitimate use of Scripture to use this passage from Ephesians to support the morality of slavery. The correct response is no. The author of Ephesians makes this statement as part of an *application* of a core teaching, not the core teaching itself. He is *applying* the core teaching (love) to the current historical and cultural setting as it is. In his cultural and historical setting, slavery was the norm.

The author of Ephesians remains silent on whether a social order that includes slavery is moral or immoral. We may wonder why this is so. Part of the reason is that the author wanted to spread the message of Christ to his society as it was, and not as it should be or could be. Remember, the author of the Letter to the Ephesians was writing in the early years of Christianity. The letter's message of universal love would take many more years to infiltrate human society. We can look to our own country as an example. Slavery was not abolished in the United States until 1865. Segregation, the legal separation of people by race, was permitted by law in schools until 1954 and was only gradually overcome in other areas of life through the leadership of Dr. Martin Luther King Jr. and many others, beginning in the 1960s. Still today racial prejudice can be a factor in our societal relationships. Moreover, slavery itself is not unheard of in many parts of the world, especially the enslavement of young women and children. The message of Christ's love has still not yet reached the hearts of all.

As we look at the individual books in the New Testament, we will explore other instances where it is important to understand the beliefs of the time and historical circumstances in which Scripture was written. ✝

Article 6 Context: Scriptural Development

In the article "An Overview of the New Testament Books," we gave a brief overview of the development of the New Testament. It notes three stages: (1) the life and teachings of Jesus, (2) the oral tradition, and (3) the written books.

The Scripture of the Jewish people, later adopted into the canon of the Old Testament, underwent a similar process in their development. This process began with Abraham around 1850 BC. The words and actions of the salvific events of the Old Testament were passed on through oral tradition and then finally written down in the various books that were accepted into the canon of the Old Testament.

Teachings in the Old Testament lay the foundation for what is revealed in the New Testament. The New Testament completes or fulfills the teachings of the Old Testament: "The Old Testament prepares for the New and the New Testament fulfills the Old; the two shed light on each other; both are true Word of God" (*CCC*, 140). Thus to truly understand Scripture, we cannot look at one small piece on its own. All must be viewed in the context of the truth God reveals to us over time throughout all of Scripture, including the New Testament, especially in the final Revelation of his Son, Jesus Christ. When we read Scripture, we read it, Old and New Testament alike, through the lens that is Christ.

© Pascal Deloche/Godong/Corbis

We owe the Jewish people a debt of gratitude for preserving the Word of God, the Sacred Scripture. Here a rabbi uses a yad (Hebrew for "pointer") to mark his place so that he will not soil or damage the scroll with his fingers.

A Fuller Understanding

Let's look at one example of a truth in Scripture that is fully revealed through the Old and New Testaments. Imagine that you are having a conversation with a friend who is a Christian, one who believes that Scripture is the Word of God and who wants to obey that Word. The two of you are discussing the way God would have us treat someone who has done us harm. The friend says: "Scripture allows us to give as good as we get. It says right here in Exodus, 'But if injury ensues, you shall give life for life, eye for eye, tooth for tooth, hand for hand, foot for foot, burn for burn, wound for wound, stripe for stripe' (21:23–25)." Has your friend proved that God would have us harm our enemy as our enemy has harmed us?

Someone who considers the process of the development of Scripture and God's full and final Revelation in Christ would say no. Why? Because, although this passage in

Exodus represents an important insight on the road to becoming loving people, the passage does not represent the fullness of truth on this subject. The meaning of the passage must be discerned in light of the whole of Scripture, especially the teaching and saving works of Jesus Christ.

The "eye for an eye" passage is certainly a positive step in the process of Revelation. This passage teaches *against* revenge. It teaches that "payback" has its limits, and that we cannot do *worse* to someone than was done to us. However, a fuller understanding of what God would have us do appears in Matthew's Gospel, in Jesus' Sermon on the Mount.

"But I Say to You"

In the Sermon on the Mount, Jesus explains that he has not come to abolish the Law and the prophets but to fulfill them (see Matthew 5:17). As an example, Jesus quotes the very passage from Exodus that we have been discussing. He says: "You have heard that it was said, 'An eye for an eye and a tooth for a tooth.' But I say to you, offer no resistance to one who is evil. When someone strikes you on [your] right cheek, turn the other one to him as well" (Matthew 5:38–39). This later teaching does not contradict the first; it stands on the shoulders of the first. It takes us another step in understanding just what is required of us in loving our neighbor.

We see, then, that it is very important that we consider the context of particular passages. If we do not consider this context, we are in danger of taking a partial truth and thinking of it as the whole truth. To receive the fullness of Revelation that is offered us through Jesus Christ, we must consider every teaching in the context of the whole Bible as well as the whole of Tradition. As we continue our study of the books of the New Testament, we will further explore the context of the truths God reveals to us over time throughout all of Scripture. ✝

Symbol of the Mountain

The Gospel writers included elements of the natural world in their presentations of the life and message of Jesus. In the Gospels, particularly in Matthew, the mountain has a symbolic meaning. Many scholars see parallels between Moses and Jesus: As Moses encounters God and receives the Law on a mountain, Mount Sinai, so Jesus teaches the New Law from the mountain; Moses teaches the Ten Commandments, and Jesus adds to them the Beatitudes of the New Law (see Matthew, chapter 5). In the Gospel of Matthew, the commissioning of the Apostles, at the end of the Gospel, takes place on a mountain.

It is symbolically significant that the Transfiguration, where Moses and Elias appear with Jesus, takes place on a mountain in all three synoptic Gospels (see Matthew 17:2, Mark 9:1–3, Luke 9:28), because in the Semitic culture, mountains symbolize closeness to God. The Mount of Olives is thought to be the mountain where Jesus wept over the city of Jerusalem. The garden at Gethsemane, where Jesus prayed before he was taken captive, is at the foot of the Mount of Olives. Mount Zion, the eastern hill of Jerusalem, was the site of David's palace and the Temple. Its elevation made it a natural fortress and a focus for the worship of God.

Article

7 Sacred Scripture: A Living Word for Today

analogy of faith
The coherence of individual doctrines with the whole of Revelation. In other words, as each doctrine is connected with Revelation, each doctrine is also connected with all other doctrines.

senses of Scripture
The senses of Scripture are the literal and spiritual senses; the spiritual senses are the allegorical, the moral, and the anagogical.

Don't get stuck on difficult passages when reading Scripture. Keep reading until you find a passage that speaks to you. You can always go back and ask a priest or teacher about passages that you found hard to understand.

So far in this part, we have discussed three ways of understanding Scripture: its literary form, its historical and cultural situation, and its development. If we ignore these three elements, we have a very good chance of misunderstanding Scripture.

Yet these three elements do not suffice for our understanding of Scripture. For a complete understanding of the meaning of Scripture, we must look to the Holy Spirit. The overarching principle of understanding and interpreting Scripture is that "sacred Scripture must be read and interpreted with its divine authorship in mind" (*Divine Revelation*, 12). Yet how can we be sure that we are interpreting Scripture as its Divine Author, the Holy Spirit, would want us to understand it? Three principles guide us in interpreting Scripture in accordance with the Holy Spirit:

1. We must recognize the unity of the whole of Scripture. Because Scripture reveals God's plan for us, and because Jesus Christ is the center of that plan, we must discern the meaning of Scripture based on the complete picture of God's plan to save us through Jesus Christ.

2. We must understand Scripture in light of the Tradition of the Church through the centuries. As the Fathers of the Church said, "Sacred Scripture is written principally in the Church's heart" (*CCC*, 113). The Church carries Scripture within her Tradition and relies on the guidance of the Holy Spirit for spiritual understanding of the Word of God.

3. We must respect the **analogy of faith**, the unity of individual doctrines, or teachings, within the whole of Revelation, and the interconnectedness between doctrines, which are congruent among themselves and also support one another. To guide us in interpreting Scripture according to the guidance of the Holy Spirit, we depend on the Magisterium of the Church—that is, the Pope and bishops in union with him who form the teaching office of the Church. The Pope and bishops continually guide our contemporary understanding of Scripture through their teachings. Only the teaching office

of the Church can make a definitive judgment on what Scripture means for our faith and moral development.

The Senses of Scripture

As we encounter Scripture at Mass or in our private reading, particular tools of interpretation can be helpful in our understanding. These tools have come down to us from the Tradition of the Church. They are called the **senses of Scripture**.

The first sense is the literal sense. The literal sense is what the words of Scripture actually mean, in the contexts we have already discussed: literary form, historical or cultural context, and the development of Scripture. The Pontifical Biblical Commission describes the literal sense as "that which has been expressed directly by the inspired human authors" and explains that "[s]ince it is the fruit of inspiration, this sense is also intended by God, as principal author" ("The Interpretation of the Bible in the Church"). All the other senses of Scripture are based on the literal meaning (see *CCC,* 116).

Because Scripture is the living Word, in addition to the literal sense, there is a spiritual sense. This spiritual sense has been developed by the Tradition of the Church and is often the reason certain Scripture passages are chosen for various celebrations or seasons of the year. The Pontifical Biblical Commission describes the spiritual sense as "the meaning

Pray It!

Pray the Psalms

One entire book of the Bible, the Book of Psalms, is essentially a book of prayers. The Psalms range from cries of lamentation to songs of praise and wonder, prayers for forgiveness, and poems of thanksgiving.

Jesus himself regularly used the Psalms for prayer. When tempted in the desert, Jesus uses Psalm 91:11–12 to rebuke the Tempter. During his Crucifixion he prays Psalm 22: "My God, my God, why have you abandoned me?" (verse 1).

When you can't find the words to pray, do as Jesus did: pray the Psalms.

- for comfort—Psalm 23
- for forgiveness—Psalm 130
- for hope—Psalm 123
- in sadness—Psalms 42–43
- for help—Psalm 121
- for guidance—Psalm 139

typology

The discernment of God's work in the Old Testament as a prefiguration of what he accomplished through Jesus Christ in the fullness of time. Typology illuminates the unity of God's plan in the two Testaments, but does not devalue the Old Covenant.

expressed by the biblical texts when read, under the influence of the Holy Spirit, in the context of the Paschal Mystery of Christ, and of the new life that flows from it" ("The Interpretation of the Bible in the Church").

Three kinds of spiritual senses can be applied to Scripture: the *allegorical* sense, the *moral* sense, and the *anagogical* sense. Using the allegorical sense of Scripture in the account of the Israelites' crossing the Red Sea, for example, the Church sees not only the literal meaning but also the added allegorical meaning of the Red Sea as an image of Baptism. We "cross over" the Red Sea into the "Promised Land" of the Church when we are baptized. The discernment of God's work in the Old Testament as a prefiguration of what he accomplished through Jesus Christ is called **typology**. As Pope Benedict XVI pointed out in his apostolic exhortation *Verbum Domini* (2010), "the entire Old Testament is a path to Jesus Christ" (38).

Using the moral sense of Scripture, the Church encourages us to act on the instructions and encouragement we find in Scripture to do good and to act justly. Using the anagogical sense of Scripture (in Greek, *anagoge* means "leading"), we are led from considering scriptural events to considering events in our lives that are significant for our eternal salvation. For example, when we read about the New Jerusalem in the Scriptures, we are led to think about the Church on earth as that New Jerusalem, leading us to the heavenly Jerusalem (see *CCC,* 117).

The meaning of Scripture always begins with the literal. However, as you read spiritual books, commentaries, and the writings of Fathers of the Church, you may meet some of these other important ways that the Church interprets Scripture.

The approach to biblical interpretation that pays attention to context in an effort to understand the literal, and therefore also the spiritual senses of Scripture, is sometimes referred to as the contextualist approach. It can be summarized as the approach through which our understanding of the literal sense of Scripture is informed by scientific and historical knowledge. This understanding informs the spiritual senses of Scripture—the allegorical, the moral, and the anagogical—with their deepest symbolic meaning. A contextualist approach simply teaches us how to relate the truths of faith to science. If Scripture is studied in a

What Did Scripture Mean to Jesus?

The Gospels present Jesus as knowing and loving Scripture. In the Gospel of Luke, Jesus, at the age of twelve, stays behind in the Temple to sit "in the midst of the teachers, listening to them and asking them questions, and all who heard him were astounded at his understanding and his answers" (2:46–47). Surely the topic of their conversations must have been the Word of God and its meaning in our lives.

In the Gospel of Matthew, when Jesus had fasted and prayed for forty days and nights in the desert and was hungry, he was tempted by the devil. Satan suggests that Jesus turn the stones into bread. Jesus replies, "One does not live by bread alone, / but by every word that comes forth from / the mouth of God" (4:4). This is almost an exact quotation of Deuteronomy 8:3.

In the Gospels of Mark and Matthew, when Jesus is on the cross, he calls out to his Father, in the words of Psalm 22, "*Eloi, Eloi, lema sabachthani?*" (Mark 15:34), which is Aramaic for, "My God, my God, why have you forsaken me?" The New Testament was written in Greek, and it is rare that Jesus is pictured speaking Aramaic, Jesus' native language. But these words attributed to Jesus in both Mark and Matthew's Gospels have been treasured through the ages.

We might note that Psalm 22 ends in triumph and victory:

> And I will live for the LORD:
> > my descendants will serve you.
> The generation to come will be told of the Lord,
> > that they may proclaim to a people yet unborn
> > the deliverance you have brought.
> > > (Verses 31–32)

We are that people. Through Jesus Christ we know that deliverance.

exegete
A biblical scholar attempting to interpret the meaning of biblical texts.

biblical exegesis
The critical interpretation and explanation of a biblical text.

contextualist manner, following the rules of sound exegesis, "there can never be any real discrepancy between faith and reason"[1] (*CCC*, 159). In other words, the truths revealed in the Bible will not conflict with the truths gleaned from science and history.

The Role of Exegetes

Biblical **exegetes** and scholars are necessary to the process of interpretation. They are scholars and teachers who study Scripture in all its aspects, seeking to discover and attend "to what the human authors truly wanted to affirm and to what God wanted to reveal to us by their words"[2] (*CCC*, 109). Their field of study is called **biblical exegesis**. This is the critical interpretation and explanation of a biblical text. In this sense, *critical* does not mean "fault-finding" but means a close and thorough investigation of a particular biblical text. Besides studying the contexts of literary form, historical and cultural situation, and development, biblical exegetes must also ground their interpretations in the Tradition of the Church and the teaching of the Magisterium in order to interpret Scripture as the living Word of God for us today.

Scripture in My Life

The following are some important questions we can ask about Scripture: Why read Scripture? How does Scripture help me in my life? in my relationship with Christ? in my faith? How does Scripture help me to live the way God wants me to live? What should be my attitude toward Scripture as I hear the Word of God read at Mass and in the Sacraments, or as I read Scripture privately?

Catholic Wisdom

Dialogue with the Word

St. Jerome said: "Ignorance of the Scriptures is ignorance of Christ." It is therefore important that every Christian live in contact and in personal dialogue with the Word of God given to us in Sacred Scripture. . . . We must not read Sacred Scripture as a word of the past but as the Word of God that is also addressed to us, and we must try to understand what it is that the Lord wants to tell us. (Pope Benedict XVI, "General Audience")

First, accept Scripture in faith for what it is: the living Word of God. The author of Psalm 119 declares, "Your word is a lamp for my feet, / a light for my path" (verse 105). We can hear the words of Scripture as living words that are addressed specifically to us. Through faith and prayer and by putting what they teach us into practice, we can learn to respond more faithfully to God's call.

Second, meditate on Scripture. Meditation, from the Latin *meditatio,* literally means "to chew over." Whether reading or listening, a few words or sentences may strike you. Try to remember them, repeat them, learn from them. As you ponder them in faith and prayer, applying them to your own life, you will grow in understanding of God's will for you and your moral obligations to him and to others. When you are looking for guidance or support, these words, the Word of God to you, will spring to your heart and mind just when you need them.

Your Spiritual Journey

You may recall the time that Jesus was reading Scripture aloud in his home synagogue. He read from the Prophet Isaiah: "The Spirit of the Lord is upon me, / because he has anointed me / to bring glad tidings to the poor" (Luke 4:18). Then he declared what these words meant to him personally: "Today this scripture passage is fulfilled in your hearing" (4:21). In other words, Jesus was saying that he is the Anointed One. Isaiah's words are living words of light that helped Jesus to name his understanding of his own mission.

You too can discern the steps in your spiritual journey by meditating on Scripture in faith and prayer and applying in your own life the truth about God and yourself that you discover along the way. God knows you through and through, and he loves you. He wants to communicate with you through the Word of Life, Christ, in Scripture. When you ponder Scripture in your heart and mind, asking "What is God calling me to do?" you will discover the Word that will give you life, purpose, and joy.

Remember, however, to consider Scripture in the light of the Church's Magisterium and in the various contexts of interpretation we have discussed. Even in private prayer and reading, no Scripture passage can be read in isolation but only in the context of the fullness of Revelation opened to us in Jesus Christ through the Church. ☩

Part Review

1. Why is it important to understand the literary forms used in Scripture?

2. What are literary conventions?

3. Why is it important to know and understand the historical and cultural contexts in which the various books of Scripture were written?

4. For what kind of answers do we look to the Scriptures?

5. Give an example of a truth in Scripture that originates in the Old Testament and is fully revealed by Jesus Christ in the New Testament.

6. What are the three criteria by which we interpret Scripture according to the Holy Spirit?

7. Who makes the definitive judgment on what Scripture means?

8. What are the three spiritual senses of Scripture?

9. What role do exegetes play in the interpretation of the Scriptures?

Part 3

The New Testament and the Church

You may remember that old conundrum, What came first, the chicken or the egg? We might revise it a little to ask, What came first, the Church or the New Testament? The answer is not as complicated as the answer to the chicken-and-egg question. The simple truth is this: The Church came first. The Church, God's People, followers of Jesus Christ, under the inspiration of the Holy Spirit, gave birth to the New Testament.

Think back for a moment about some of the things you have learned about the Church, from a broad viewpoint: founded by Jesus Christ, sent to evangelize the nations, sent to spread the Good News of God's love and his salvation, headed by Jesus Christ who is risen from the dead, and guided by the Holy Spirit until the end of time.

This is the Church that, after the death and Resurrection of Christ, recalled all that Jesus had done and taught, and told and retold the events of his life, death, Resurrection, and Ascension until they were saved in writing. This is the Church that, under the leadership of the bishops, gathered the accounts together, verified them as authentic, read them in the liturgy, organized them into chapters and verses, saw that they were copied and saved by countless anonymous monks and nuns, and guarded them carefully through the centuries. This is the Church that when the printing press was invented, printed the Word of God, translated it, distributed it, carried it to far-off lands, and continues to teach it and preach it to this day. Yes, the Church, led by the Holy Spirit, gave birth to the New Testament and has placed it in your hands. As you read the articles in this part, tracing the relationship between the Church and the New Testament, you may ask yourself: How will I respond to this New Testament? How will I pass along its teachings in my life?

The articles in this part address the following topics:

43

Article 8 Jesus Christ, the Word of God

Word of God

The entire deposit of truth revealed by God throughout history and transmitted through Scripture and Tradition, under the guidance of the Holy Spirit. Through all the words of Sacred Scripture, God speaks of the Word, Jesus Christ, the fullness of Revelation and the Eternal Son of God. Jesus Christ became man (the Word incarnate) for the sake of our salvation.

incarnate

From the Latin, meaning "to become flesh," referring to the mystery of Jesus Christ, the Divine Son of God, becoming man. In the Incarnation, Jesus Christ became truly man while remaining truly God.

In the previous articles, we briefly introduced all of Scripture as the inspired **Word of God**. We then focused on the New Testament and briefly explained its development. We also discussed the role of Apostolic Tradition and its relationship to Scripture and to the New Testament in particular.

Now let us take a step back, and consider what (or, we might better ask, who) is the source of both Scripture and Tradition, the source of both the Old and the New Testaments, and of the Apostolic Tradition, which the Church has preserved through the centuries? The answer is this: Jesus Christ, the Word of God. A more detailed answer would be: Jesus Christ, the *preexistent* and *incarnate* Word of God.

What does it mean to say that Jesus Christ is *preexistent*? If you recall what you already know about the Mystery of the Holy Trinity, you will remember that God (the Father, the Son, and the Holy Spirit) existed from all eternity. The Son of God existed as the Word of God but without a human nature. It was only at the Annunciation, when Mary consented to be the Mother of God, that the Word of God, sent from the Father, took on a human nature through the power of the Holy Spirit, became **incarnate** (from the Latin *caro*, meaning "flesh"), and was named Jesus, meaning "God saves." Both Scripture and Tradition bear witness to this preexistent Word of God who became incarnate for our sake.

We declare our belief in the preexistent Word of God every time we proclaim the Nicene Creed. We assert in faith:

> I believe in one Lord Jesus Christ,
> the Only Begotten Son of God,
> born of the Father before all ages.
> God from God, Light from Light,
> true God from true God,
> begotten, not made, consubstantial with the Father;
> through him all things were made.
> For us men and for our salvation
> he came down from heaven,
> and by the Holy Spirit was incarnate
>   of the Virgin Mary,
> and became man.
>
> *(Roman Missal)*

Celebrating the Incarnation

During what season of the year do we celebrate the Incarnation? We focus on celebrating the great mystery of the Incarnation of the Word of God at Christmas and during the Christmas season. The prayers of the Christmas Masses constantly remind us of the wonder of the Word Made Flesh and what it means to us. In this preface for Christmas, we pray to the Father:

For in the mystery of the Word made flesh
a new light of your glory has shone upon the eyes of our mind,
so that, as we recognize in him God made visible,
we may be caught up through him in love of things invisible.

(*Roman Missal*, "Preface I of the Nativity of the Lord")

The love of God does not end at the end of the Christmas season, for Jesus, the Word of God, is with us always.

Compare this proclamation of faith with the beginning (prologue) of the Gospel of John:

In the beginning was the Word,
and the Word was with God,
and the Word was God.
He was in the beginning with God.
All things came to be through him,

and without him nothing came to be.
What came to be through him was life,
    and this life was the light of the human race;
the light shines in the darkness,
    and the darkness has not overcome it.

(1:1–5)

© Manfred Konrad / iStockphoto.com

In these first five verses, the Gospel of John introduces us to the preexistent Word of God, describes his life on earth as "the light of the human race" (1:3), and declares his Resurrection as the light that shines in the darkness, "and the darkness has not overcome it" (1:5). The scholarship of biblical exegetes indicates that this prologue to John's Gospel (see 1:1–14) is, for the most part, an early Church hymn that was sung when Christians gathered for the breaking of the bread. You may want to read these fourteen verses for yourself, and recall them when you receive Communion, as you too are receiving the very Word of God in the Eucharist. ✝

Article 9 The Bible and the *Lectionary*

When we listen to the Word of God proclaimed at the Eucharist each Sunday, are we listening to readings from the Bible or from the *Lectionary*? Actually, we are listening to readings from both, because the readings from the **Lectionary**, the official liturgical book from which the readings during the Liturgy of the Word at Mass are taken, are also readings from the Bible. The *Lectionary* is a collection of readings that have been selected from the Bible for proclamation during the Church's liturgies throughout the year. These scriptural readings proclaimed at Mass, and also in the other Sacraments, are short excerpts from the various books of the Bible, chosen to commemorate the various seasons of the liturgical year and the mysteries of Christ they celebrate. To understand the relationship between the Bible and the *Lectionary,* we need to understand the structure of the liturgical year.

The Liturgical Year

The **liturgical year** is the annual cycle of religious feasts and seasons that forms the context for the Church's worship. It can be compared to a great wheel, a wheel that carries us through the Church's seasons and into the mysteries of Christ of which we become a part. Each season of the liturgical year focuses on and celebrates a different aspect of the mystery of Christ. The liturgical year begins on the First Sunday of Advent. During the seasons of Advent and Christmas, we celebrate the mystery of the Incarnation of Christ. The Christmas season continues to the Solemnity of the Baptism of the Lord and is followed by Ordinary Time. During Ordinary Time, named because the weeks of this season are named with ordinal numbers (1st, 2nd, 3rd, and so on), we celebrate the mystery of Christ in all its aspects. Lent follows this period of Ordinary Time. Lent is the season of preparation for the Solemnity of Easter, the pinnacle of the Church year. The Easter season continues until Pentecost, which ushers in a longer period of Ordinary Time. The liturgical year ends with the Solemnity of Christ the King. The following Sunday, the beginning of Advent, the liturgical year begins again.

Lectionary

The official liturgical book containing the readings of the Mass, the Gospels, the Responsorial Psalms, and the Gospel Acclamations.

liturgical year

The Church's annual cycle of religious feasts and seasons that celebrates the events and mysteries of Christ's birth, life, death, Resurrection, and Ascension, and forms the context for the Church's worship.

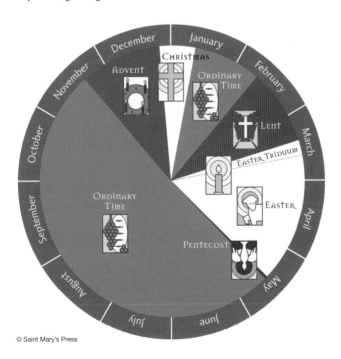

© Saint Mary's Press

What season of the year is the Church celebrating now? In what season of the liturgical year does your birthday fall? the birthdays of friends and family? How do you celebrate each season in your home?

How deeply we enter into the mysteries of Christ, how closely we assimilate them into our hearts and minds, is our own choice. The wheel of the liturgical year, year after year, brings us into contact with Christ through the liturgy. We can choose to participate on the surface, or we can plunge into the life-giving cycle set before us.

The Readings of the Liturgical Year

We might expect that year after year we would have the same readings for the same Sundays as we celebrate the same mysteries of Christ. But this is not the case. The *Lectionary* has been constructed to provide us with a rich and full selection of readings, year after year, in a three-year cycle. In each year of the cycle, we proclaim semicontinuous readings from the Gospels. (Semicontinuous means that we read from the same Gospel, in the order written, but some parts are skipped.) On the Sundays of cycle A, the Gospel readings come mainly from the Gospel of Matthew; in cycle B, from Mark; and in cycle C, from Luke. The Gospel of John is proclaimed during Lent, Holy Week, and in the Easter season in all three cycles and on five Sundays in cycle B.

On weekdays the *Lectionary* is organized in a two-year cycle, year I (odd-numbered years) and year II (even-numbered years). There are usually only two readings (an Old or New Testament reading and the Gospel) proclaimed at Mass on weekdays.

Live It!

Understanding Scripture

Sometimes passages in Scripture can be confusing. The author of the Second Letter of Peter admitted that some of Saint Paul's writings could be challenging: "In them there are some things hard to understand" (2 Peter 3:16). If you are having troubling "getting" the meaning of a verse, try reading another translation. Sometimes all it takes is a slightly different word to make the entire passage suddenly come alive for you.

The translation we use in the Mass is the New American Bible, but other translations include the Jerusalem Bible, the New Revised Standard Version: Catholic Edition, and the Good News Translation: Catholic Edition. You can also use a parallel Bible that has several Catholic translations printed side-by-side for easy comparison.

The proclamation of the Gospel is the high point of the Liturgy of the Word. On Sundays two other readings lead up to the Gospel. The first is from the Old Testament (except during the Easter season, when this reading is from the Acts of the Apostles). This reading is selected to prepare us for the theme of the Gospel. The second reading is from a New Testament book other than the Gospels. This reading witnesses to the faith of the early Christians, and how they appropriated and lived out the Gospel in their own lives and in their own settings. We, of course, are called to do the same.

The *Sunday and Feast Day Lectionary*

The *Sunday and Feast Day Lectionary* was compiled by the Catholic Church. However, in recent years, thirteen churches and faith communities in North America (including Episcopalian, Lutheran, Presbyterian, Methodist, and Disciples of Christ churches) have developed their own cycle of Sunday and feast day readings, called the Revised Common Lectionary, based on this lectionary. The *Revised Common Lectionary* is not a separate bound book. It is simply a list of the biblical references to the readings for Sundays and feast days, many of them identical or similar to those given in the *Sunday and Feast Day Lectionary*. During the service the readings themselves are read directly from the Bible.

Because of these similarities, we now share the same calendar, liturgical seasons, and three-year-cycle of readings with these thirteen churches and faith communities. We read almost exactly the same Gospel readings on each Sunday. In addition, we all hear three readings proclaimed each Sunday. Because of the similarities in our liturgical readings, we enjoy much more unity at the table of God's Word than we have in the past.

A Gift from the Church

The *Lectionary* is a great gift from the Church to all her faithful. Listening to Scripture at Mass, in the thoughtful arrangement the *Lectionary* provides, is a great privilege. However, familiarity with the *Lectionary* is not the same as familiarity with the Bible. Why? Because the *Lectionary* is selective. Bible passages are chosen to help us to reflect on certain themes and events in the life of Christ. They are necessarily presented in small excerpts suitable for public reading.

Reading a book of the Bible, on the other hand, helps us to put these familiar passages into the wider context of the entire book from which they come. Understanding the larger context of the selected reading deepens our understanding of why the readings were selected and the truths they reveal for our lives. Because the *Lectionary* is not the entire Bible, knowledge of the Bible becomes an essential component to our fuller understanding of the Word of God. ✝

Pray It!

The Bible and Personal Prayer

You may have a family Bible that has been carefully preserved through many years or generations. Such an heirloom is precious, because it is the Word of God and because it may contain treasured family records and mementos.

But the Word of God is above all meant to be heard and read; it is a living Word, and it can give us guidance, direction, encouragement, and hope in our everyday lives. One way to make the Bible a part of your daily life is to read passages as a personal prayer by using *I* and *me* in place of *we* and *us*. Making the words deeply personal gives them an urgency and a relevance that sometimes gets lost when they become too familiar.

Try this with the prayer Jesus taught us, the Lord's Prayer (see Matthew 6:9–13). We pray this as "we" and "us" because Jesus taught us that we are all brothers and sisters in him, but at times you might want to pray some of the lines of the prayer in this way:

My Father . . . your kingdom come to me . . . your will be done by me. . . . Give me today my daily bread, and forgive me my trespasses as I forgive those who have trespassed against me. And lead me not into temptation, but deliver me from evil. Amen.

© David Lees/CORBIS

This *Road to Emmaus* is an altarpiece by Duccio di Buoninsegna (c. 1255–1319). Jesus is being invited into the inn. What makes Jesus look like a traveler? Why would the front of an altar be an appropriate place for this art?

Article 10 Scripture and the Eucharist

You may remember this incident from the Gospel of Luke: Two friends were traveling from Jerusalem to Emmaus. Their leader, Jesus, had just been crucified, and they were leaving the city with heavy hearts. Suddenly, a stranger joined them, explained God's plan to them, and "interpreted to them what referred to him in all the scriptures" (Luke 24:27). At the end of the day, they invited the stranger to stay with them. At table the stranger broke the bread, and suddenly "their eyes were opened and they recognized him" (24:31). He was Jesus, crucified and now risen. Suddenly, he vanished from their sight. The two friends exclaimed, "Were not our hearts burning [within us] while he spoke to us on the way and opened the scriptures to us?" (24:32). The friends returned to Jerusalem to tell the Apostles and disciples about their encounter with the Risen Christ and "how he was made known to them in the breaking of the bread" (24:35).

This encounter on the road to Emmaus illustrates the intimate connection between Scripture and the Eucharist. Along the road it is Jesus himself who explains Scripture to the friends. Later, at table, Jesus once more breaks the

Eucharist, the
The celebration of the entire Mass. The term sometimes refers specifically to the consecrated bread and wine that have become the Body and Blood of Christ.

bread and offers it to them as his own Body and Blood. The friends identify Jesus in both actions: opening up Scripture and breaking the bread. This intimate connection between Scripture and the Eucharist has been fostered by the Church ever since. From the earliest liturgies of the Church, the celebration included both the reading of Scripture—writings from the Old Testament as well as the apostolic writings (the letters of Paul and the other Apostles)— and the Eucharist. It is the same today. In every Eucharist, in both the Word and in the Sacrament, we encounter the Risen Christ.

The Eucharist: Heart and Summit

The Eucharistic celebration is the memorial of Christ's Passover, his work of salvation won for us mainly through his Passion, death, Resurrection, and Ascension. This work does not merely remain in the past. It is a *living* remembrance continuing into the present in the liturgy because, for God, all time is eternal and all time is now.

The Eucharist is offered by Christ himself, as the eternal high priest of the New Covenant, acting through the ministry of the priest. In **the Eucharist**, we proclaim the Word of God and give thanks to the Father for all his blessings, especially for the gift of his Son. The offerings of bread and wine are consecrated, and we are invited to receive the Body and Blood of Christ. Every Eucharistic celebration includes all these elements, forming one single act of worship.

For all these reasons, the Eucharist is "the heart and summit of the Church's life" (*CCC,* 1407). Moreover, in the Eucharist, Christ invites each and all of the members of his Church, his family, to join with him in the sacrifice of praise and thanksgiving that he offered to his Father once and for all on the cross. In the Eucharist, the living memorial of this sacrifice, Christ continues to pour out his saving love and grace upon his Body, the Church.

Scripture in the Mass

The Mass is made up of four parts: the Introductory Rites, the Liturgy of the Word, the Liturgy of the Eucharist, and the Concluding Rite. As we explore each of these parts, we will discover how Scripture both shaped the Eucharistic celebration from its beginnings and is essential to it.

The Introductory Rites

The Introductory Rites begin with an entrance antiphon that is always taken from either the Old Testament or the New Testament. (On Sundays this antiphon is usually replaced with a gathering song.) Except during Advent and Lent, the Glory to God *(Gloria)* is also part of the Introductory Rites. The words of this song of praise originated in the Gospel of Luke, at the angel's announcement of the birth of Jesus to the shepherds:

> And suddenly there was a multitude of the heavenly host with the angel, praising God and saying:
> > "Glory to God in the highest
> > and on earth peace to those on whom his favor rests."
>
> (Luke 2:13–14)

At the Eucharist we join in this song of heavenly praise.

The Liturgy of the Word

Following the Introductory Rites and the Opening Prayer, we celebrate the Liturgy of the Word. The Liturgy of the Word is integral to the Eucharist and indeed to every Sacrament. Through Scripture we are led to respond in faith to the meaning of the sacramental action, proclaimed and expressed by the Word of God. As stated in *Divine Revelation,* promulgated by the Second Vatican Council, "The church has always venerated the divine scriptures as it has venerated the Body of the Lord, in that it never ceases, above all in the sacred liturgy, to partake of the bread of life and to offer it to the faithful from the one table of the word of God and the Body of Christ" (21).

Catholic Wisdom

Scriptural Art

Scripture has inspired great art. During the Middle Ages, the great stories and messages of Scripture were "translated" into stained-glass windows so that everyone could "read the Bible" by looking at the pictures in the windows. Abbot Suger of the Abbey of Saint Denis, near Paris, who lived in the twelfth century, called stained-glass windows "sermons that reached the heart through the eyes instead of entering through the ears." The same can be said for beautiful scriptural and religious art today.

The words "the one table of the Word of God and the Body of Christ" remind us that Christ is present not only in the Eucharist but also in the Word of God proclaimed. This truth is explicitly stated in the Vatican II document *Constitution on the Sacred Liturgy* (*Sacrosanctum Concilium*, 1963): "He [Christ] is present in his word since it is he himself who speaks when the holy scriptures are read in the Church" (7).

In addition to the three readings on Sundays (the last and most prominent one from the Gospel), a psalm is read or sung. This is called the Responsorial Psalm. Then, before the Gospel, a Gospel acclamation is read or sung, with an Alleluia (suppressed during Lent). Both the Responsorial Psalm and the Alleluia verse (or the acclamation verse in Lent) are taken from Scripture.

In the liturgy, reverence toward the Gospel is expressed by the acclamation verse that precedes it, by standing for the Gospel reading, and often by a Gospel procession to the lectern or ambo, accompanied by candles and incense.

Following the Gospel, a homily is given by the priest or deacon. A homily is not the same as a sermon. A sermon can be given on any religious topic; a homily is centered on Christ and based on the readings from Scripture or another scriptural text from the Mass. The function of a homily is to insert the Scripture readings of the day into the life of the gathered community, to teach the Word of God here and now. It must also lead the listening community to an active participation in the Eucharist. The homily invites us, like the disciples at Emmaus, to recognize Jesus in the opening up of Scripture and in the breaking of the bread.

The Liturgy of the Eucharist

The most solemn part of the Mass is the Liturgy of the Eucharist. At the beginning of the Eucharistic Prayer, we are invited by the celebrant to join the angels and saints as they sing, "Holy, Holy, Holy Lord God of hosts" (*Roman Missal*). This acclamation is based on the Prophet Isaiah's description of the heavenly throne room (see Isaiah 6:3) and on the crowd's welcoming Jesus as he entered Jerusalem (see Mark 11:9–10).

This acclamation is a good example of the spiritual sense of the verse "Blessed is he who comes in the name of the Lord" (Mark 11:9). In its literal meaning, the crowds are greeting Jesus as a prophet who speaks for God. But when

we proclaim this verse at Mass, we have the benefit of knowing that this same Jesus died and rose for us and is with us
now, and will shortly come to us in the Eucharist. And so we
say, "Blessed is he who comes" to me personally, very soon
now, in the Body and Blood of Christ!

In the Eucharistic Prayer, the blessing of the Holy Spirit,
invoked by the priest upon the essential signs of wheat bread
and grape wine, is accompanied by the words of **Consecration**
that the priest pronounces. These words ("This is my Body
. . ." and "This is the chalice of my Blood . . ." *[Roman Mis-
sal]*) are based on words spoken by Jesus at the Last Supper
and found in passages in the **synoptic Gospels**, the Gospels
of Mark (see 14:22–26), Matthew (see 26:26–30), and Luke
(see 22:19–20). (The word *synoptic* comes from the Greek,
meaning "seeing the whole together" and refers to the basic
unity of vision shared by these three Evangelists. All three
follow the same synopsis or general view of Jesus' life, Passion, death, Resurrection, and Ascension. We will study the
synoptic Gospels more closely in upcoming articles in this
student book.)

Then, before receiving the Eucharist, we unite in prayer
as sons and daughters of the Father, brothers and sisters of
Jesus, as we pray the Lord's Prayer, based on Matthew 6:9–13
and Luke 11:2–4. The Communion Rite includes within it
the short litany, the Lamb of God *(Agnus Dei)*, which has its
sources in John 1:29 and Revelation 5:6–13. During this part
of the Mass, we also pray a prayer based on the words of the
centurion to Jesus, found in the Gospel of Matthew:

> Lord, I am not worthy
> that you should enter under my roof,
> but only say the word
> and my soul shall be healed.
>
> *(Roman Missal)*

You might like to read the entire incident on which this
prayer is based in Matthew 8:5–13. This will give you a
wider context in which to appreciate this short prayer we say
before receiving the Body of Christ.

The Concluding Rite

As we are dismissed, we accept the gift of peace that the
Risen Christ offered to his disciples as he commissioned
them to go forth and to share that peace with the world:

**consecrate,
Consecration**

To declare or set
apart as sacred or to
solemnly dedicate to
God's service; to make
holy. At Mass the
Consecration occurs
during the Eucharistic
Prayer when the priest
recites Jesus' words
of institution, changing
the bread and wine
into the Body and
Blood of Christ.

synoptic Gospels

From the Greek for
"seeing the whole
together," the name
given to the Gospels
of Matthew, Mark, and
Luke, because they
are similar in style and
content.

"Peace be with you. As the Father has sent me, so I send you" (John 20:21; see also John 20:19).

Our place of the Eucharist—our parish church, our school chapel, even an auditorium or a stadium—has been our "Upper Room," where we shared Christ's Word and his Body and Blood. In our own time and place, we have

The Institution of the Eucharist

When we think of Jesus' institution of the Eucharist, the first passages that might come to mind are the accounts in Mark (14:22–25), Matthew (26:26–29), and Luke (22:15–20). These describe the words and actions of Jesus as he shared the Last Supper with his disciples. However, the earliest written account is found in the First Letter to the Corinthians. In that letter the Apostle Paul writes:

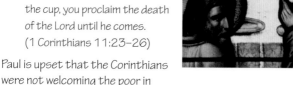

© Richard Cummins/CORBIS

> For I received from the Lord what I also handed on to you, that the Lord Jesus, on the night he was handed over, took bread, and, after he had given thanks, broke it and said, "This is my body that is for you. Do this in remembrance of me." In the same way also the cup, after supper, saying, "This cup is the new covenant in my blood. Do this, as often as you drink it, in remembrance of me." For as often as you eat this bread and drink the cup, you proclaim the death of the Lord until he comes.
> (1 Corinthians 11:23–26)

Paul is upset that the Corinthians were not welcoming the poor in their midst when they celebrated the Eucharist. Paul is insisting that the Corinthians recognize the Body of Christ in the Eucharist and also in the Church, especially in the poor. In other words, he is reminding the Corinthians that they cannot accept Christ in his Body and Blood and then reject him in those who are poor.

encountered his saving love. We are strengthened by his Word—not only in the readings but also woven throughout the celebration of the Eucharist. We are also strengthened by his Sacrament, going forth to bring him, in his life and love, to others, through our own. ✟

Part Review

1. What does it mean to say the Word of God, Jesus Christ, is preexistent?

2. What is the relationship between Scripture and Tradition?

3. What role does the Magisterium play in the interpretation and teaching of Scripture and Tradition?

4. Why are the Gospels of Matthew, Mark, and Luke called the synoptic Gospels?

5. How is the *Lectionary* similar to the Bible? How is it different from the Bible?

6. Describe the role of Scripture in the Mass. Give three examples.

The Synoptic Gospels and the Acts of the Apostles

Part 1

What Is a Gospel?

"**D**o not be afraid; for behold, I proclaim to you good news of great joy that will be for all the people. For today in the city of David a savior has been born for you who is Messiah and Lord" (Luke 2:10–11). With these words, the angel of the Lord announced to the shepherds the birth of Christ. And with these words, this anonymous angel encapsulated for the shepherds and for us the very meaning of *Good News:* You have a Savior. Your Messiah and Lord has come.

Gospel means "good news." In these verses we are told that Jesus Christ is the Good News. Jesus Christ is the Gospel. But of course, our study in this book is of the four written Gospels of Matthew, Mark, Luke, and John. The purpose of these written Gospels, the inspired Word of God, is to lead us directly to the Good News of Jesus Christ.

In this next part, we look closely at the relationship between Jesus himself and the Gospels that witness to him and to his message. The Gospels we study today are an end result of a long process. Of course they began with the life and teaching of Jesus, but how did they come to be written in the first place? Why are the synoptic Gospels (Matthew, Mark, and Luke) so similar and yet different from one another? (Remember that *synoptic* means "seeing the whole together.") And for whom were they written? What were their target audiences in the first centuries of the Church?

There are only two articles in this part, but they lay the groundwork for a detailed study of each of the synoptic Gospels to be studied in the rest of this section.

The articles in this part address the following topics:

- Article 11: "The Formation of the Gospels" (page 60)
- Article 12: "An Overview of the Synoptic Gospels" (page 65)

Article 11 The Formation of the Gospels

What exactly is a Gospel? How did it come to be? Is a Gospel one person's eyewitness account? Has the author written a kind of diary, jotting down his own observations as he witnesses events? Or has he written a research paper, gathering information together from various sources?

The answers to these questions are very important because understanding the purpose and the process of the formation of the Gospels helps us to understand why the Gospels are both similar to and different from one another, and what the inspired authors are teaching.

The inspired author of a Gospel is not claiming to be an eyewitness. Rather, he is relying on a variety of trustworthy accounts from other people. As he does so, under the guidance of the Holy Spirit, he thinks about the significance of these events. He tries to find the best way to communicate that significance to his audience.

For example, the author of the Gospel of Luke addresses the question of Gospel formation directly. As he begins his Gospel, he tells us how he went about writing it:

> Since many have undertaken to compile a narrative of the events that have been fulfilled among us, just as those who were eyewitnesses from the beginning and ministers of the word have handed them down to us, I too have decided, after investigating everything accurately anew, to write it down in an orderly sequence for you, most excellent Theophilus, so that you may realize the certainty of the teachings you have received. (Luke 1:1–4)

By beginning in this way, the author of Luke's Gospel explains that his finished product is the result of a three-stage process, a process that began with events in the life of Jesus Christ.

First Stage: The Life and Teachings of Jesus

At the core of each of our Gospels are the events in the life and teachings of Jesus. You are undoubtedly familiar with many of them: Jesus' public ministry, preaching, powerful actions, Passion, death, Resurrection, post-Resurrection appearances, and Ascension. The events of the life of Jesus, his preaching and his miracles, are themselves the message

This painting, by William Brassey Hole (1846–1917), depicts the Risen Jesus waiting for his disciples on the shore of the Sea of Galilee. Peter is jumping in! Read about this post-Resurrection appearance in John 21:1–14.

© Look and Learn / William Brassey Hole / Private Collection / The Bridgeman Art Library

of salvation, "the bottom line" of the Gospels (see *Catechism of the Catholic Church [CCC]*, 126.)

The post-Resurrection appearances are part of this message and are indispensable to the message and mission of Christ because they confirm the reality of the Resurrection. Without the post-Resurrection appearances, the accounts of the life of Jesus would be a poignant record of a man who, for a short time, brought light and goodness to the world, yet seems to have been defeated in the end. However, Jesus was not defeated; he was victorious. He was raised from the dead. He met with his disciples. He commissioned them to spread this Good News to the whole world. Because of the Resurrection, the events in the life of Jesus took on an entirely new and powerful meaning. The Gospel accounts reflect an understanding of Jesus that takes into account not only his earthly life but also his Resurrection.

It is important to note that none of the Gospels was written at the same time as the events it describes. The Evangelists were not news reporters or bloggers, constructing a day-by-day picture of the life of Jesus. Rather, the Gospels were written many years after the death and Resurrection of Christ. The Gospel of Mark is thought to be the first Gospel to have been written, and it dates to between AD 65 and 70, thirty-five to forty years after the death of Jesus.

What, then, occurred in those years between the Resurrection of Christ and the time an early Christian could have read (or heard proclaimed) the Gospel of Mark?

Second Stage: Oral Tradition

The Good News about Jesus' life, death, Passion, Resurrection, and Ascension was first passed on through **oral tradition**. The Apostles and disciples of Jesus went forth proclaiming and teaching the Good News in both word and deed. Accounts that later would appear in the Gospels were told and retold by those who were witnesses to them. More and more people heard and believed the Good News. These new believers, in turn, shared what they had learned and the Good News continued to spread. In this way the followers of Jesus grew in faith and attracted others to their company (see *CCC*, 126).

During this time in which the life and teachings of Jesus were spread by oral tradition, the sharing of the message of salvation took many forms, including the following:

Catholic Wisdom

One Saint, Two Books

Studying Scripture is a solemn matter, but it doesn't have to make you solemn. Saint Philip Neri, who lived in Rome in the sixteenth century, always carried a Bible with him. But he also carried another book in his pocket—a joke book. Philip Neri was well known for his practical jokes and his sense of humor, saying, "A joyful heart is more easily made perfect than a downcast one."

- **Preaching to nonbelievers, those who had not witnessed or previously heard the Good News** This basic message of salvation—the life, death, Resurrection, and Ascension of Jesus—was called the **kerygma**, a Greek word meaning "proclamation." *Kerygma* refers both to the message of salvation itself and to the proclamation of that message.

- **Preaching to believers, to strengthen the faith of those who had accepted Jesus and the message of salvation** This teaching inspired the followers of Jesus to remain true to their new way of life and was known as **didache**, a Greek word meaning "teaching."

- **Communal worship *(liturgia)*, especially the celebration of the Eucharist** When the early Church gathered, the people would share the Body and Blood of Christ and recount the events and teachings of Jesus' life. In the breaking of bread and in the sharing of the Good News of salvation, the early believers were strengthened and nourished. Gradually they began to collect accounts of Jesus' sayings. Ritual language developed as the Church worshiped together and new members of the community were baptized.

oral tradition
The handing on of the message of God's saving plan through words and deeds.

kerygma
A Greek word meaning "proclamation" or "preaching," referring to the announcement of the Gospel or the Good News of divine salvation offered to all through Jesus Christ. *Kerygma* has two senses. It is both an event of proclamation and a message proclaimed.

didache
A Greek word meaning "teaching," referring to the preaching and instruction offered to all who have already accepted Jesus.

Third Stage: Written Gospels

In time the early followers of Christ realized that the saving events of his life, death, Resurrection, and Ascension, as well as his teachings, must be written down. Why? One reason was that the early disciples of Jesus, the original witnesses, had begun to die. The Church would need a record of the life and teachings of Christ so that nothing might be lost from memory. Also, there was a growing understanding among early Christians that the second coming of Jesus was not going to happen as quickly as they had originally thought, so there was a need to preserve his teachings for future generations. Preserving Jesus' teachings in writing would keep them free of distortion by heretical teachings.

These various written accounts were used by the four inspired authors of the Gospels as source material. We know that written traditions were part of the heritage of the author of Luke's Gospel because he says so: "Since many have undertaken to compile a narrative of the events," he writes, "I too have decided . . . to write it down" (Luke 1:1,3). In fact, Scripture scholars conclude that Mark's Gospel was one of

Canonical or Apocryphal?

The narratives that were accepted by the Church as authentic and genuine accounts of the truth of God's Revelation are called **canonical**. Among the canonical books of the New Testament are the four Gospels of Matthew, Mark, Luke, and John. They were accepted into the canon of the New Testament because they met the criteria of acceptance. The four Gospels we have today were in standard use in the early Church by the end of the second century. The entire New Testament was in place, accepted as canonical, by the end of the fourth century. However, the canon was not officially closed until the sixteenth century. At that time the Council of Trent, in response to questions brought up by the Protestant Reformation, declared that no book would be added to the canon, and no book would be taken away.

Other narratives in existence were not accepted into the canon. Many of these are called apocryphal books. (The Greek word **apocrypha** means "hidden, unknown.") These were writings that were not accepted as valid accounts by the Church because they distorted in some way the truth about Jesus or about the Christian message. For example, the Infancy Gospel of Thomas includes a fanciful story of the child Jesus forming birds out of clay, and then bringing them to life. This story distorts the reality of Jesus, who is both truly *God* and truly *man*, the Word of God who became flesh and lived among us, "tested in every way, yet without sin" (Hebrews 4:15), and who used his divine powers in service to the Kingdom of God and its message of salvation.

the written sources that the authors of both Luke and Matthew consulted and included in their own accounts.

Thus the inspired human authors of the Gospels, the Evangelists, can be seen as *editors* as well as authors. They carefully went over the inherited oral and written traditions about the events, and wrote "an orderly sequence" (Luke 1:3) to meet the needs of the audience to whom each was writing. The Evangelists were not trying to teach history, even though at the core of their accounts are historical events. As Luke tells us, they were trying, under the guidance of the Holy Spirit, to help others to grow in faith, to "realize the certainty of the teachings [they] have received" (Luke 1:4) and to encourage their readers and hearers to live out the Gospel in a variety of different circumstances (see *CCC*, 126). ☥

canonical
When referring to Scripture, *canonical* means included in the canon—that is, part of the collection of books the Church recognizes as the inspired Word of God.

apocrypha
Writings about Jesus or the Christian message not accepted as part of the canon of Scripture.

Article 12 An Overview of the Synoptic Gospels

Mark, Matthew, and Luke's Gospels, the synoptic Gospels, can be "seen together" because they contain common points of view and have many similarities. They all proclaim the Good News of Jesus Christ and convey the same truth about him. However, they also differ from one another in various ways. In this overview of the synoptic Gospels, we discuss the reasons for both the similarities and the differences. Both are important as we strive to understand the fullness of

Catholic Wisdom

The Baptism of Jesus

Every synoptic Gospel contains an account of the Baptism of Jesus (see Mark 1:9–11, Matthew 3:13–17, Luke 3:21–22), and, in the Gospel of John, John the Baptist testifies to it. The Church celebrates the Solemnity of the Baptism of the Lord on the Sunday after January 6. On this Sunday we also celebrate the mystery of the Trinity, for at Jesus' Baptism, the presence of all three Persons of the Trinity—the Father, the Son, and the Holy Spirit—was made known: The Father's voice was heard from the cloud, and the Holy Spirit descended in the form of a dove upon Jesus, revealed as the Son of God. The mystery of the Trinity is the central mystery of our faith and of our Christian life, and only God reveals this to us by making himself known as Father, Son, and Holy Spirit.

The Synoptic Gospels

Gospel	Date Written (Approximate)	Audience	Theme	Organization
Mark	AD 65–70	persecuted Roman Christians	Suffering and death lead to eternal life.	begins with Baptism and public ministry, recounts acts of power and controversies with Pharisees
Matthew	AD 85	primarily Jewish Christians	Jesus is the Messiah who continues the Jewish tradition.	begins with infancy narrative, including genealogy beginning with Abraham, placing Jesus in the context of the Israelites' salvation history
Luke	AD 80–90	Gentile Christians	God's covenant love is universal.	begins with infancy narrative, includes genealogy going back to Adam, and structures the Gospel around a journey to Jerusalem, the center of Jewish faith.

Revelation the Church faithfully passes on from generation to generation.

Sources

One of the reasons the synoptic Gospels are so similar is that, as mentioned earlier, Mark is believed to have been a source for both Matthew and Luke. If you were to take a scissors and cut out of Matthew and Luke what also appears in Mark, you could almost reproduce Mark by rearranging the cut-out parts.

Matthew's and Luke's Gospels, with Marcan material removed, still have a great deal of common material consisting mostly of things Jesus said. Biblical scholars have surmised that Matthew and Luke had a second common source, a hypothetical written collection of Jesus' sayings and teachings known as "Q" or the **Q Source**. (Its name comes from the German word *quelle,* meaning "source." It is *hypothetical* because it is assumed to have existed.) Matthew's and Luke's use of both Mark and Q is the reason the synoptic Gospels have so much in common.

Q Source
A hypothetical written collection of the teachings of Jesus shared among the early followers of Christianity surmised by Scripture scholars to be a source for both Matthew and Luke.

Audiences and Themes

One of the reasons the synoptic Gospels differ is that they were written for different audiences. We all know that we describe events differently depending on the audience to whom we are speaking. For example, if you were asked to write directions for sending a text message, the steps and descriptions you would include would be influenced by who was going to be reading the directions. You would describe the process one way to someone who is familiar with cell phones and another way to a person who has never used a cell phone. Your description would be influenced by what you think that particular person needs to hear. You would, however, be describing the same process. The same is true with the Gospels. In sharing the same truths about Jesus,

Live It!

Faith

It is tempting to think that the people of Jesus' time found it easier to believe in him and to follow his teachings than we do because they were with him when he was alive on earth. But that's not really true. Without television, phones, photographs, and movies, only a relatively few people actually got to see or hear Jesus. Unless a person happened to be in a particular village at the exact time Jesus was teaching or performing a miracle, he or she would have had to rely on what others had seen and heard—just like we do.

The calming of the storm at sea, in both the Gospels of Matthew and Mark, addresses the need for faith in the midst of uncertainty and even danger.

In Mark we read about Jesus "asleep on a cushion" (Mark 4:38) as the waves were pouring into the boat. The Apostles woke Jesus and asked, "Teacher, do you not care that we are perishing?" (4:38). Jesus immediately said to the sea, "Quiet! Be still!" (4:39), and there was a great calm. Jesus then asked them, "Why are you terrified? Do you not yet have faith?" (4:40). Then the Apostles said to one another, "Who then is this whom even wind and sea obey?" (4:41).

This powerful miracle does not mean that our faith in Jesus will spare us from every danger or from death itself. But it assures us that Jesus, who died and was raised, will bring his followers with him, beyond death and terror, into eternal life.

each Gospel author is responding to the needs of his particular audience.

Mark's Gospel is believed to have been written between AD 65 and 70 in Rome during a persecution of Christians. Mark's audience was asking, "Why should we suffer for our belief in Christ?" Mark responds to this question by presenting a narrative of Jesus' life that helps his community to make sense of its suffering and persecution. The narrative teaches that Jesus didn't want to die, but still chose fidelity to his Father's will. Because of this, death, rather than being an end, leads to eternal life.

Matthew was written approximately AD 85 to settled Jewish Christians, probably in Antioch, Syria, who were adjusting to the presence of Gentile Christians in their midst. They were asking, "Is becoming a disciple of Jesus Christ an act of fidelity to my ancestors' two-thousand-year covenant relationship with God or not?" Matthew highlights Jesus as the fulfillment of many Old Testament hopes and prophecies. Matthew wanted his Jewish Christian readers to know that believing in Jesus was not a break with their tradition. Rather, he wanted them to see it as a continuation of their tradition. At the same time, he wanted to make clear that Gentile disciples of Jesus were also welcome to join the community.

Luke was writing to Gentiles between the years AD 80 and 90. Luke's Gentile audience had questions related to

Pray It!

Help My Unbelief!

Even though our faith is the cornerstone of our lives, we all have times when we struggle to believe. In those moments it's okay to wonder and question because, as Blessed Cardinal John Henry Newman said, "Ten thousand difficulties do not make one doubt." If he, who is on his way to canonized sainthood, could struggle with his faith, so can the rest of us.

When you are facing a challenge to your faith and wonder what to do, it can help to remember Jesus' healing of a boy who had seizures. When the boy's father asked Jesus if he could heal his son, Jesus said, "Everything is possible to one who has faith" (Mark 9:23). The father immediately cried out, "I do believe, help my unbelief!" (9:24).

The next time you face a difficulty in your faith, make this your prayer: "Lord, I do believe, help my unbelief!"

their non-Jewish heritage: "Is the salvation offered by Jesus restricted to the Jewish people, or are we, as Gentiles, welcome too?" Luke emphasized the universal nature of God's invitation to covenant love: Everyone is invited. In a society in which the rich had special privileges and the poor were often oppressed and overburdened, Luke makes clear that Jesus is the compassionate Savior who welcomes all. In several ways he emphasizes that Jesus is a friend to the outsider, and to those who are poor or marginalized in some way.

Thus Luke gives us a particular insight into the many ways we might follow Jesus. We too are challenged to be compassionate and to reach out to the marginalized in our midst.

Organization

Each author's audience and theme affects the organization of his Gospel. Mark starts his account at the time of Jesus' public ministry with the witness of John the Baptist and Jesus' baptism. To help early Christians make sense of suffering and persecution, Mark encourages them to look forward to the final victory of the Kingdom by recounting Jesus' acts of power. Because the early Christians in Mark's audience are being persecuted, Mark's Gospel reminds them that Jesus dealt with adversaries who opposed him, in his controversies with the Pharisees. Mark then describes in great detail the greatest trial of all, followed by the greatest victory: Jesus' Passion, death, and Resurrection.

Matthew, to highlight Jesus as the fulfillment of many Old Testament hopes and prophecies, starts his account with a genealogy, beginning with Abraham, that places Jesus within the context of the Israelites' salvation history. After accounts of Jesus' birth, Matthew inserts five sections, reminiscent of the Jewish Law (or the five books of the Pentateuch), before his account of Jesus' Passion, death, and Resurrection. Luke also includes a genealogy, but his goes back not to Abraham but to Adam. After his accounts of Jesus' birth, Luke structures his Gospel around a journey: Jesus' ministry in Galilee, his journey to Jerusalem, and his ministry in Jerusalem before his Passion, death and Resurrection. As we read and discuss each Gospel, we will discover how particular points are emphasized for particular audiences. We will also see that although the Gospels offer different accounts of the life of Jesus, they are faithful and without error in sharing the Good News of Jesus Christ. We are the beneficiaries of a much richer understanding of our faith because we have a number of accounts of the Good News. ✝

Attribution

Each of the Gospels is titled "The Gospel According to . . ." with the name inserted: Matthew, Mark, Luke, or John. However, none of these men associated with the four Gospels identifies himself within the Gospel text. The names we associate with each Gospel are attributions to Apostles or apostolic men, often established by early Church fathers.

Papias, a bishop in Asia Minor, attributed Matthew's Gospel to Matthew, Jesus' Apostle. Papias also attributed Mark's Gospel to John Mark, a companion of Barnabas and Paul whom we read about in the Acts of the Apostles. Irenaeus, a bishop in Gaul, attributed the Gospel of Luke to Luke, a fellow traveler of Paul. Irenaeus also attributed the Gospel of John to John, an Apostle of Jesus.

The attribution of a Gospel to a respected and revered teacher was considered a great compliment to that teacher and in itself a proclamation of the authenticity of the account. It may also have been a tribute to the person to whom a particular faith community owed the origins of its faith in Jesus. "Authorship by attribution" was common in the ancient world, in which personal intellectual property was less important than recognition of the origins of a body of thought.

Part Review

1. What are the three stages in the formation of the Gospels?

2. Explain some of the forms that the preaching of the Gospel message took during the oral tradition stage.

3. What is the difference between a canonical Scripture text and an apocryphal account?

4. Why are there similarities among the synoptic Gospels?

5. Why are there differences among the synoptic Gospels?

6. When reading a passage from one of the Gospels, why is it helpful to know something about the Evangelist's audience?

7. What is the meaning of *attribution* in our understanding of the authorship of the Gospels?

Part 2

The Gospel of Mark

It was early morning, before dawn. Jesus, who was living in Capernaum, a seaside town on the shores of the Sea of Galilee, left his house and went off to a quiet spot and prayed. Simon Peter and the other disciples followed him, and, when they found him, Simon Peter said to Jesus, "Everyone is looking for you" (Mark 1:37).

Who is this Jesus that everyone was looking for—and still seeks today? The Gospel of Mark gives us a compelling picture of an energetic, compassionate, powerful man who is, at the same time, the Divine Son of God.

As we have learned previously, the Gospel of Mark is the earliest Gospel. From the very first line, this account calls itself "the gospel of Jesus Christ, the Son of God." From the beginning this account identifies itself as the Good News about Jesus, the Christ (meaning "Anointed One" or "Messiah"), Son of God. Mark affirms the truth that Jesus is both true God and true man. The self-offering of Jesus, in suffering and death, results in his glorious victory—of Resurrection, Ascension, and eternal life—and ours.

The articles in this part unfold the various aspects of Mark's Gospel and the ways he, under the inspiration of the Holy Spirit, communicated the Good News about Jesus to his community of persecuted Christians who were being asked to die for their faith in Jesus.

The articles in this part address the following topics:

© Manolis Grigoreas / Private Collection / Malva Gallery / The Bridgeman Art Library

An Overview of the Gospel of Mark

The Gospel of Mark	
Inspired author:	a Jewish Christian, traditionally attributed to a disciple of Peter named John Mark
Approximate date of writing:	AD 65–70. This was the first written Gospel.
Location of writing:	most likely Rome
Audience:	non-Jewish Christians in Rome who were experiencing persecution for their belief in Jesus
Image of Jesus:	healer and miracle worker who accepts suffering as the cost of following God's will
Genealogy:	none
Themes:	Jesus as Suffering Servant and Messiah, Son of Man and Son of God, miracles and controversies with Pharisees
Sources:	oral and written tradition
Symbol of Gospel:	lion, a desert animal with a loud roar, because the Gospel begins with the quote from Isaiah, "a voice of one crying out in the desert" (1:3) (meaning John the Baptist)

A Glance at the Gospel
Mark 1:1–13: preparation for the public ministry of Jesus
Mark 1:14—8:26: the mystery of Jesus
Mark 8:27—9:32: the mystery begins to be revealed
Mark 9:33—16:8: the full revelation of the mystery
Mark 16:9–20: the longer ending
Mark 16:20: the shorter ending

Article 13 The Miracles in Mark's Gospel

Of the sixteen chapters in the Gospel of Mark, each of the first ten includes one or more *miracles* of Jesus, such as healing people who are lame or restoring sight to those who are blind. The Greek word that Mark, as well as the other Evangelists, used for these miraculous events is *dynameis*, the root word for our word *dynamite*. These miracles, or "acts of power," as *dynameis* is often translated, were events through which people encountered the power and presence of God. Jesus demonstrated that he had power over illness, evil spirits, forces of nature, even over death itself.

Miracles were part and parcel of Jesus' preaching about the coming of the Kingdom of God. In Mark, when Jesus begins his public ministry, the first words he says are: "This is the time of fulfillment. The kingdom of God is at hand. Repent, and believe in the gospel" (1:15). Then Mark tells us that Jesus cured a man possessed by unclean spirits, as well as Simon Peter's mother-in-law and many others in the town. Jesus' miraculous acts of power as he confronted evil and illness gave authority to his words.

However, these acts of power were sometimes a distraction to the message of Jesus. Some people wanted only to be healed, not to hear and believe in the Good News of the Kingdom. For Jesus the preaching itself was more important. After healing many in his hometown of Capernaum, Jesus slipped off before dawn to find a deserted place to pray. His disciples come to look for him and say to him, "Everyone is looking for you" (Mark 1:37). Jesus does not go back to Capernaum; rather, he says: "Let us go on to the nearby villages that I may preach there also. For this purpose have I come" (1:38).

Often Jesus tells people not to talk about his miracles. Why might this be? For instance, Jesus tells a leper whom he has cured to "tell no one" (Mark 1:44). However, the man "spread the report abroad so that it was impossible for Jesus to enter a

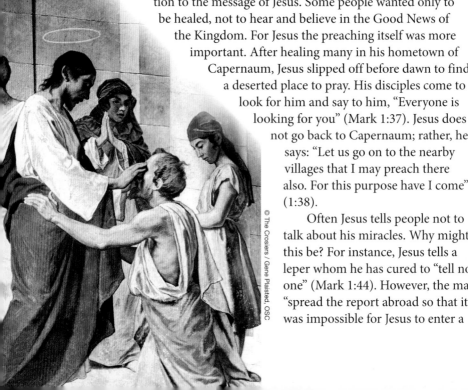

Jesus' healing acts announced the presence of the Kingdom of God. Jesus reaches out to heal the blind man; the blind man reaches out to Jesus also. This painting is from Saints Peter and Paul Cathedral, in Pozna'n, Poland.

© The Crosiers / Gene Plaisted, OSC

town openly" (1:45). When "word of mouth" is at work, the crowds get so great (and perhaps so demanding of his healing power) that Jesus is unable to preach. Thus sometimes the reputation of Jesus as a miracle worker interferes with his opportunity to spread his message of the Kingdom.

Although Jesus performed his miracles as part of his announcement of the coming of the Kingdom of God, the synoptic Gospels recount these miraculous events to center the audience's attention on the identity of Jesus Christ. Accounts of miracles, like many literary genres, have a set form. In these accounts a problem is clearly stated, the problem is brought to Jesus' attention, Jesus is described as solving the problem, and the crowd reacts to Jesus' powerful act. It is in this reaction that our attention is focused on the identity of Jesus Christ as the **Messiah** and Son of God.

For instance, early in his ministry, Jesus is asked to cure a man who is paralyzed. Such a crowd had gathered that the friends of the man could only bring him to Jesus by lowering him through the roof of the house where Jesus was teaching. Jesus' first words are, "Child, your sins are forgiven" (Mark 2:5). This statement causes some **scribes** to ask: "Why does this man speak that way? He is blaspheming. Who but God alone can forgive sins?" (2:7). With this question the scribes put the focus squarely on the identity of Jesus Christ. The dilemma is clear: either Jesus *is* God and *can* forgive sins, or he is only claiming to be able to forgive sin, a blasphemous act.

Jesus responds in a lighthearted manner. He asks which is easier to say: "Your sins are forgiven," or "Rise, pick up your mat and walk" (Mark 2:9). Obviously anyone can *say* either. The question is not what is easier to say but whether one's words have power. Does Jesus have the divine power

Messiah

Hebrew word for "anointed one." The equivalent Greek term is *Christos*. Jesus is the Christ and the Messiah because he is the Anointed One.

scribes

People associated with the Pharisees or Sadducees who were skilled copyists, professional letter writers, and interpreters and teachers of the Law.

Catholic Wisdom

True God and True Man

In our human minds, we might wrongly picture Jesus as divided in half, part God and part man, or as two persons, one human and the other God. We must change our picture to the true one: Jesus Christ is true God and true man, united in one Divine Person. "For this reason he is the one and only mediator" between God and the human race (CCC, 480). This union of the divine and human natures in the one Person of the Word of God is called the mystery of the Incarnation.

to forgive sins? If so, who is this Jesus? After Jesus asks his question, he says, "But that you may know that the Son of Man has authority to forgive sins on earth" (2:10). He continues by saying to the paralytic, "Rise, pick up your mat, and go home" (2:11). When the paralytic does rise and pick up his mat, the crowd reacts with astonishment, saying, "We have never seen anything like this" (2:12). Jesus has proven his spiritual authority and power (to forgive sins) by manifesting his authority and power over nature (by healing a paralysis). If Jesus can heal, then he can also forgive sins. But

Son of God and Son of Man

Have you ever asked yourself why, if the Gospels are teaching that Jesus Christ is the Son of God, Jesus is so often referred to by the title **Son of Man**? In the synoptic Gospels, this is the only messianic title Jesus uses in reference to himself. As he begins his Gospel, Mark writes, "The beginning of the gospel of Jesus Christ [the Son of God]" (Mark 1:1). In Mark's account of the healing of the paralytic, we read Jesus' words: "But that you may know that the Son of Man has authority to forgive sins on earth" (2:10). Thus, in the Gospel of Mark, we find both titles, Son of God and Son of Man, referring to Jesus. What do these titles mean?

The title Son of God describes a unique relationship Jesus has with the Father. This title teaches that Jesus is God's only Son and that Jesus is God himself. The title Son of Man is a messianic title taken from the Book of Daniel (see 7:9–14). This Son of Man comes on the clouds of Heaven, receives glory and kingship from God, and is given everlasting dominion. The title Son of Man signals that, no matter what his sufferings for the sake of the Kingdom, Jesus will ultimately triumph.

The Feast of Christ the King, celebrated on the last Sunday of Ordinary Time, includes, in cycle B, this very reading from the Book of Daniel (see 7:13–14). This feast was instituted to remind us that earthly glory will pass away, but the glory and kingship of Jesus Christ, Son of God and Son of Man, will last forever.

only God can forgive sins. So, if Jesus can do what only God can do, Jesus must be divine.

As you read about the miracles in Mark's Gospel, indeed in all three of the synoptic Gospels, notice the form. (The miracles in the Gospel of John take a different form because they have a different purpose, which we will discuss when we discuss that Gospel.) Notice the crowd's reaction. Ask yourself, What does this account teach me about the identity of Jesus Christ? It teaches Jesus' true identity as the Son of God, truly God and truly man, and that his miraculous acts of power have been handed down from the Apostles to every generation, under the guidance of the Holy Spirit, until Christ returns in glory. ✝

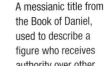

Son of Man
A messianic title from the Book of Daniel, used to describe a figure who receives authority over other nations from God; the only messianic title in the Gospels used by Jesus to describe himself.

Article 14 The Parables in Mark's Gospel

Of the three synoptic Gospels, Mark's has the fewest number of parables. On the whole, Mark's Gospel tells us far less about what Jesus taught than do the Gospels of Matthew and Luke. Most of the sayings of Jesus that Mark does include are in the context of Jesus' controversies with the Pharisees. These controversies give a partial answer to a question central to Mark's Gospel: Why did Jesus have to die?

However, Mark does give us a few of Jesus' parables, enough to give us the opportunity to learn the definition of a parable, why there is some confusion about the difference between a parable and an allegory, and why knowing the difference is important. This knowledge is essential to not only our understanding of Mark's Gospel but also to our understanding of the Gospels of Matthew and of Luke.

What Is a Parable?

In the context of the New Testament, a **parable** is a story that Jesus tells his listeners in order to call them to self-knowledge and conversion. This kind of story uses everyday images, or comparisons and metaphors, to teach a particular message or to invite a response from the listener. A parable is always told in the middle of a conversation. In order to correctly understand what Jesus is teaching through a parable, we must notice to whom

In this modern stained-glass art by Susan Pratt-Smith, Jesus is teaching a diverse group of people—all ages and all races. Try writing your own parable for this group.

© The Crosiers / Gene Plaisted, OSC

parable

A story intended to call a particular audience to self-knowledge and conversion through an implicit comparison of the audience to someone or something in the story; the use of parables as invitations to choose the Kingdom of God was a central feature of Jesus' teaching ministry.

allegory

A literary form in which something is said to be like something else, in an attempt to communicate a hidden or symbolic meaning.

Jesus is speaking, what has already been said, and how that particular audience compares to someone or something in the parable. The lesson of the parable will be drawn from that comparison.

For instance, Jesus tells the Parable of the Sower to a large crowd (see Mark 4:1–8). In this parable a sower sows seed in all kinds of ground: some rocky, some weedy, some fertile. To interpret the parable, we identify the audience: a crowd. We ask, To what in the story does the audience compare? The crowd compares to the soil that has different degrees of receptivity. Jesus is teaching his listeners to be good soil, to let his Word take root in them so they can bear much fruit.

What Is an Allegory?

An **allegory** is a story or literary genre in which more than one level of meaning must be grasped in order to understand the story's literal sense. Understanding the literal sense is the basis for understanding the spiritual sense of Scripture. In an allegory the plot elements express one level of meaning, but all of the elements stand for something else. In order to understand what an author intends to convey through allegorical writing, this additional deeper level of meaning must be discerned. It is important to recognize that the literary genre referred to as "allegory," which you have no doubt studied in English class, is distinct from the spiritual sense of Scripture referred to as the allegorical sense, which discerns in the Old Testament prefigurations of what God has accomplished in Jesus Christ (see article 7, "Sacred Scripture: A Living Word for Today").

In Mark's Gospel the Parable of the Sower is interpreted as though it were an allegory (see 4:14–20). The original meaning of the parable is that the crowd to whom Jesus was speaking was being challenged to be good soil. In the allegory each element of the parable is given a specific symbolic meaning: the seed stands for the Word of God; rocky ground stands for people who at first accept the Word with joy, but when persecution comes, they fall away; thorny soil stands for people who want other things more than they want the Good News of the Gospel; rich soil stands for those who receive the Word and bear much fruit.

Scripture scholars think that when parables passed through oral tradition many of them were separated from their original contexts. Allegorical sermons were built on parables, and some of these allegorical interpretations of parables were included in the Gospels and attributed to Jesus. Obviously many parables lend themselves to allegorical interpretation. The Parable of the Sower is an obvious example, and such an interpretation helps the audience to understand its meaning.

The Parable of the Tenants in the Vineyard

At the same time, some parables do not lend themselves to allegorical interpretation, and when people allegorize them, much harm can be done. Why? Let us look to the Parable of the Tenants (see Mark 12:1–9) as an example. If this parable

Teaching in Parables

Teaching in parables was part of Jesus' Semitic tradition. The famous parable told to King David by the Prophet Nathan in the Old Testament shows that this tradition was at least a thousand years old. King David had committed adultery with Uriah's wife, Bathsheba, and then made sure that Uriah, a soldier in David's army, would be killed in battle. The Prophet Nathan confronted David with these terrible sins, telling him the Parable of the Rich Man, about a rich man who stole and slaughtered his poor neighbor's only ewe lamb in order to offer hospitality to the rich man's guest (see 2 Samuel 12:1–14). David, not realizing that the story was about him, was outraged. He replied in anger: "As the LORD lives, the man who has done this deserves death! He shall make fourfold restitution for the lamb because he has done this and was unsparing" (12:5–6). Nathan then told David, "You are the man!" (12:7). David understood and repented.

Another reason for Jesus' teaching in parables is that it is a wonderful way to call a defensive audience to self-knowledge and conversion. Why? Because initially the listeners do not realize that the story is about them, so they pass judgment on the characters. Only in hindsight do they realize they have passed judgment on themselves.

© Adrian Burke/Corbis

is interpreted allegorically, the vineyard owner in the story is seen to stand for God, and the owner is cruel. Such a misinterpretation leaves one with a negative image of God.

Jesus tells this parable to the chief priests, scribes, and elders who are questioning his authority (see Mark 11:27–33). In this parable the vineyard owner, concerned about his vineyard, sends his servants to take care of it. But the tenants kill the servants. Finally, the owner sends his own beloved son, thinking, "They will respect my son" (12:6). But the tenants give the son no respect at all. In fact, they kill him too, and expect to receive his inheritance. Jesus then asks, "What [then] will the owner of the vineyard do? He will come, put the tenants to death, and give the vineyard to others" (12:9). The chief priests, scribes, and elders realize the parable is addressed to them (see 12:12). What is Jesus teaching them?

The wicked tenants who kill the son of the vineyard owner compare to the audience, the adversaries of Jesus. But the vineyard owner who simply kills the tenants cannot be compared to God. This parable is not intended to define God but rather to warn the specific audience to whom Jesus is speaking about the consequences of rejecting God's Son and his message. If we used this parable as an allegory to define God, this allegorical interpretation would be harmful to our understanding of God.

In fact, Jesus is spending time teaching his enemies, those who want to silence him, and by that very act is lovingly inviting them to repent and choose the Kingdom, just as he is lovingly inviting everyone else to repent and choose the Kingdom. Jesus is also teaching his adversaries that by their own actions, they are rejecting both him and the Kingdom of God. Those who reject Jesus and his message will be left outside the Kingdom. But this is the result of the choices they themselves have made. ✝

In *The Denial of Saint Peter* (1879), by Ferdinand Graf von Harrach, Peter bows his head in stubbornness and shame, turning his back on Jesus, as Jesus looks on sadly. Note the rooster in the tree and see Mark 14:30.

Article 15 Mark's Passion Narrative

As you know, one of the reasons for the uniqueness of each Gospel is that the Gospels have different audiences. As you've already read, Mark's Gospel was most probably written in Rome, around the years AD 65–70, to Christians who were facing persecution. Imagine that you were a Christian living in Rome at that time, faced with a choice between denying your faith or being persecuted, jailed, or even martyred. Can you imagine saying to yourself: "I don't think Jesus would really want me to die for him. After all, Jesus healed people. He said that it is what is in the heart, not just what is on the lips, that is important. If I deny Jesus with my lips, Jesus will know I am not denying him with my heart. Martyrdom is really too much to ask. It wasn't as hard for Jesus as it would be for me because Jesus was God."

If you were to think this way and then to read Mark's Gospel, you would know that you were wrong. You would realize that to abandon Jesus by denying your faith in him is wrong. You would realize that your idea—Jesus' accepting death was easier for him because he was God—was wrong. Mark teaches all these truths, which are responsive to the needs of his audience, by the way he describes the Paschal Mystery of Jesus—his Passion, death, Resurrection, and Ascension.

Abandoned by His Disciples

As Mark tells it, Jesus is abandoned by all as he faces his Passion and death. Judas, the betrayer, is not the only one

Catholic Wisdom

The Jews and the Gospels

Though the Gospels speak of some of "the Jews" as rejecting Christ, they give us no reason to accuse all Jews of sharing in responsibility for the death of Jesus. The United States bishops remind us of our common purpose: "It is the mission of the Church, as also that of the Jewish people, to proclaim and to work to prepare the world for the full flowering of God's Reign, which is, but is 'not yet'. . . . Both Christianity and Judaism seal their worship with a common hope: 'Thy kingdom come!'" (USCCB, God's Mercy Endures Forever, 11)

Abandoned by God?

Did Jesus feel abandoned even by God as he was dying on the cross? At first glance we might be inclined to say yes. However, that answer fails to take into consideration the fact that "My God, my God, why have you forsaken me?"(Mark 15:34) are the first words of Psalm 22, which is a lament. A lament is a distinct literary form. Laments begin with a call to God and a cry for help, but they then move on to an expression of trust, a petition, and a song of praise or a promise to praise God.

Psalm 22 follows this pattern. After the call to God and a cry for help, the psalmist remembers:

> Yet you are enthroned as the Holy One;
>> you are the glory of Israel.
> In you our fathers trusted;
>> they trusted and you rescued them.
>
>> (Verses 4–5)

As the psalm ends, the psalmist proclaims:

> The generation to come will be told of the Lord,
>> that they may proclaim to a people yet unborn
>> the deliverance you have brought.
>
>> (Verse 32)

Rather than portraying Jesus as feeling abandoned, Mark portrays Jesus as beginning a prayer to his Father that ends in trust and praise.

© Sandro Vannini/CORBIS

who abandons him. All of the Apostles do. During his agony in the garden, Jesus tells Peter and John that his "soul is sorrowful even to death" (Mark 14:34) and asks them to watch and pray with him. Three times they fail to do this. Jesus is so distraught that he falls on the ground, begging his Father: "Take this cup away from me, but not what I will but what you will" (14:36). When the arresting soldiers arrive, all of Jesus' disciples flee (see 14:50). One disciple is anxious to get away from Jesus so quickly that his clothing comes undone and he runs away naked (see 14:51–52).

Sanhedrin

An assembly of Jewish religious leaders—chief priests, scribes, and elders—who functioned as the supreme council and tribunal during the time of Jesus.

Abandoned by the Courts and the Crowds

All the members of the **Sanhedrin** abandon Jesus. They do not try to find the truth and do what is right; rather, "the chief priests and the entire Sanhedrin kept trying to obtain testimony against Jesus in order to put him to death" (Mark 14:55). After listening to false testimony, "they all condemned him as deserving to die" (14:64). It is in the courtyard of the high priest that Peter denies Jesus three times. The third time "he began to curse and to swear, 'I do not know this man about whom you are talking'" (14:71).

Pilate, the crowds, and the soldiers all abandon Jesus. Pilate does not find Jesus guilty of sedition (or treason—for claiming to be the Messiah, and thus a king and rival to the Roman emperor), but, in order to please the crowd, Pilate

Pray It!

Facing the Hard Times

Lord, you really *do* know what it is like to be beaten, teased, pushed around, and rejected. If you could put up with this torment, then maybe there is hope for others who feel the same way at times—those who are made fun of or rejected because of the way they look or act or for what they believe in, or those who feel all alone or that no one understands what they are feeling.

I know that you understand, Lord, when I feel these things. You walked this difficult path even before we did. You have been there. You show us a way through these tough times.

Lord, give me the strength to overcome despair. Give me faith to abandon myself into the Father's hands as you did. Give me the courage to talk to a trusted adult when I am in pain or confused. Give me hope to see a new life beyond these moments of pain and hopelessness. Amen.

centurion

The commander of a unit of approximately one hundred Roman soldiers.

turns Jesus over to be crucified. The soldiers mock Jesus as "King of the Jews." The crowd passing by reviles him. The chief priests taunt him. They wonder why, if Jesus has so much power that he can save others, he cannot save himself. They tempt Jesus by saying, "Let the Messiah, the King of Israel, come down now from the cross that we may see and believe" (Mark 15:32). Not a single person offers Jesus any kind of support or comfort.

Jesus obviously finds this total abandonment very painful. As Jesus dies he cries out, "My God, my God, why have you forsaken me?" (Mark 15:34). It is only after Jesus has died that words of faith are spoken, and they come from a most unlikely source. A Roman **centurion** who was standing at the foot of the cross says, "Truly this man was the Son of God!" (15:39). Mark also tells us: "There were also women looking on from a distance. . . . These women had followed him when he was in Galilee and ministered to him" (15:40–41). Joseph of Arimathea asks for Jesus' body to bury it. However, all these courageous and supportive people and actions are reported only after Jesus has died, died with a deep feeling of abandonment.

By describing Jesus' Passion and death in this way, Mark is teaching his audience that God calls them to remain faithful and accept suffering, even death if necessary, just as Jesus did. Why? Because death is not the end of life. Because of Jesus, death leads to resurrection. ✝

Article 16 The Suffering Messiah

Mark's Gospel addresses one of life's great mysteries: Why was it necessary for Jesus to suffer in order to redeem us? Why was it necessary for Mark's audience to suffer just as Jesus did? Why is suffering part of our lives? Are we too called to accept suffering?

Mark's Gospel does not explain why suffering seems to be unavoidable.

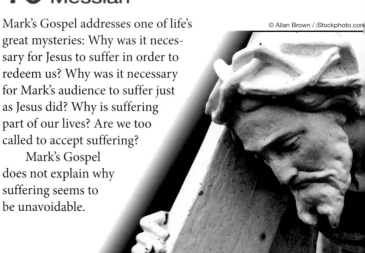

© Allan Brown / iStockphoto.com

However, the Gospel does give purpose to suffering, because Jesus was an innocent person who suffered, and his suffering did not end in death but in eternal life. Mark is encouraging his persecuted audience to follow Jesus through suffering and death so that they too may have eternal life.

Mark's purpose, to teach that the cross was not a defeat but a victory, shapes his Gospel in many ways. In taking on a human nature, Jesus embraces all of human life—both its joys and its sorrows. In bringing God's Kingdom to the world, Jesus opens himself to not only the rejection of his enemies but also the misunderstanding of his friends. Yet this human path of suffering—the path that Jesus, the Son of God, walked—led not only to death but also to ultimate victory, the victory of Resurrection. This is our path as well, and, with Jesus, it will be our victory.

The Humanity of Jesus

There is no question that Mark teaches Jesus' divinity. We have already discussed how he teaches Jesus' divinity from the first sentence, by calling Jesus "the Son of God" (Mark 1:1). Mark also includes the miracles of Jesus as part of this teaching. At the same time, Mark, more than any other Gospel, stresses Jesus' humanity—the ordinary actions and feelings that give human life meaning. Jesus' humanity shows in his compassion to those he heals through his miracles. It is also evident in the way he puts his arms around a child he placed in the midst of the Twelve (see 9:36) and when he embraced the children that had been brought to him to be blessed (see 10:16). Yet Jesus could be irritated with his Apostles' lack of understanding (see 4:13); he could be angry, as he is with those who are buying and selling in the Temple area—to the point of overturning tables and chairs (see 11:15.) He could also be indignant, as when the disciples tried to prevent the children from approaching him (see 10:14), and exasperated, as he is when he curses the fig tree for not bearing fruit (see 11:12–14), even though, as Mark explains, it was not the season for fruit!

The Self-Emptying of Jesus

At the same time, Jesus begins to reveal his identity as Messiah and Son of God to his disciples. While walking down the road to Caesarea Philippi, Jesus asks his disciples, "Who do people say that I am?" (Mark 8:27). The disciples reply that some people think he is John the Baptist (who had been killed by King Herod), others think he is the Prophet Elijah (who by Tradition is to come to announce the Messiah), and yet others think he is one of the prophets. Jesus persists: "But who do you say that I am?" (8:29). Peter is the first to speak up: "You are the Messiah" (8:29).

Then Jesus immediately tells them what kind of Messiah he is. He will be a Messiah who suffers. He will be the Suffering Servant Messiah foreshadowed by the Prophet Isaiah (See Isaiah, chapters 49–55). He will be the kind of Messiah and Christ who will not cling to his divine privileges but who will accept his humanity even to suffering and death. Actually, throughout his ministry Jesus had warned the disciples that he would be put to death. But immediately after Peter's identification of Jesus as Messiah, Jesus explains again that "the Son of Man must suffer greatly and be rejected by the elders, the chief priests, and the scribes, and be killed, and rise after three days" (Mark 8:31).

This was not just terrible news to the disciples; it was incomprehensible. Jesus was using a messianic title in referring to himself as the Son of Man. The Son of Man was the one to whom God would give authority over other nations: "His kingship . . . shall not be destroyed" (Daniel 7:14).

Live It!

Your Way of the Cross

What does "taking up the cross" mean in our Christian lives? It means denying the sometimes misguided ways of the world and embracing the way of Jesus. It means tough self-sacrifice and a willingness to suffer for what is right.

But what does it mean to deny ourselves and take up our own crosses? It means we cannot be fooled by mistaken notions of what it means to be truly alive. We hear too many messages suggesting that happiness comes from wealth, power, prestige, or selfish pleasure. But those things actually make us feel less alive and more anxious.

Taking up our own crosses means being willing to cling to the right things—love, forgiveness, justice, service, and compassion for those who are poor and those who are unpopular—even if it brings us suffering and pain. Being committed to Jesus and these virtues or "right things" will bring us real life, true freedom, joy, and inner peace.

Jesus was supposed to conquer the Romans, not be killed by them! What kind of Son of Man was this?

Peter does not accept this Suffering Messiah, a messiah who would be rejected and then give up his very life. Taking Jesus aside, Peter challenges him and "began to rebuke him" (Mark 8:32). Can you imagine this conversation? Can you imagine Peter's explaining to Jesus that this idea of a Suffering Servant Messiah is all wrong? When Peter argues with him, Jesus says to Peter: "Get behind me, Satan. You are thinking not as God does, but as human beings do" (8:33). (The root of the word *Satan* is the Greek word for "obstacle.") Why would Jesus speak so harshly to Peter? Evidently Jesus experienced Peter's words as a temptation. Jesus did not want to suffer and die, but he knew that avoiding such treatment would mean failing in his mission to proclaim the Good News and to redeem us from sin and death. Jesus had to continue his preaching, accompanied by his miracles, and accept the consequences.

Jesus then teaches his disciples that they must do the same. Jesus says: "Whoever wishes to come after me must deny himself, take up his cross, and follow me. For whoever wishes to save his life will lose it, but whoever loses his life for my sake and that of the gospel will save it" (Mark 8:34–35). Mark has placed this scene right in the middle of his Gospel. It is his core message for his persecuted audience. In order to save their lives, they too must pick up their crosses and follow Jesus.

The Disciples: Failing to Understand

Mark continues to emphasize the disciples' complete inability to understand as he portrays Jesus' warning them two more times that he is going to be killed. With the second warning, Mark tells us that the disciples "did not understand the saying, and they were afraid to question him" (Mark 9:32). The third time Jesus tells the Twelve about his Passion, death, and Resurrection, the Apostles get in an argument with one another, wanting positions of power when Jesus comes into his glory. One can only imagine the exasperation Jesus felt as he explained to the Apostles that whoever wants to be first among them must be a servant (see 10:32–45).

Why would Mark emphasize Jesus' humanity, especially his suffering and death, as well as the Apostles' inability to understand what Jesus had tried so hard to teach them? Despite all his efforts, what had Jesus accomplished? Even his chosen friends, his handpicked messengers of the Kingdom, had completely failed to understand his mission. Why would Mark stress such failure?

Mark wants his persecuted audience to be able to identify with Jesus. Like Jesus, they too may be suffering the frustration of having to face death before they have accomplished what they wanted to accomplish in their lives. These persecuted Christians, like Jesus, faced death every day, and

The Ending of Mark's Gospel

The work of biblical scholars indicates that Mark's *Gospel* originally ended with chapter 16, verse 8, and that the longer ending, which includes the appearance to Mary Magdalene, the commissioning of the Twelve, and the Ascension, was added later, sometime before the second century. (This longer ending is a summary reflecting traditions found in Luke and in John.) Why would Mark's *Gospel* have ended originally by telling us that Mary Magdalene and her companions "said nothing to anyone" (Mark 16:8) about the empty tomb and the news that Jesus had been raised? This is all the more unusual, as they had been specifically instructed by the angel at the tomb to tell Jesus' disciples and Peter to go to Galilee where they would see Jesus themselves.

Perhaps Mark ended his *Gospel* so abruptly in order to leave his persecuted readers with a challenge. Because they are Christians, they too are called to be witnesses to Jesus Christ. Will they, out of fear for their lives also say "nothing to anyone" (Mark 16:8), or will they proclaim their faith in Christ, remain faithful to him, be witnesses of the Good News, and follow Jesus through death to life?

And what of ourselves? What keeps us from proclaiming and living our faith in Christ? fear of criticism? indifference? laziness? How are we called to follow Jesus from death to life?

possibly faced, like Jesus, the misunderstanding and rejection of others for being so foolish as to give up their lives for the Kingdom of God. Mark wants these faithful Christians to look beyond the "failure" of death and misunderstanding to see the victory Jesus won for them in his Resurrection. Now, after the Resurrection, Mark wants his audience to believe and, finally, to understand.

This failure to understand persists to our own day, and we can recognize it in ourselves as well. We do not understand how suffering and death can lead to life. We do not understand why suffering continues to be a part of our lives and the lives of those we love. Nevertheless, in the midst of the joys and sorrows of human life, we, like Jesus, are called to trust in God's boundless love. Jesus trusted his Father, accepted death, and did, indeed, rise on the third day. He promises us the same glorious ending, if we take up our cross, our own sufferings, large or small, and follow him. ✝

Part Review

1. Why did Jesus perform miracles?

2. Why did the early Church repeat accounts of Jesus' performing miracles?

3. What is a parable?

4. What is an allegory?

5. Why is it sometimes misleading to interpret a parable as an allegory?

6. To whom is Mark writing? What questions are on Mark's audience's mind?

7. What does Mark emphasize in his Passion narrative? How is this emphasis responsive to the needs of his audience?

8. In what way does Mark's Gospel give purpose to suffering?

Part 3

The Gospel of Matthew

The Gospel of Matthew is the first book of the New Testament, but we know now that the Gospel of Mark was the first Gospel written. Why, then, does Matthew's Gospel retain its place of honor?

The Gospel of Matthew is the opening book of the New Testament because at one time it was thought to have been the first written, but also because, at its beginning, it connects the life and teachings of Jesus most immediately to the writings of the Old Testament through the genealogy. In addition, this Gospel captures for the Church a picture of Jesus, the Son of God and Teacher of the New Law, that has been highly esteemed through the centuries. Of the four Gospels, this was the most popular Gospel in the early Church.

In the Gospel of Matthew, Jesus is the New Moses, who teaches God's Law of love and forgiveness. In this Gospel, Jesus is the Teacher who, in word and action, in discourses, parables, and miracles, points to the presence of the Kingdom of God here and now, and also urges his listeners to prepare for the coming of the Kingdom of God in the future. This is the Teacher whose words and actions—especially through his suffering, death, and Resurrection—point to the divine power and authority alive in him.

The articles in this part trace the themes of the Gospel of Matthew from their beginnings, through the teaching of the New Law of the Kingdom, to the authority of Jesus and, finally, to the summary of these themes in the account of the Passion, death, and Resurrection of Jesus.

The articles in this part address the following topics:

An Overview of the Gospel of Matthew

The Gospel of Matthew	
Inspired author:	unknown; most likely a Jewish Christian; traditionally attributed to the Apostle Matthew
Approximate date of writing:	AD 85
Location of writing:	probably Antioch, the capital of Syria
Audience:	a mixed community of primarily Jewish Christians, with Gentiles
Image of Jesus:	Jesus as the New Moses and Teacher of the New Law
Genealogy:	traced Jesus back to Abraham, the father of the Jewish nation
Themes:	In bringing a New Covenant, Jesus, who is the Messiah, fulfills the Old Covenant. Jesus has authority from God to initiate the New Covenant, and he passes this authority on to his Apostles.
Sources:	The Gospel of Mark, Q, and the M Source (Matthew's independent source)
Symbol of Gospel:	a man, symbolizing the genealogy of Jesus' human origins with which the Gospel begins

A Glance at the Gospel
Matthew 1:1—2:23: the infancy narrative
Matthew 3:1—7:29: the proclamation of the Kingdom
Matthew 8:1—11:1: ministry and mission in Galilee
Matthew 11:2—13:53: opposition from Israel
Matthew 13:54—18:35: Jesus, the Kingdom, and the Church
Matthew 19:1—25:46: ministry in Judea and Jerusalem
Matthew 26:1—28:20: the Passion and Resurrection

Article 17 Matthew's Infancy Narrative

© Anyka / Shutterstock.com

In Matthew's Gospel, the Magi, as Gentiles, did not know Scripture. Yet they found the Messiah through knowledge of creation. We celebrate the "showing" of the Savior to the Gentiles on the Solemnity of the Epiphany.

When Matthew wrote his Gospel, he did not think, "I am writing a Gospel for the New Testament." Matthew was a Jewish Christian. His audience was also made up of Jewish Christians, but Gentiles were becoming more prominent in this community. Matthew wanted to demonstrate that being a disciple of Jesus Christ was completely compatible with being a faithful Jew because Jesus was the fulfillment of God's promises to the Israelites. Matthew also wanted to help his fellow Jews to accept that Gentiles were welcome to become followers of Jesus and to join the community.

One way Matthew conveys the universality of Jesus' call is through an **infancy narrative**, which captures known historical elements and combines them with interpretation that teaches us the identity and significance of Jesus from a post-Resurrection perspective. This infancy narrative is another literary form of the kind discussed in section 1. It is written after someone has died, to teach the significance of that person's life.

Two of the Gospel writers, Matthew and Luke, include infancy narratives in their Gospels. The infancy narratives teach the significance of Jesus' birth as it was understood in light of the Resurrection. Both the writers and the audience already know that Jesus is the Son of God who died and rose for their salvation; the infancy narratives help the audience to deepen their understanding of Jesus' human and divine natures.

Matthew's infancy narrative includes a genealogy and the announcement of the birth of Jesus to Joseph. It also includes some details that appear in no other Gospel: the Magi who follow the star, the flight into Egypt, the massacre of the infants, and the return from Egypt.

Genealogy

In order to teach that Jesus is truly the son of Abraham and son of David, Matthew ties his Gospel to the Old Testament by beginning with a genealogy: "The book of the genealogy of Jesus Christ, the son of David, the son of Abraham" (Matthew 1:1). Abraham, who lived about 1850 BC, is, of course, the Israelites' father in faith. His covenant with God begins the saving acts of God toward the Chosen People, and this people's promise of faithfulness, about which we read in the Old Testament (see Genesis, chapters 12–25).

infancy narratives
The accounts of Jesus' birth and early life.

It is important for this Gospel to note that Jesus is a true descendant of King David and thus a "son of David." For this reason Matthew, spanning Israelite history, names fourteen patriarchs, fourteen kings, and finally fourteen other men, ending with Joseph. Although this genealogy traces the ancestry of Joseph (who was of the house and family of David), it does not present Joseph as the biological father of Jesus. The genealogy concludes with this: "Jacob the father of Joseph, the husband of Mary. Of her was born Jesus who is called the Messiah" (Matthew 1:16). Joseph adopted Jesus by taking him into his home as his son and naming him, thus making Jesus a descendant of David. For this reason Jesus is of the house of David, and thus the Son of David. Jesus is the fulfillment of the promises God has made to Abraham, to David, and to the whole people of Israel throughout their history.

In his genealogy Matthew also names five female ancestors of Jesus, four from the Old Testament: Tamar, Rahab, Ruth, Bathsheba (Uriah's wife), and Mary. Only Matthew includes these women in his genealogy. Of these five women, the first three were Gentiles, the fourth was married to a Gentile, and only Mary is Jewish. Matthew may have included these women to prepare his audience to accept Gentile converts into the Christian community. If Gentiles were ancestors of Jesus, they certainly could be welcomed into the Christian faith.

The Annunciation to Joseph

When we refer to the annunciation, we usually mean the Annunciation by the Angel Gabriel to Mary that she had been chosen to be the Mother of God. That Annunciation is recounted in the Gospel of Luke. Matthew's birth narrative includes an annunciation, or announcement, to Joseph. Mary does not come on stage; we simply hear about her. In this announcement Joseph (who was disturbed to learn of Mary's pregnancy) is told by an angel that Mary has conceived her child through the Holy Spirit, that he is to take Mary into his home, and is to name the child Jesus "because he will save his people from their sins" (Matthew 1:21). The name Jesus means "God saves." Joseph is assured that all this is happening for God's good reasons, to fulfill the words of the Prophet Isaiah: "'Behold, the virgin shall be with child and bear a son, / and they shall name him Emmanuel,' / which means 'God is with us'" (Matthew 1:23).

Here Matthew cites one of the many Old Testament passages—Isaiah 7:14—fulfilled by Jesus Christ. The inspired authors of the infancy narratives drew on the Old Testament in order to convey important truths about Jesus. Around their accounts of the events of Jesus' birth, these inspired authors wove elements that are allusions to Old Testament texts. When we recognize the allusions, we gain a deeper understanding of the significance of Jesus' birth.

For instance, the account of the Magi (from Gentile nations) who follow a star, bringing gifts of gold, frankincense, and myrrh is an allusion to the Book of the Prophet Isaiah, chapter 60, in which God's People (at the time exiled in Babylon) are assured that people from all over the world will come to honor them:

Arise! Shine, for your light has come,
the glory of the LORD has dawned upon you.

Nations shall walk by your light,
kings by the radiance of your dawning.

the wealth of nations shall come to you.

All from Sheba shall come
bearing gold and frankincense,
and heralding the praises of the LORD.

And you shall know that I, the LORD, am your savior,
your redeemer, the Mighty One of Jacob.

(Isaiah 60:1,3,5,6,16)

Matthew's Use of the Old Testament

The other elements unique to the birth narrative in Matthew include allusions to the Old Testament. Joseph, saving his family by fleeing to Egypt, recalls a previous Joseph, the patriarch who was sold into slavery in Egypt by his brothers and who later saved his whole family from starvation (see Genesis, chapters 37–50). The reason for the flight into Egypt (the massacre of the children) recalls the massacre of the children at the time of Moses' birth (see Exodus 1:1—2:10). Matthew's infancy narrative makes clear that Jesus is the New Moses who was saved from Herod's decree of death, just as Moses was saved from pharaoh's decree that all male Jewish infants should be killed.

Matthew's account of the flight into Egypt also shows that Jesus fulfills God's promises to his people. The account states that Joseph, with the child and his mother, stayed in Egypt until King Herod's death, "that what the Lord had said through the prophet might be fulfilled, 'Out of Egypt I called my son'" (Matthew 2:15). Here Matthew quotes from Hosea 11:1. The quote from Hosea referred to the people of Israel as "God's son." With this citation Matthew identifies Jesus with the people of Israel. Like them, he too was led into the desert, symbolic of the Exodus experience of the people of Israel, then called out of it by God. The sonship of Jesus, however, is not as part of a nation that claims God as their Father. The sonship of Jesus is unique. As unique Son of God, Jesus will represent God's People and thus save them. The meaning of this sonship is gradually elucidated throughout the Gospel.

By alluding to the history of Israel and the Israelite's great ancestors in faith, Matthew is teaching his Jewish audience what was fully understood only after the Resurrection: As son of Abraham, son of David, son of Joseph and Mary, and especially as Son of God, Jesus is the fulfillment of the history of his people. All of God's promises to Israel have been fulfilled through this child, born in Bethlehem.

By alluding to Isaiah in the infancy narrative, Matthew is teaching that God's promises to Israel have been fulfilled in Jesus Christ. Herod and all those troubled by the message of the Magi foreshadow the ultimate rejection of Jesus as Messiah by the majority of the Jewish nation and his ultimate acceptance by the Gentiles ("the nations" symbolized by the Magi). Through Jesus, who was an Israelite, all nations (Gentiles) have come to recognize their Lord. ✝

Article 18 The Kingdom in Matthew's Gospel

In Matthew's Gospel, Jesus begins his public ministry by preaching: "Repent, for the kingdom of heaven is at hand" (4:17). In the parallel passage in Mark, Jesus says: "This is the time of fulfillment. The kingdom of God is at hand. Repent, and believe in the gospel" (1:15). Matthew's *kingdom of heaven* and Mark's *kingdom of God* are referring to the same reality. Mark, writing for Gentile Christians, refers to God by name. Matthew, out of respect for his fellow Jews' deep reverence for God and their hesitation to mention God directly, uses the phrase *kingdom of heaven*. What does Jesus mean by using the word *kingdom*?

The word *kingdom* is a metaphor, a comparison. Metaphors are often used to explore mysteries that are beyond our comprehension. By comparing the reality he is proclaiming to a kingdom, Jesus is relying on his listeners' knowledge of earthly kingdoms. Based on their own experience of their kingdom under King David, they know that a kingdom is the place where the king's rule reigns. Their idea of a kingdom is a geopolitical reality, not a spiritual reality. In using the word *kingdom*, Jesus is preparing his listeners and his disciples, then and now, to make the leap from this geopolitical reality to the reality of God's Kingdom.

Jesus used everyday images from the natural world in his teaching. To find his teachings using the image of a mustard seed, or of fields ready for harvest, read Matthew 13:1–9, 18–23, 24–30, and 31–32.

© melhi / iStockphoto.com

Kingdom in the Lord's Prayer

Jesus was not preaching about a kingdom like David's, but about God's Kingdom. God's Kingdom would be a place where his will would reign. Jesus makes this clear when he teaches his disciples how to pray. He teaches them a prayer that has been treasured by the Church ever since, called the Lord's Prayer or the Our Father.

In this prayer Jesus addresses God not as his Father alone but as Father to all. We can call on God as "Father" because the Son has revealed him to us.

"Our Father in heaven . . . / your kingdom come, / your will be done" (Matthew 6:9–10).

The lines "your kingdom come" and "your will be done" are an example of **synonymous parallelism**, a common literary device used in Hebrew poetry in which the same idea is expressed in two adjacent lines but in different words. Jesus is teaching that God's Kingdom is present where his will is done. In addition, Jesus teaches that this Kingdom can be present both on earth and in Heaven. The Apostles are to pray: "Your kingdom come, / . . . on earth as in heaven" (Matthew 6:10).

synonymous parallelism

A device used in Hebrew poetry in which the same idea is expressed in two adjacent lines but in different words, thus expanding and emphasizing the idea in a balanced composition.

Pray It!

A Lord's Prayer Reflection

Jesus taught his followers the Lord's Prayer as an alternative to hypocritical and empty prayer. Yet because the Lord's Prayer is so familiar to us, we may need to make an effort to pray it sincerely. Look up these verses in the Gospel, and consider these thoughts when you pray the Lord's Prayer:

- **Matthew 5:9** How do I honor God as the Creator of all things? How do I honor God in my thoughts, words, and actions?
- **Matthew 5:10** How does my life reflect God's Kingdom of love, justice, and peace? Do I put too much emphasis on material things?
- **Matthew 5:11** Can I trust God to provide for my daily physical, emotional, and spiritual needs?
- **Matthew 5:12** When I have sinned, do I admit my wrong, ask God's forgiveness, and start anew? When people have wronged me, do I hold a grudge? Am I able to forgive them as God forgives me?
- **Matthew 5:13** What are the temptations I face in life? How do I rely on God for the strength to resist them?

commission

To commission someone is to send him or her on a mission. Jesus commissioned the Apostles to carry out his mission to the world.

The object of these first three petitions is the Father's glory: reverence toward his holy name, the coming of his Kingdom, and the doing of his will. The four remaining petitions lift up our own needs to the Father who loves us and all his children. We pray for nourishment, for the forgiveness and healing of sin, and for victory in our everyday struggle over evil.

When we pray the Lord's Prayer, we join with Jesus in praying to "our Father" and so share in his dignity of sonship as his own brothers and sisters. This prayer brings us into communion with God the Father and God the Son and increases our will to become like Jesus, our Brother. Each time we pray this prayer, we grow in humility and in trust of the Father who will always love and care for us.

Because of its themes of respect for God's name, longing for God's Kingdom and his will on earth, forgiveness from God as we forgive others, and a final petition to be delivered from temptation and evil, this prayer is "the summary of the whole Gospel"[1] (*CCC*, 2774) and "the quintessential prayer of the Church" (2776).

Parables of the Kingdom

> Particularly in the Gospel of Matthew, Jesus is presented as a teacher. Like the best teachers, he taught in many ways and with his whole being. He taught by word and by example. He taught through his powerful miracles and his quiet prayer alone with his Father. Above all, he taught by his love and respect for all people, especially for those who were poor and powerless. The teaching of Jesus is emphasized in Matthew's Gospel, which for that reason, as well as for its clear organization and memorable images, has been treasured by the Church. (Based on Raymond E. Brown, *Introduction to the New Testament*, page 171)

Following the Resurrection, at the end of this Gospel, Jesus **commissions** his Apostles to become teachers themselves: "Make disciples of all nations . . . teaching them to observe all that I have commanded you" (Matthew 28:19–20).

In teaching his disciples and the people about the Kingdom of Heaven, Jesus tells many stories, or parables, about it. Some of the parables of Matthew can be found in Mark and in Luke. Some may have come from the Q Source we discussed in article 12, "An Overview of the Synoptic Gospels." Some others, unique to Matthew, may have come from a source known only to Matthew, called by scholars the M Source. As we read and listen to these parables, we find ourselves more and more drawn into mystery and paradox—seemingly contradictory statements or situations that expose an underlying truth.

These parables confront certain questions about the Kingdom of Heaven. For instance, what will happen at the end of time? Is the coming of the Kingdom a future startling event that will be seen by everyone, or is it a present subtle growth process that is more easily recognized in hindsight? It seems to be both.

For example, at the end of the Parable of the Weeds among the Wheat, Jesus explains that a judgment is coming: Those who cause others to sin, and all evildoers, will be punished, but "the righteous will shine like the sun in the kingdom of their Father" (Matthew 13:43). But Jesus also compares the coming of the Kingdom to the growth of a mustard seed and to the effect of yeast on a loaf of bread (see 13:31–33). The coming of the Kingdom is not just a spectacular end-time event of judgment but also a slow process of growth in which weeds are growing along with the wheat (see 13:24–30,36–43).

Two additional questions the parables confront are these: How can we enter the Kingdom? Is entrance into the

Live It!

Conversion of Heart

How should one act in order to accept the invitation to the Kingdom? One must repent. Accepting the Kingdom requires a conversion of heart. A conversion is a "turning around," a turning away from sin and evil and a turning toward God—the Father, Son, and Holy Spirit. Action is required: "Not everyone who says to me, 'Lord, Lord,' will enter the kingdom of heaven, but only the one who does the will of my Father in heaven" (Matthew 7:21).

Through the story of the judgment of the nations, Jesus teaches just what is the will of his Father. Read Matthew 25:31–46. Choose one positive action described there. How will you live out that action this week? It is the people who love one another and who live out the Beatitudes (see 5:3–11) who will be welcomed into the Kingdom as true disciples.

Kingdom a gift, or is entrance into the Kingdom something a person must earn? Again we are involved in paradox. Jesus tells the Parable of the Workers in the Vineyard (see Matthew 20:1–16) to Peter as an answer to Peter's question: "We have given up everything and followed you. What will there be for us?" (19:27). In this parable the workers who arrive last and work only one hour are given the same reward as the ones who started early in the morning and worked all day. We, along with the original audience of the parable, might judge this as unfair. Yet Jesus is making a particular point. He is teaching Peter that the Kingdom is not earned. It is a gift to those who follow him as his disciples and do his Father's will on earth.

Still one must respond to the invitation. Through the Parable of the Wedding Feast (see Matthew 22:2–14), Jesus teaches the chief priests and Pharisees, who are rejecting him, that they are refusing the invitation to the Kingdom. These chief priests and Pharisees are also being invited to the Kingdom (the wedding feast), but by refusing to come, they are rejecting Jesus and rejecting the Kingdom.

Another question concerns timing: When will this Kingdom come? The answer again is mysterious and paradoxical. We glimpse the Kingdom here, now, when we follow Jesus as disciples and do the Father's will. But it is not yet fully here. We look forward to the full realization of the Kingdom at the end of time. We see then that the Kingdom that Jesus proclaimed is both an actual Kingdom that is present when we follow him as his disciples and do the Father's will "on earth as it is in heaven," when we care for others, when we choose to forgive. But God's Kingdom is not a material or physical kingdom. It is not a physical place one can point to or journey toward. It is a spiritual and eternal

Catholic Wisdom

The Doxology

A doxology literally means "a word of praise." During the Eucharist we add an ancient doxology to the Lord's Prayer. After we pray the Lord's Prayer together, the priest prays a prayer for peace, for freedom from sin and anxiety, and for hope in the coming of our Savior, Jesus Christ. Then we all join in the doxology: "For the kingdom, the power and the glory are yours, now and for ever" (Roman Missal).

The Kingdom and the Church

The Kingdom of God is the Reign of God, the rule of God, both on earth and in Heaven. The Church, as a gathering of God's People around Jesus Christ, the Son of God, is the "seed and beginning"[2] of this Kingdom (*CCC*, 541), and we enter it through Baptism. Baptism, first and foremost, forgives our sins. It unites us to Christ, who died and was raised for us, and who gave us the Holy Spirit to be our Advocate and Guide. Baptism opens the door to the Church, to the Sacraments, and to the Kingdom of God.

The Church is herself a sign and sacrament of salvation, the means by which God gathers his people together around Christ, his Son. For this reason entrance into the Church through Baptism, birth into the new life of Christ, is necessary for salvation, for all salvation comes from Christ, the Head, through his Body, the Church. We know, however, that this does not mean that only Christians can be saved. All who seek the truth and God's will with sincerity, even if they do not know Christ, are saved through Christ "in a way known to God"[3] (*CCC*, 1260).

Each Sacrament—instituted by Christ and given to the Church—is an efficacious sign of grace, and the visible rites of each Sacrament signify and make present that grace. Through the Sacraments, beginning with Baptism, we are continually strengthened with God's life. If we receive the Sacraments with faith, that life grows within us and bears fruit in loving actions. So, each in our own way, we plant more seeds of the Kingdom of God's love, peace, and joy on earth.

Kingdom. We enter this Kingdom when God's will truly reigns in our lives.

Miracles

In Matthew's Gospel, as in Mark's, Jesus reinforces his teaching about the coming of God's Kingdom and its salvific effect by performing miracles. In addition, Jesus commissions his Apostles to preach the Kingdom with authority just as he does, saying to them: "As you go, make this proclamation: 'The kingdom of heaven is at hand.' Cure the sick, raise the dead, cleanse lepers, drive out demons" (Matthew 10:7–8). Jesus' and the Apostles' miracles, or acts of power, were evidence of the authority with which they preached the Kingdom. We continue this discussion of the authority of Jesus and his extension of that authority to his Apostles in the next article. ✝

Article 19 The Question of Authority

The question of Jesus' authority and the Apostles' authority is important to Matthew and his audience. After all, Matthew is writing to faithful Christian Jews who are coming to terms with the fact that a number of Gentiles are also becoming Christians. These Gentiles don't obey the Jewish Law. Who has the authority to free them of this responsibility?

To make matters more complicated, Jesus, a Jew, was condemned by the Jewish leaders and handed over by them to a Roman court for crucifixion. If Jesus was truly the fulfillment of God's covenant promises to the Israelites, why was the Sanhedrin so disapproving of him? Obviously, Jesus threatened some of the Jewish leaders' authority and their interpretation of the Law of Moses. Who was Jesus to reinterpret the Law, to criticize their interpretation? Where did he get his authority to do this? Where did the early Church leaders get their authority?

Matthew, throughout his Gospel, responds to these questions by addressing the question of authority. Matthew presents Jesus as the New Moses, who has authority from God to promulgate the New Law. We have already seen Jesus' identity as the Son of God expressed through the infancy narrative (see Matthew, chapters 1–2). In addition, the allusions to Moses begin in the infancy narrative, especially with Matthew's reference to the slaughtering of the innocents, an event that accompanied Moses' birth.

The Sermon on the Mount

The allusions to Moses continue with the Sermon on the Mount. Here Jesus proclaims the Beatitudes, which "teach us the final end to which God calls us: the Kingdom" (*CCC*, 1726). Matthew specifically depicts Jesus' proclaiming his New Law from a mountain (see Matthew 5:1, Luke 6:17), an allusion to Moses' proclaiming the Law that he received on the mountain during the Israelites' time in the desert (see Exodus, chapters 19–20).

© Laura James / Private Collection / The Bridgeman Art Library

In this contemporary painting, Jesus is out of proportion to the crowd. Why is he portrayed so much larger than everyone else?

Successors of the Apostles

Christ chose the Apostles and their successors to proclaim the faith and to inaugurate his Kingdom on earth. The Pope and the bishops are the successors to the Apostles and share in Christ's own mission just as the Apostles did. From Christ, the Pope and the bishops receive the power to act in the person of Christ on earth. As successor to Saint Peter, to whom Christ entrusted the keys of the Kingdom and whom he made the visible 'rock' on which the Church stands, the Pope is the Vicar (representative) of Christ, pastor (shepherd) of the universal Church, and head of the college (assembly) of bishops. Through Apostolic Succession the teaching and authority of the Apostles has been handed on directly to all bishops through the laying on of hands when a bishop is ordained in the Sacrament of Holy Orders. Because they succeed the Apostles, the bishops are the "visible source and foundation of unity" in their own particular Churches, or dioceses. (*Dogmatic Constitution on the Church [Lumen Gentium, 1964]*, 23)

During the Sermon on the Mount, Jesus spells out his relationship to the Law. He says: "Do not think that I have come to abolish the law or the prophets. I have come not to abolish but to fulfill" (Matthew 5:17). Then Jesus refers to a number of commandments in the Mosaic Law and shows that his teaching is built on that Law. But he asks more of people, not less. Jesus says: "You have heard . . ." and then he quotes the Law. Next he says, "But I say to you . . ." and he teaches something more demanding than the Law. For example, the Law teaches that people must not kill, but Jesus teaches: "Whoever is angry with his brother will be liable

The Beatitudes

In the **Beatitudes** (see Matthew 5:3–12), Jesus draws a word-picture of the Kingdom, a vision of God's will and the path that leads us to eternal life. The word *beatitude* is often translated as "blessed" or "happy"; thus these proclamations respond to the desire for happiness God has placed in our hearts and fulfill the promises God made to Abraham: "I will bless you abundantly . . . and in your descendants all the nations of the earth shall find blessing" (Genesis 22:17,18). In the Beatitudes, all of these promises are ordered to the Kingdom of Heaven.

However, the Beatitudes do not conform to some popular ideas of happiness—either then or now. In the Beatitudes, Jesus makes clear that more possessions, more prestige, more power, more status do not equal happiness. We find true happiness only in God. The Beatitudes call us to be grateful for what we have, to give to others in sadness and joy, to grow in patience and self-control, to work for justice, to show mercy, to make room for God in mind and heart, to seek

© JLP/Jose L. Pelaez/Corbis

peace, and to face persecution with courage. These qualities bring us into the Kingdom of God here on earth. The Beatitudes also teach us the final end to which God calls us: participation in the divine nature and full communion with him in the eternal Kingdom of Heaven.

to judgment" (5:22). Similarly, the Law teaches that people must not commit adultery, but Jesus teaches that someone who looks at another with lust "has already committed adultery" (5:28) in the heart. People have heard that an eye for an eye is a fair punishment, but Jesus teaches: "Offer no resistance to one who is evil. . . . Love your enemies" (5:39,44). Jesus is not abandoning the Law; he is making it more demanding in the direction of loving one's neighbor. Jesus teaches that obedience to the Law begins in the heart.

The Keys of the Kingdom

Matthew makes clear that Jesus delegates authority to the Apostles in his account of Jesus' first commissioning of the Twelve. Jesus tells them to go to the lost sheep of the house of Israel and "As you go, make this proclamation: 'The kingdom of heaven is at hand.' Cure the sick, raise the dead, cleanse lepers, drive out demons" (Matthew 10:7–8). The Apostles' ability to perform miraculous acts of power added authority to their preaching.

Matthew also shows his great interest in authority when he gives an account of Jesus' first prediction of his Passion, of Peter's profession of faith, and of Jesus' rebuke of Peter. After Peter's profession of faith, but before his rebuke, Matthew describes Jesus' telling Peter that he is blessed. Jesus then says: "You are Peter, and upon this rock I will build my church, and the gates of the netherworld shall not prevail against it. I will give you the keys to the kingdom of heaven. Whatever you bind on earth shall be bound in heaven; and whatever you loose on earth shall be loosed in heaven" (Matthew 16:18–19).

These verses also highlight Peter's place among the Apostles as the first in authority. Here Jesus extends Peter's authority to the Church and even to the Kingdom of Heaven (see *CCC,* 552–553.) (Keys are a symbol of authority because, even in our own day, only responsible people are given keys to things of value.) By "binding and loosing" (*CCC,* 553) is meant the authority in the Church, given to the Apostles and particularly to Peter, to absolve sins, to formulate doctrine, and to make decisions regarding Church order and discipline.

Beatitudes
The teachings of Jesus that begin the Sermon on the Mount and that summarize the New Law of Christ. The Beatitudes describe the actions and attitudes by which one can discover genuine happiness, and they teach us the final end to which God calls us: full communion with him in the Kingdom of Heaven.

Amen
A Hebrew word that expresses agreement. When used at the beginning of a teaching, as Jesus uses it, the word adds authority to what follows.

Later Jesus gives the disciples as a whole the power to bind and to loose. Jesus says: "**Amen**, I say to you, whatever you bind on earth shall be bound in heaven, and whatever you loose on earth shall be loosed in heaven" (Matthew 18:18). This emphasis on authority is once more evident when Jesus commissions his disciples after his Resurrection, saying to them, "All power in heaven and on earth has been given to me" (28:18). Jesus gives Peter and the other Apostles the authority to carry on Jesus' mission to the world. ✝

Article 20 The Paschal Mystery According to Matthew

The account of the Passion, death, and Resurrection of Christ in the Gospel of Matthew is the summit, or high point, of his Gospel. This account can be found in chapters 26, 27, and 28 of Matthew's Gospel. Matthew's account is quite similar to Mark's. It includes the betrayal by Judas; the Last Supper; the agony in the garden; the trial before Jewish leaders; the trial before Pilate; and the Crucifixion, burial, and Resurrection of Jesus. However, Matthew includes some extra information, details that address the question in the minds of Matthew's audience: Is God's authority with Jesus or not? A closer look at this question will give us important insights about Jesus and about our own Christian discipleship.

Prophetic Fulfillment

Matthew continues to emphasize that God's plan for the human race is being carried out through Jesus by pointing out that the events in Jesus' life are fulfilling the words of the prophets. When Jesus is arrested in the garden of Gethsemane, he comments: "But all this has come to pass that the writings of the prophets may be fulfilled" (Matthew 26:56). When the chief priests use the thirty pieces of silver that Judas flung at them to buy the potter's field, Matthew says, "Then was fulfilled what had been said through Jeremiah, the prophet, 'And they took the thirty pieces of silver . . . and they paid it out for the potter's field'" (27:9). Judas regrets his betrayal and gives the money to the Temple, and the chief priests use this "blood money" for a charitable

© Gianni Dagli Orti/CORBIS

Detail of *Anastasis* (Greek for "Resurrection"), a fresco painting in the Kariye Camii (once a church, now a museum) in Istanbul. Here the Risen Jesus visits the realm of the dead and brings Adam and Eve with him into Paradise.

purpose (see 27:3–7.) The fact that Jesus is fulfilling the words of the prophets is evidence that God's purposes for his people are being achieved through his Son, Jesus Christ, who is himself God.

Jesus' Divine Identity

In Matthew's account of the Passion of Jesus, all those who have religious or civil authority act reprehensibly, but their abuse of their authority cannot thwart God's will. His authority is with the innocent Jesus, his only Son. Matthew emphasizes Jesus' innocence by portraying Pilate's wife, after her dream, warning her husband, "Have nothing to do with that righteous man" (Matthew 27:19), and Pilate's washing his hands before the crowd saying, "I am innocent of this man's blood" (27:24). Nevertheless, Pilate turns Jesus over to be crucified.

In Matthew's account, in addition to the veil of the Temple ripping immediately after Jesus dies, there is an earthquake (see Matthew 27:51). Earlier in Matthew's Gospel, when Jesus was describing the coming of the end of the age, Jesus warned that there would be earthquakes (see 24:7). Matthew also reports an earthquake when the women go to the tomb and discover it empty (see 28:2). This is Matthew's way of saying that Jesus' death and Resurrection are of cosmic, earth-shaking importance and of affirming Jesus' identity and authority as divine.

Matthew also tells us that when Jesus died "tombs were opened, and the bodies of many saints who had fallen asleep were raised. And coming forth from their tombs after his resurrection, they entered the holy city and appeared to many" (Matthew 27:52–53). The expectation that the dead would rise at the end of the age had previously appeared in the Book of Daniel: "Many of those who sleep / in the dust of the earth shall awake" (12:2). By proclaiming that the dead had risen from their tombs, Matthew is teaching that Jesus, the Son of God, is initiating a new age.

Burial and Resurrection

Matthew's account of the burial of Jesus makes clear that Jesus really died and was really buried. The death of Jesus was witnessed even by the Gentile centurion and the soldiers at the cross (see Matthew 27:54) and by the women from Galilee (see 27:56). These women would later become important as witnesses, along with the other disciples and Apostles, to the Resurrection of Jesus. In these ways Matthew emphasizes the historicity of the death and burial of Jesus, so that his Resurrection, attested to by these same witnesses, would be believed.

The chief priests and Pharisees try to prevent any claim of resurrection by asking Pilate to post a guard at the tomb. Pilate gives permission: "So they . . . secured the tomb by fixing a seal to the stone and setting the guard" (Matthew 27:66). Of course, they had no authority to prevent the Resurrection. After being thwarted, the chief priests and elders

Catholic Wisdom

Jesus Descended to the Dead

In the Apostles' Creed, we proclaim that Jesus "was crucified, died, and was buried. He descended into hell; the third day he rose again." This means that after his death, Jesus, in his human soul united to his Divine Person, visited the dead, opened the gates of Heaven, and assured the just of salvation.

A poignant Resurrection icon in the tradition of the Eastern Churches shows Christ's conquering the underworld, extending his hands to Adam and Eve to bring them with him to Paradise.

bribe the guards to lie about what has happened, and to say that the disciples stole the body in order to claim a resurrection (see 28:14).

Mary Magdalene and her companions, who discover the empty tomb, are instructed by an "angel of the Lord" (Matthew 28:3) to tell Jesus' disciples to go to Galilee where they will see the Risen Christ (see 28:7). Along the way they meet the Risen Jesus himself, who reassures them, "Do not be afraid" (28:10) and repeats the instruction to tell the disciples to go to Galilee to meet him. But then, unlike Mark, Matthew presents the appearance of Jesus and the commissioning of the Apostles taking place on a mountain: "The eleven disciples went to Galilee, to the mountain to which Jesus had ordered them" (28:16). This is, of course, to remind us once more that Jesus is the New Moses.

When Jesus commissions the disciples, he reminds them that "all power in heaven and on earth has been given to me" (Matthew 28:18). It is God's authority that Jesus is passing on to his disciples. Jesus then commissions his disciples to "make disciples of all nations, baptizing them in the name of the Father, and of the Son, and of the holy Spirit" (28:19). This Trinitarian form for Baptism is unique to Matthew's Gospel.

The last words that Jesus spoke to the Apostles on earth, "And behold, I am with you always, until the end of the age" (Matthew 28:20), bring Matthew's Gospel full circle. These words bring us back to the beginning, to the meaning of the name of Jesus given to Joseph in a dream, the name that will fulfill the prophecy of Isaiah: "And they shall name him Emmanuel,' which means 'God is with us'" (1:23). Yes, in the Risen Jesus, God is with us always. ✝

Samaritan

An inhabitant of Samaria. The Samaritans, an interreligious and interracial people (Jewish and Assyrian), rejected the Jerusalem Temple and worshipped instead at Mount Gerizim. The hostility between Jews and Samaritans is often recounted in the New Testament.

Calling All Nations!

In Matthew's Gospel, when Jesus initially commissions the Twelve, he tells them not to "go into pagan territory or enter a **Samaritan** town. Go rather to the lost sheep of the house of Israel" (Matthew 10:5–6). However, at the commissioning after the Resurrection, Jesus tells his Apostles to baptize "all nations . . . in the name of the Father, and of the Son, and of the holy Spirit" (28:19). Remember, this distinction concerning *all nations* would be important to Matthew's primarily Jewish Christian audience, who are accepting that Gentiles are now being invited into covenant love. Matthew's Gospel has emphasized this theme from the first, with its genealogy, which included both Jewish and Gentile ancestors of Jesus.

Perhaps you recognize in these words of commissioning the words from the rite of Baptism. As you may recall, the essential rite of Baptism consists of immersing a candidate in water (or pouring water over the head) while saying: "I baptize you in the name of the Father, and of the Son, and of the Holy Spirit" (*Rite of Baptism for Children,* 97). Through faith and through Baptism, all are called to become part of the new People of God, to form one family and one people. This is the invitation that both begins and ends the Gospel of Matthew.

© FRANCIS R. MALASIG/epa/Corbis

Part Review

1. What is the function of Matthew's genealogy? What is unusual about it?

2. What is an infancy narrative?

3. What details are unique to Matthew's infancy narrative? What is their significance?

4. What is another name for the Kingdom of Heaven? Where might one find this Kingdom?

5. What paradoxes about the Kingdom do we learn through the parables?

6. Why is the question of authority so important to Matthew's audience?

7. What is Jesus' relationship to the Jewish Law? Give examples.

8. Name four ways Matthew addresses the question of Jesus' authority in his Passion narrative.

9. What is significant about Jesus' last spoken words in Matthew's Gospel?

Part 4

The Gospel of Luke

Why did the inspired human author of Luke write his Gospel? He answers this question at the very beginning: "I too have decided, after investigating everything accurately anew, to write it down in an orderly sequence for you, most excellent Theophilus, so that you may realize the certainty of the teachings you have received" (Luke 1:3–4).

Of the three synoptic Gospels, Luke's is the only one to include such a prologue, or introduction. Luke proposes to organize the teachings of Jesus and the events of his life, Passion, death, Resurrection, and Ascension "in an orderly sequence" for someone called Theophilus. (The Acts of the Apostles, also written by Luke and considered a second volume to this Gospel, is also addressed to Theophilus.)

But who is Theophilus? The name Theophilus means "friend of God" or "lover of God." Theophilus may have been a real person or perhaps a symbolic stand-in for all the "friends and lovers of God" who would read or listen to this Gospel.

It is not surprising then that in this Gospel, Luke presents Jesus himself as a friend and a lover of all people, especially those who are lost and forgotten. Jesus is the Son of God and Savior who comes among us with a deep and compassionate love for those who are poor and in need, for those who live on the edges of society, and for all sinners who feel far from the love of God. In this Gospel we are each invited, in following Jesus, to be another Theophilus, extending our love of God to the entire human race.

The articles in this part address the following topics:

© Manolis Grigoreas / Private Collection /
Malva Gallery / The Bridgeman Art Library

ὉΆΓΙΟΣ   ΜΌΣΧΟΣ

An Overview of the Gospel of Luke

The Gospel of Luke	
Inspired author:	a Gentile Christian named Luke, traditionally thought to be a disciple of Paul
Approximate date of writing:	AD 80–85
Location of writing:	Greece
Audience:	Gentile (Greek) Christians represented by Theophilus (see Luke 1:3)
Image of Jesus:	merciful, compassionate, with a special concern for poor people, women, and non-Jews
Genealogy:	goes back to Adam, to emphasize that Jesus is the Savior of the entire human race
Themes:	portrait of Mary, God's love for all (especially those who are poor or marginalized), presence of the Holy Spirit, use of meal as symbol of the Kingdom of God
Sources:	The Gospels of Mark, Q, and L Source (a source unique to Luke)
Symbol of Gospel:	the ox, an animal used in sacrifice, recalling the beginning of the Gospel; Zechariah is offering a sacrifice in the Temple

A Glance at the Gospel

Luke, chapters 1–2: introduction; accounts of Jesus' birth and early childhood

Luke 3:1 — 9:50: Jesus' ministry in Galilee

Luke 9:51 — 19:27: parables and miracles on the way to Jerusalem

Luke 19:28 — 21:38: Jesus in Jerusalem; conflict with the religious authorities

Luke, chapters 22–24: accounts of Jesus' Passion, death, Resurrection, and Ascension

Article 21 Luke's Infancy Narrative

The Gospel of Luke is the third synoptic Gospel. As you recall, the synoptic Gospels of Mark, Matthew, and Luke are similar, as they maintain a similar approach to the proclamation of the Good News of Jesus Christ. However, as we have seen in the Gospels of Mark and Matthew, the Gospels differ in the details they record because each was written at a different time, in a different place, and for a different audience. The Gospel of Luke, drawing on the Gospels of Mark and Q as its sources (as well as its own independent source that has been labeled the L Source), seeks to proclaim the Good News to Greek-speaking Gentile Christians.

Luke, like Matthew, includes both an infancy narrative and a genealogy in his Gospel. In the Gospel of Matthew, the genealogy is part of the infancy narrative (the first part), whereas in Luke's Gospel the genealogy follows the infancy narrative. Also, like Matthew, Luke includes a number of descriptions in his infancy narrative that are found only in his Gospel: the Annunciation to Mary, the narratives surrounding John the Baptist's birth, Mary's visit to Elizabeth, Jesus' being born in a stable and placed in a manger, the announcement of Jesus' birth to the shepherds, the presentation, and the finding of Jesus in the Temple as a young boy. Once more, to understand the full significance of these unique descriptions, we must recognize the biblical allusions that are woven around the accounts of events to teach the significance of those events. Additionally, we must remember that the infancy narratives were written after the Resurrection of Jesus, and so, even though they are about his infancy, they carry the post-Resurrection understanding of Jesus as Savior and Son of God.

The Annunciation, by William Brassey Hole. The Gospel of Luke includes a narrative of the early years of Jesus; the Mother of God is a prominent figure in this Gospel. Mary's yes to God's plan makes her the perfect disciple.

© Lebrecht Music & Arts/Corbis

Mary in Luke's Gospel

Because Luke's is the Gospel in which we fully meet Mary, we will look first at Luke's accounts of both the Annunciation and the Visitation. We will see that many of our beliefs about Mary find their roots in Luke's Gospel.

Luke tells us that after Mary was engaged to Joseph, but before they lived together, the angel Gabriel appeared to her. The angel's greeting is: "Hail, favored one! The Lord is with you" (Luke 1:28). The angel tells Mary that she will conceive through the Holy Spirit and bear a son. The angel then describes the significance of Jesus' birth. In response to the angel's words, Mary says: "Behold, I am the handmaid of the Lord. May it be done to me according to your word" (1:38).

The doctrine that Mary, "the most excellent fruit of redemption" (*Constitution on the Sacred Liturgy [Sacrosanctum Concilium]*, 103), was free from Original Sin from the moment of her conception (the Immaculate Conception) finds its roots in the angel's words to her. From all the human race, Mary was chosen by God to be the mother of his Son. Mary was "favored" and the "Lord was with her" from the moment of her conception, not just at the Annunciation. Mary's "May it be done unto me," also called her ***fiat***, expresses her complete cooperation with God's saving activity, not only for the Incarnation but also for the complete mission her Son was to fulfill. This *fiat,* plus Elizabeth's words to Mary at the Visitation—"Blessed are you who believed that what was spoken to you by the Lord would be fulfilled" (Luke 1:45)— are the reason Mary is understood to be the preeminent disciple of Jesus Christ, the model in holiness for all of us.

In addition to naming Mary's profound faith, Elizabeth calls her "the mother of my Lord" (Luke 1:43). She does this after her child, John the Baptist, leaps in her womb at Jesus' presence (see 1:41–44). Mary is the mother of Jesus, who is

fiat
Latin for "let it be done," words Mary spoke to the angel at the Annunciation.

Catholic Wisdom

The Hail Mary

We call Mary "full of grace" for, from the first moment of her conception, she was kept free from Original Sin and from all personal sin throughout her life. We praise her: "Blessed are you among women" because God chose her from among all women to be the Mother of his Son. She is thus "the most excellent fruit of redemption" (*Sacred Liturgy*, 103). As Mary is the mother of the Eternal Son of God made man (Jesus) who is God, she is truly *Theotokos*, the Mother of God. As the handmaid of the Lord in her whole being, she is both mother and ever-virgin. And so we ask her intercession "now, and at the hour of our death. Amen."

true man and true God. For that reason she is truly Mother of God. In the Eastern Churches, Mary, as true Mother of God, is often called *Theotokos,* a Greek term meaning "God bearer."

The Firstborn Son

In Luke's Gospel we read that Mary "gave birth to her first-born son. She wrapped him in swaddling clothes and laid him in a manger, because there was no room for them in the inn" (Luke 2:7). As we have said, to understand the full significance of these words, we must recognize the biblical texts to which they are alluding.

No Room in the Inn

Luke tells us that Jesus was born in a stable, "because there was no room for them in the inn" (2:7). This is another allusion to the Old Testament, one that teaches a profound truth. In Jeremiah we read: "Hope of Israel, LORD, / our savior in time of need! / Why should you be a stranger in the land, / like a traveler stopping only for a night?" (14:8).

Jesus is born in a stable, not an inn, and laid in a manger, because he is not "a traveler stopping only for a night" (Jeremiah 14:8). Jesus is the Savior who has come to be nourishment for his people, and who has come to dwell with them. Jesus, the firstborn from the dead, will remain with his people forever.

The word *firstborn* does not imply that Mary had other children; rather, it is a title given to Christ, as the firstborn of all creation (see Colossians 1:15–20, Hebrews 1:5–6) and the firstborn of the dead (see Revelation 1:5). Luke teaches that Jesus is divine. Yet this Divine Person is wrapped in swaddling clothes like every other human baby. This is an allusion to the Book of Wisdom, where **Solomon** describes himself as an infant: "In swaddling clothes and with constant care I was nurtured. / For no king has any different origin or birth" (7:4–5).

Solomon
David's son, a king of Israel renowned for his wisdom.

In comparing Jesus to Solomon, Luke teaches that Jesus is fully human. Mary places her child in a manger. A manger is a feeding trough, a place where one puts food for the flock. This is Luke's way of teaching that Jesus is the Bread of Life. The Good News of the Savior's birth is announced to the shepherds (see Luke 2:8–11). The shepherds are told to look for the sign: "an infant wrapped in swaddling clothes and lying in a manger" (2:12). They rush to Bethlehem, see the sign (see 2:16), and recognize their Savior.

After his infancy narratives, Luke includes the preaching of John the Baptist, the Baptism of Jesus by John, and then a genealogy. Matthew's genealogy goes back to Abraham, but Luke's goes back to Adam. This is Luke's way of placing the significance of Jesus' saving actions not just in the context of the Israelites' history but in the context of the whole human race. Jesus is Savior for all. The invitation to the Kingdom is universal. ✝

Article 22 The Universal Nature of Covenant Love

As you know, Luke is writing to Gentiles. Luke's Gentile audience has entirely different needs than Mark or Matthew's audiences. Luke's audience has questions like these: Do we have to become Jewish in order to become Christian? What should be our Christian attitude toward those who are poor and marginalized? How can we ourselves follow Jesus in our lives? In responding to his Gentile audience, Luke emphasizes that everyone, absolutely everyone, is invited to the Kingdom.

Christ and Mary Magdalene, by Jacopo Tintoretto (1518–1594), shows Jesus pardoning a sinful woman who shows great love. In Luke's Gospel, Jesus often shares meals with sinners and often teaches while conversing at a meal.

© Cameraphoto Arte, Venice / Art Resource, NY

Come to the Feast

In the Gospel of Luke, the teaching of Jesus stresses that everyone is invited to the Kingdom of God. As a dinner guest in a Pharisee's home, Jesus responds to a comment another guest has made (see Luke 14:15–24). The guest remarks: "Blessed is the one who will dine in the kingdom of God" (14:15). Jesus tells everyone a parable. A man decides to give a feast, but one by one, those he invites refuse his invitation. The host is so enraged that his handpicked guests have not accepted his invitation to dine that he tells his servants to *force* strangers from the highways and byways to come in (see 14:23). Jesus is teaching that there is no problem with being invited to the Kingdom. The invitation is offered to all. The problem is that many who are invited refuse the invitation.

Luke's Gospel has many accounts of people being included and of people being forgiven that appear in no other Gospel. One example is Zacchaeus, a despised tax collector. Zacchaeus is anxious to see Jesus. Because he is short, he climbs a sycamore tree. As Jesus passes by, he sees this marginalized man in the tree. Jesus calls out: "Zacchaeus, come down quickly, for today I must stay at your house" (Luke 19:5). Zacchaeus is completely converted by being in Jesus' presence and promises to give half of his wealth to the poor. Jesus tells him: "Today salvation has come to this house. . . . For the Son of Man has come to seek and to save what was lost" (19:9–10).

Forgiveness for All

In the Gospel of Luke, Jesus is particularly interested in reaching out to sinners with compassion and forgiveness. Of the synoptic Gospels, only Luke has the Parable of the Prodigal Son (see 15:11–32). Jesus tells this parable to the Pharisees and scribes who are complaining that Jesus "welcomes sinners and eats with them" (15:2). In response, Jesus tells them the story of a man who has two sons. The younger son asks for his inheritance, wastes it, returns home, and is forgiven. The older son, who has always obeyed and kept the rules, is angry that his father has forgiven the younger son and has even thrown a banquet in the younger son's honor. This turns the tables. Who is the sinner now? The older son is because he is failing to love his brother. The father explains why he is overjoyed to welcome back his younger son, a sinner, and then invites the older brother to the party. Jesus is teaching the Pharisees and scribes (the "elders" of the Jewish people who are sincere in their observance of the Law) that they too are invited to the Kingdom, but to accept the invitation, they must learn to forgive other sinners. All repentant sinners will be welcomed into the Father's Kingdom.

The Holy Spirit in the Gospel of Luke

As you know, the Holy Spirit is the Third Person of the Blessed Trinity. Just as the People of God expected a Messiah to inaugurate a new Kingdom of God, so they expected the Spirit of God to descend anew, the Spirit of whom Isaiah spoke when he prophesied: "But a shoot shall sprout from the stump of Jesse, / and from his roots a bud shall blossom. / The spirit of the LORD shall rest upon him" (11:1–2).

Luke's Gospel consistently shows that the Holy Spirit, like the Father himself, is with Jesus and guides Jesus in all that he does. It is important to realize that whenever God the Father sends his Son, he always sends the Holy Spirit with him. Both the Son and the Holy Spirit share one inseparable mission: to bring us back to God.

As we have seen from studying the infancy narrative in Luke's Gospel, the life of Jesus begins with the coming of the Holy Spirit upon Mary (see 1:35). It ends with Jesus' asking his Apostles to wait in Jerusalem until they are "clothed with power from on high" (Luke 24:49). This verse prepares us for

the coming of the Holy Spirit on Pentecost, recounted in the
Acts of the Apostles, chapter 2. Between these two points,
Luke refers to the Holy Spirit as present with Jesus at two
other significant times: at his Baptism (see 3:22) and at the
beginning of his ministry, when he goes to Galilee "in the
power of the Spirit" (4:14) and reads from Scripture in his
hometown synagogue, "The Spirit of the Lord is upon me"
(4:18). Jesus also teaches that the Holy Spirit will be with his
disciples as well, in his teaching on prayer and the gift of the
Holy Spirit (see 11:13) and in his assurance that the Holy
Spirit will teach the disciples what to say when undergoing
persecution (see 12:12). This emphasis on the Holy Spirit
anticipates the prominent role the Holy Spirit takes in the
early Church, as recounted in Luke's subsequent book, the
Acts of the Apostles.

Closely connected to his emphasis on the Holy Spirit
is Luke's emphasis on prayer. In Luke's Gospel, Jesus prays
(and so gets in touch with the Father and the Holy Spirit)
at significant points in his life. It was when Jesus "had been
baptized and was praying" (Luke 3:21) that the Holy Spirit
descended upon him. Before choosing the Twelve Apostles,
Jesus "spent the night in prayer to God" (6:12), and he gave
praise to his Father when the mission of the Apostles proved
successful (see 10:21). Luke's two parables on prayer (see
18:1–14) are unique to Luke, and they teach us, whatever our
difficulty or our situation, to persist in humble and faithful
prayer.

The Passover Meal: A New Covenant

A group of students was asked to read the entire Gospel of
Luke and then to offer their impressions to the class. One
student raised his hand: "It seems to me," he began, "that
Jesus and the disciples are always eating." The teacher con-
gratulated that student for noticing an important element in
Luke's Gospel: the sharing of the meal.

In the Gospel of Luke, the banquet, the shared meal,
foreshadows the heavenly banquet to which all are invited.
In the Gospels of Matthew and Mark, Jesus' miracles,
through which the blind see and the lame walk, are signs of
the coming of the Kingdom. In the Gospel of Luke, so are
Jesus' meals with sinners. Zacchaeus's change of heart, and
Jesus' offer to stay (and, with customary Semitic hospitality,

The Gentleness of Luke

As Luke presents Christ constantly offering forgiveness to sinners and inviting them to a shared meal, he models himself on Christ by being a gentle and merciful narrator. Over and over Luke recounts events described in the Gospel of Mark in such a way that he refrains as much as possible from putting others in a bad light.

For instance, when Luke retells Mark's account of Peter's profession of faith and of Jesus' warning the disciples about his coming death, Luke simply omits the fact that Peter remonstrated with Jesus or that Jesus said, "Get behind me, Satan" (Mark 8:33). When, in Mark, Peter, James, and John fail three times to stay awake and support Jesus with their prayer, Luke mentions their failure only once and then adds that they were "sleeping from grief" (Luke 22:45). As you read Luke, you will notice again and again that Luke simply refrains from speaking unkindly about others whenever he can.

© Arte & Immagini srl/CORBIS

eschatological meal

The Eucharist, which anticipates the heavenly banquet that Jesus will share with the faithful when the Kingdom of God is fully realized at the end of time. The word *eschatological* derives from *eschaton*, meaning "the end of time."

most likely dine) at his house, are just as much manifestations of the truth of Jesus' proclamation of the power and presence of the Kingdom of God as are Jesus' powerful acts of physical healing. As you read Luke's Gospel, you will notice that Luke constantly emphasizes that sinners are called and forgiven. All are invited to dine with Christ, both in this life and the next.

Jesus makes this symbolism explicit at his last meal with his disciples. Jesus says that he has "eagerly desired to eat this Passover with you before I suffer, for, I tell you, I shall not eat it [again] until there is fulfillment in the kingdom of God" (Luke 22:15–16). When Jesus offers the cup, he says, "For I tell you [that] from this time on I shall not drink of the fruit of the vine until the kingdom of God comes" (22:18).

It is on this occasion that Jesus gives new reality and new meaning to the bread and wine of the Passover meal by instituting the Eucharist. The bread becomes Jesus' Body, and the wine becomes Jesus' Blood. Jesus says, "This cup is the new covenant in my blood, which will be shed for you" (Luke 22:20). In this offering of his Body and Blood, Jesus offers himself for the salvation of all, and at the same time makes his offering truly present. Jesus tells his disciples to "do this in memory of me" (22:19), thus establishing the **eschatological meal** on earth. ✝

Pray It!

The Signs of the Eucharist

When Jesus gave the Apostles his Body and Blood at the Last Supper, he used the bread and wine of the Passover meal. These two essential elements remain today the essential signs of the Sacrament of the Eucharist: wheat bread and grape wine, upon which the blessing of the Holy Spirit is invoked and the priest says in these words: "This is my Body which will be given up for you. . . . This is the chalice of my Blood. . . ." (*Roman Missal*) (see *CCC*, 1412). This consecration brings about the Transubstantiation of the bread and wine into the Body and Blood of Christ. Under this consecrated species of bread and wine is Christ himself, "present in a true, real, and substantial manner: his Body and his Blood, with his soul and his divinity" (*CCC*, 1413).

The next time you receive the Eucharist, spend some time thanking Jesus for being really present with you, and then take him to everyone you meet.

Article 23 Luke's Passion Narrative

Pope Saint John Paul II, in his apostolic exhortation *Catechesi Tradendae*, states:

© Brian Dunne / Shutterstock.com

> The whole of Christ's life was a continual teaching: his silences, his miracles, his gestures, his prayer, his love for people, his special affection for the little and the poor, his acceptance of the total sacrifice on the Cross for the redemption of the world, and his Resurrection are the actualization of his word and the fulfillment of Revelation." (9, in *CCC*, 561)

The truth of this statement is nowhere more evident than it is in Luke's account of Jesus' Passion and death. Instead of depicting Jesus as the abandoned victim, as does Mark, Luke depicts Jesus actively involved in his mission to invite sinners into the Kingdom and to make visible the coming of the Kingdom of God through his miraculous acts of power even as he is being arrested and crucified.

That is not to say that Luke changes the basic outline from Mark's account. He does not. Judas still betrays Jesus. Peter still denies him. Jesus still appears before both the Sanhedrin and Pilate, although Luke describes Herod as also being involved. Pilate still turns Jesus over to be crucified, even though he finds no guilt in him. Jesus is still crucified with two criminals and dies on the cross. But Luke, in keeping with his compassion and gentleness, does change some details.

For instance, the spotlight on the Apostles' inability to understand is lessened. In fact, at the Last Supper, Jesus says to them: "It is you who have stood by me in my trials; and I confer a kingdom on you, just as my Father has conferred one on me, that you may eat and drink at my table in my kingdom" (Luke 22:28–30). Luke refrains from mentioning that all the disciples deserted Jesus.

Luke also portrays the behavior of the Sanhedrin as being less reprehensible. They condemn Jesus for not denying that he is the Son of God (see Luke 22:70–71), but they do not purposely bring forward false witnesses.

Yet Luke does not omit Jesus' terrible suffering. During his agony in the garden, Jesus prays to be relieved of his cup (see Luke 22:42). Luke tells us that Jesus "was in such agony and he prayed so fervently that his sweat became like drops

Red-Letter Words

Have you ever seen a red-letter New Testament—that is, a New Testament that prints all the words attributed to Jesus in red ink? This emphasizing of Jesus' words seems to suggest that the words are exact quotations. However, Scripture scholars do not claim that Jesus' words are exact quotations. There are several reasons for this. First, Jesus spoke in Aramaic, and the Gospels were originally written in **Koine Greek**. (The Greek word *koine* means "common" in the sense of "for all people." It is also called "biblical Greek" and, at the time of the writing of the New Testament, it had become the common language of Israel.) A translation cannot be an exact quotation. Second, the Gospels are the fruit of oral tradition. Oral tradition can never be proven to quote exactly. Finally, at the time Jesus lived, people did not have ready access to paper and pens. They did not have recording devices. Yet, through their communal memory, they passed on what they had learned from Jesus. We treasure the words of Jesus that have come to us through the New Testament, because they bring to us the thoughts, actions, and the very presence of Jesus, the Word of God.

of blood falling on the ground" (22:44). But at the same time, Jesus is still constantly thinking of others and continues to try to teach his disciples by his every action.

Jesus Heals

Even during his betrayal and arrest, Jesus shows his saving compassion. When one of the disciples defends Jesus with a sword, cutting off the ear of the high priest's servant, Jesus immediately stops this behavior. Then "he touched the servant's ear and healed him" (Luke 22:51).

In Luke, Jesus is not abandoned by the crowd as he is in Mark's account. Luke tells us that "a large crowd of people followed Jesus, including many women who mourned and lamented him" (23:27). Jesus seems to be more concerned about the women and their children's welfare than he is about his own. Jesus says, "Daughters of Jerusalem do not weep for me; weep instead for yourselves and for your children" (23:28).

Jesus Forgives

Jesus' ministry of seeking out the lost continues even on the cross. Two criminals are crucified with Jesus. One criminal reviles Jesus, but the other defends him. That criminal then says to Jesus, "Remember me when you come into your kingdom." Jesus responds, "Amen, I say to you, today you will be with me in Paradise" (Luke 23:42–43). Scripture

Koine Greek
The dialect of the Greek language most commonly used from around 300 BC to AD 300, and the language in which the New Testament books were originally written.

Live It!

Compassionate Presence

As we have learned, the Gospel of Luke is particularly attentive to those who lived on the margins of society at the time of Jesus: those who were poor, sick, or in need. In this Gospel the response of Jesus to human need is compassion.

At its root, the word *compassion* means "to suffer with." You may have experienced how difficult it is to be with someone who is hurting or in pain, and to feel helpless in the face of that hurt. Yet you are there. You are "suffering with" that person, who, because of you, is not facing a painful experience alone. Even though you may feel you cannot "do" anything, your very presence is healing. And the compassion expressed by your presence is a great gift. Without saying a word, you can bring God's love to someone who needs it, just by being there.

scholars suggest that by portraying Jesus saying "Paradise" rather than "my kingdom," Luke is teaching that through his death Jesus is reversing the sinful state of human beings that resulted in their being separated from Paradise (see Genesis 3:22–23). Because God the Father loved us and sent his Son to save us, Jesus is redeeming the human race from sin and is "reconciling the world to himself" (2 Corinthians 5:19).

Jesus even forgives the Roman soldiers at the very moment they are crucifying him. Jesus prays: "Father, forgive them, they know not what they do" (Luke 23:34). Finally, Jesus' last words on the cross express not a feeling of abandonment, as they did in Mark, but a great sense of trust. Jesus says, "Father, into your hands I commend my spirit" (23:46). Jesus dies peacefully, knowing that he has forgiven and invited all into the Kingdom of God. ✝

Article 24 Luke's Post-Resurrection Appearance Narratives

As expected, the accounts of post-Resurrection appearances of Jesus in the synoptic Gospels are similar. Luke, like Mark and Matthew, has both an empty tomb narrative and narratives about Jesus' post-Resurrection appearances. However, Luke's post-Resurrection appearance accounts are unique to his Gospel and continue the themes that we have been tracing throughout the Gospel: all are invited to the Kingdom, all are offered forgiveness, and a shared meal both foreshadows and becomes an eschatological banquet at which Christ, himself, is present.

In *The Supper at Emmaus,* by Trophime Bigot (c. 1595–1650), the surprise on the faces of the supper companions is obvious, and even the waiter is drawn into "the breaking of the Bread." Jesus is with us in Word and Sacrament.

On the Road to Emmaus

Mark, Luke's source, tells us that the Risen Christ appeared to two disciples as they were walking along, but Mark gives us no details. Luke fleshes out Mark's statement into a wonderful narrative that responds to the question: Where is the Risen Christ? (see Luke 24:13–35).

In the Gospel of Luke, two disciples are walking along the road talking about Jesus when Jesus himself joins them. However, the disciples fail to recognize Jesus in this fellow traveler. (This failure to recognize Jesus is a common theme in post-Resurrection appearance accounts.) The two are downcast. They had placed their hopes in Jesus, and now they think he is dead. They are downcast because they simply do not believe the women who have been to the empty tomb and have told them Jesus is alive.

The stranger (that is, Jesus) who has joined the two disciples tells them that they have failed to believe what the prophets spoke. He then asks, "Was it not necessary that the Messiah should suffer these things and enter into his glory?" (Luke 24:26). Jesus then "interpreted to them what referred to him in all the scriptures" (24:27). As the two disciples approach the village, they invite the stranger to stay with them. While they are at table together, the stranger "took bread, said the blessing, broke it, and gave it to them" (24:30). These words are obviously an allusion to Jesus at the Last Supper when Jesus "took the bread, said the blessing, broke it, and gave it to them" (22:19). Luke then tells us: "With that their eyes were opened and they recognized him" (24:31).

If we ask ourselves, Where was the Risen Christ present in the two disciples' lives? we will have the answer to the question, Where is the Risen Christ present in our lives? Christ was present when the two were gathered together in his name. Christ was present in the stranger on the road. Christ was present in the living Word. Christ was present in the Eucharist.

Once the two disciples recognize the presence of Christ in their lives, they become witnesses of this Good News. They immediately return to Jerusalem where they tell the eleven and some others with them that Christ "was made known to them in the breaking of the bread" (Luke 24:35).

Passover

The night the Lord passed over the house of the Israelites marked by the blood of the lamb, and spared the firstborn sons from death. It also is the feast that celebrates the deliverance of the Chosen People from bondage in Egypt and the Exodus from Egypt to the Promised Land.

Stay in Jerusalem

Unlike the Gospels of Mark and Matthew, Jesus' appearances to the eleven and their companions in the Gospel of Luke are in Jerusalem, not Galilee. As we mentioned in our overview of the Gospels, Luke organizes his Gospel geographically, around a journey. Luke's Gospel starts in Jerusalem with the announcement of John the Baptist's birth. Jesus has a ministry in Galilee, a trip to Jerusalem, and a ministry in Jerusalem, which is also the city in which Jesus died, was buried, and was raised. In the post-Resurrection appearances of Jesus, the Gospel ends where it began—in Jerusalem.

In this way we are prepared for the second half of Luke's work, the Acts of the Apostles. In this book Luke continues his account of the Good News of salvation by describing the spread of the Church under the influence of the Holy Spirit. This book is also structured around a journey, a journey that begins in Jerusalem. (Because the Acts of the Apostles is linked to the Gospel of Luke, we will study the Acts of the Apostles in the next section.)

After his Resurrection, when Jesus appears in Jerusalem to the eleven, they think he is a ghost. Jesus shows them his hands and feet. This is so that they can see his wounds and know that the person who is appearing to them, the Son of God made man, is the person who was crucified and died. Jesus also asks for something to eat and eats it. This too is to emphasize the bodily presence of the Risen Christ.

At this meeting, when Jesus commissions the Apostles, he says: "Thus it is written . . . that repentance, for the forgiveness of sins, would be preached in his name to all the nations, beginning from Jerusalem" (Luke 24:47). This is the commissioning of the Apostles, the sending forth of these witnesses to Christ into the world. Only in Luke does the commissioning have this emphasis on repentance and forgiveness, which, as we have seen, are significant themes in the Gospel of Luke.

The disciples are told to stay in Jerusalem until they receive the Spirit, "the promise of my Father" . . . until [they] are "clothed with power from on high" (24:49). The Gospel then ends where the second half of Luke's two-volume work will begin, with Jesus' Ascension into Heaven.

The Apostles then return to Jerusalem "with great joy, and they were continually in the temple praising God" (Luke

24:52–53). The Gospel that opened with a priest of the Old Covenant, Zechariah, offering a sacrifice in the Temple, now ends in that same Temple, with the custodians of the New Covenant praising God for all he has done through the gift of his Son, Jesus. ✝

Heart and Summit

The *Catechism* reminds us that "the Eucharist is the heart and the summit of the Church's life, for in it Christ associates his Church and all her members with his sacrifice of praise and thanksgiving offered once for all on the cross to his Father; by this sacrifice he pours out the graces of salvation on his Body which is the Church" (1407).

When we look back on our study of Luke's Gospel, we realize that the Eucharist is the beginning, the heart, and the summit of Luke's account.

However, Luke uses a number of different narrative forms to probe the mystery of Christ as the Bread of Life. First, Luke places the Christ child in the manger, the place where one puts the food for the flock. Then Luke describes Jesus' last **Passover** meal with his disciples where Jesus institutes the Eucharist. Finally, Luke describes the disciples on the road to Emmaus recognizing the Risen Christ in the breaking of the bread. Luke puts this emphasis on the Eucharist because he wants his audience, including us, to be able to recognize Christ in the breaking of the bread too.

Part Review

1. What beliefs about Mary find their roots in Luke's Gospel?

2. What is Luke teaching by calling Jesus the firstborn son, who was wrapped in swaddling clothes and laid in a manger (see Luke 2:7)?

3. Name three ways Luke teaches that everyone is offered forgiveness and everyone is invited to the Kingdom.

4. At what points in his Gospel does Luke note the presence and work of the Holy Spirit?

5. How does Jesus give new reality and new meaning to the bread and wine of the Passover meal?

6. Name four ways Jesus continues to be a healer and a forgiver during his Passion and Crucifixion.

7. Why can we not claim that the words attributed to Jesus in the Gospels are exact quotations?

8. In what ways was the Risen Christ present to the two disciples on the road to Emmaus?

9. What does Luke emphasize in his account of Jesus' appearance to the eleven in Jerusalem?

10. Name three ways Luke probes the mystery of Jesus as the Bread of Life.

Part 5

The Acts of the Apostles

At the beginning of the Acts of the Apostles, we find Luke once again writing to his friend (or to his readers) called Theophilus. Luke's "first book" was his Gospel, and he begins this second book where he ended the first, with the Ascension of Jesus:

> In the first book, Theophilus, I dealt with all that Jesus did and taught until the day he was taken up, after giving instructions through the holy Spirit to the apostles whom he had chosen. He presented himself alive to them by many proofs after he had suffered, appearing to them during forty days and speaking about the kingdom of God. (Acts of the Apostles 1:1–3)

Luke then recalls the instructions of Jesus, to stay in Jerusalem until the Holy Spirit would come upon them. Luke goes on to recount the Ascension of Jesus into Heaven. His last words to them are, "You will be my witnesses . . . to the ends of the earth" (Acts of the Apostles 1:8).

An angel interrupts them as they stare into the sky, asking, "Men of Galilee, why are you standing there looking at the sky?" (Acts of the Apostles 1:11). So they returned to Jerusalem, having been told that it was time to start doing, time to start witnessing, time to start *acting*. And so begins the Acts of the Apostles and the account of their witness to Jesus Christ in Jerusalem, in Judea and Samaria, and yes, to the ends of the earth.

The articles in this part address the following topics:

- Article 25: "Witness to Christ in Jerusalem" (Acts of the Apostles, Chapters 1–7) (page 133)

- Article 26: "Witness to Christ in Judea and Samaria" (Acts of the Apostles, Chapters 8–12) (page 138)

- Article 27: "Witness to Christ to the Ends of the Earth" (Acts of the Apostles, Chapters 13–28) (page 141)

© Francis G. Mayer/CORBIS

An Overview of the Acts of the Apostles

The Acts of the Apostles	
Inspired author:	often identified as Luke, who also wrote the Gospel of Luke
Approximate date of writing:	AD 85
Location of writing:	Greece
Audience:	Gentile (Greek) Christians represented by Theophilus
Purpose:	to show how the Christian faith spread from Jerusalem to "the ends of the earth" (represented by Rome)
Themes:	the work of the Holy Spirit in the Church; authority and unity in the Church
Sources:	Luke himself, while traveling with the Apostle Paul; other sources unknown

A Glance at the Acts of the Apostles

Acts of the Apostles 1:1—2:13: preparation for the Christian mission
Acts of the Apostles 2:14—8:3: the mission in Jerusalem
Acts of the Apostles 8:4—9:43: the mission in Judea and Samaria
Acts of the Apostles 10:1—15:35: the inauguration of the Gentile mission
Acts of the Apostles 15:36—28:31: the mission of Paul to the ends of the earth

Article 25 Witness to Christ in Jerusalem (Acts of the Apostles, Chapters 1–7)

As we read the second half of Luke's two-volume work, we learn how Christianity moved beyond Jewish circles and how Christ became the light of the world for Gentiles.

What we already know about the formation of a Gospel is important information as we read the Acts of the Apostles. Acts too is an edited account of inherited written and oral traditions about events. We do not know exactly what Luke's sources were. There is a real possibility that one source was an account of events that occurred when Luke was Paul's traveling companion. During some of the journey narratives, the narrator's voice occasionally changes from third person, talking about Paul, to first-person plural: "We . . ." (see Acts of the Apostles 16:10–17, 20:5–15, 21:1–18, 27:1—28:16).

The Acts of the Apostles is often called the Gospel of the Holy Spirit. It is the Holy Spirit who precipitates all the *acts* that are described. The book begins as Luke's Gospel ends, with the Ascension of Jesus Christ. As was true at the empty tomb, an angel explains the significance of the event: "This Jesus who has been taken up from you into heaven will return in the same way as you have seen him going into heaven" (Acts of the Apostles 1:11).

In *The Miracle of Pentecost,* by Luis de Morales (Church of the Asuncion, Caceres, Spain), the three most prominent figures are Mary, Peter (to her right), and John (to her left). What does this say about the apostolic Church?

Remain in Jerusalem

Before his Ascension, Jesus tells his disciples to remain in Jerusalem where they will soon be baptized with the Holy Spirit (see Acts of the Apostles 1:5). Jesus also tells them: "You will be my witnesses in Jerusalem, throughout Judea and Samaria, and to the ends of the earth" (1:8). Here Luke gives us the geographic organization of the Acts of the Apostles: chapter 2–7 tell of the disciples' witness in Jerusalem, chapters 8–12 of their witness in Judea and Samaria, and chapters 13–28 of their witness to the ends of the earth (Rome).

Deacons in the Early Church

Although Luke's descriptions of community life among the Christians in Jerusalem are sometimes idyllic, Luke also tells us that there was division in the community. The **Hellenists** complained against the **Hebrews** that their "widows were being neglected in the daily distribution" (Acts of the Apostles 6:1). This accusation is taken seriously by the Twelve. They must devote themselves to the Word of God, but also realize that tending to the temporal needs of those in their community is important work as well. Therefore, the Twelve tell the Hellenists to "select from among you seven reputable men, filled with the Spirit and wisdom, whom we shall appoint to this task" (6:3).

The Hellenists do just that. They select seven men, and the Apostles "prayed and laid hands on them" (Acts of the Apostles 6:6). These men came to be called deacons, from a Greek word meaning "servant." We see here the beginning of the division of roles and the formal selection and del-

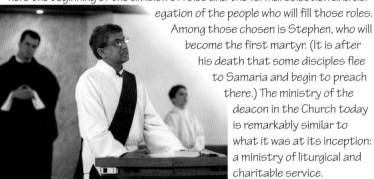

egation of the people who will fill those roles. Among those chosen is Stephen, who will become the first martyr. (It is after his death that some disciples flee to Samaria and begin to preach there.) The ministry of the deacon in the Church today is remarkably similar to what it was at its inception: a ministry of liturgical and charitable service.

The community that waits and devotes itself to prayer includes Mary, Jesus' mother, as well as some other women (see Acts of the Apostles 1:14). While they wait, under Peter's leadership, they replace Judas, who has met a gruesome death. Judas is the only one of the Twelve who is replaced upon his death. It is important as the Apostles begin their ministry of being Christ's witnesses to the world that there are twelve of them, evidently to reflect the Twelve Tribes of Israel. The Twelve Apostles are foundational. It is on the Twelve's apostolic witness that the Church will be built. The final choice is made by lot. Just as Jesus appointed the Twelve, so does the Holy Spirit appoint Matthias to replace Judas. The mission of Christ and the mission of the Spirit are joined together and inseparable.

Hellenists
Greek-speaking Jewish Christians.

Hebrews
In some New Testament writings, Hebrew-speaking Jewish Christians.

Baptized by the Holy Spirit

In the Acts of the Apostles, the Holy Spirit comes upon the disciples on Pentecost. Pentecost was already a feast for the Jews, the day on which they celebrated their covenant with God and his giving Moses the Law on Mount Sinai (see Exodus 19:16–19). A large group is in one room when "suddenly there came from the sky a noise like a strong driving wind. . . . Then there appeared to them tongues as of fire, which parted and came to rest on each one of them" (Acts of the Apostles 2:2–3). Wind and fire are also the signs of God's presence on Mount Sinai. Notice that the tongues of fire rest on each person, not just on a chosen few. The effect of the Holy Spirit's presence is that the disciples are filled with power. They begin to speak in different tongues so that people of many languages are able to understand them. This is Luke's way of describing the effect that the disciples' witness will have. People from all over the world will hear the Good News of Jesus Christ in every language under the sun.

The *Kerygma*

Peter, now emboldened, with no sign of his former weaknesses, then stands up to speak. He preaches the most basic content of the apostolic witness. (Remember that, just as in the Gospels, the Acts of the Apostles is not claiming that speeches are exact quotations; speeches were based on oral tradition, then shaped by the author and attributed to the historical person in order to teach the audience.)

The content of Peter's talk is called the *kerygma,* which, as you may recall from an earlier article, means "proclamation" or "preaching." Its function is not to explain, apply, or exhort; it simply proclaims the most basic truths of the Good News of salvation through Jesus Christ. Throughout the first half of the Acts of the Apostles, Peter repeats this *kerygma* over and over. The *kerygma* includes five main points, four of which appear in this initial speech:

- Jesus fulfills the words of the prophets.
- Jesus suffered, died, and was raised from the dead.
- Jesus is the Messiah. (As you will recall, *Messiah* and *Christ* both mean "the Anointed One," a reference to the one for whom the Israelites hoped.)
- Jesus calls everyone to repentance.
- Jesus will come again.

Live It!

The Gifts of the Holy Spirit

At Confirmation, the bishop prays this prayer for the candidates:

All-powerful God, Father of our Lord Jesus Christ,
by water and the Holy Spirit
you freed your sons and daughters from sin
and gave them new life.
Send your Holy Spirit upon them
to be their Helper and Guide.
Give them the spirit of wisdom and understanding,
the spirit of right judgment and courage,
the spirit of knowledge and reverence.
Fill them with the spirit of wonder and awe in your presence.
We ask this through Christ our Lord.

(Rite of Confirmation, 25)

Which of these seven gifts do you recognize in your life? Which ones do you need more of? Do you pray to the Holy Spirit as you make decisions in your life?

The Gifts of the Holy Spirit are strengthened through prayer and especially by the reception of the Sacraments. If you have not been confirmed, talk with your parents or parish priest about receiving this Sacrament.

The Holy Spirit and Confirmation

Before conferring the Sacrament of Confirmation, the bishop may offer remarks similar to these: "In our day the coming of the Holy Spirit in confirmation is no longer marked by the gift of tongues, but we know his coming by faith. He fills our hearts with the love of God, brings us together in one faith but in different vocations, and works within us to make the Church one and holy" (*Rite of Confirmation*, 22).

In the early centuries of the Church, the Sacrament of Confirmation, which confers the Gifts of the Holy Spirit upon us today, was celebrated with Baptism. Although this Sacrament is now celebrated separately in the Western Church, it retains its meaning as the completion of Baptism. The Sacrament of Confirmation brings baptismal grace to perfection. Through the Holy Spirit, we are rooted more deeply in Christ as children of God. Our bond with the Church and her mission is strengthened, and we are made ready to bear witness to our faith, with the help of the Holy Spirit, in word and action.

The Sacrament of Confirmation, like Baptism, confers an indelible character, or mark, on the soul. For this reason this Sacrament can be received only once. The essential rite of Confirmation is anointing the forehead of the baptized with Sacred Chrism (in the East, other sense organs as well), together with the laying on of the minister's hand and the words "Be sealed with the Gift of the Holy Spirit" (*Rite of Confirmation*, 27).

As was true during Jesus' public ministry, the disciples' preaching of this *kerygma* has added authority because they perform many wonders and signs. The Christian community also witnesses to this Good News of salvation in everyday life, for Luke tells us, "They devoted themselves to the teaching of the apostles and to the communal life, to the breaking of the bread and to the prayers" (Acts of the Apostles 2:42).

Their life together included sharing with one another and caring for those in need: "All who believed were together and had all things in common; they would sell their property and possessions and divide them among all according to each one's need" (Acts of the Apostles 2:44–45). This communal life remains today a model for Christian living and is the template on which religious communities today still shape their lives. ♱

Article 26 Witness to Christ in Judea and Samaria (Acts of the Apostles, Chapters 8–12)

Because of persecution, Philip, one of the seven chosen during the disagreement between the Hellenists and the Hebrews, leaves Jerusalem and goes to Samaria to spread the Good News of Jesus Christ.

Find the following places on this map: Bethlehem, Nazareth, Cana, Capernaum, Bethany, Jerusalem, Samaria, Gaza, and Damascus. Can you recall events from the Gospels and the Acts of the Apostles associated with these places?

Philip in Samaria

As you read the Acts of the Apostles, notice that Luke wants his audience to be assured that the Holy Spirit leads the Church. For example, Luke is careful to tell us that Philip, in doing something as revolutionary as going to the "unclean" people of Samaria, was not being a loose cannon. Philip was being led by the Holy Spirit, and was staying in touch with the Church in Jerusalem. When the Apostles in Jerusalem heard that Philip was baptizing Samaritans, they sent Peter and John down to check things out. Peter and John approved of what they saw, laid hands on the Samaritans, and they received the Holy Spirit (see Acts of the Apostles 8:17).

Next, an angel of the Lord directs Philip to take a road headed for Gaza on which he meets an Ethiopian **eunuch**. The eunuch is reading a passage from Isaiah: "Like a sheep he was led to the slaughter, / and as a lamb before its shearer is silent" (Acts of the Apostles 8:32). The eunuch asks Philip if the prophet is speaking about himself or someone else.

This interchange is a perfect example of how the Church, both then and now, understands the Scriptures

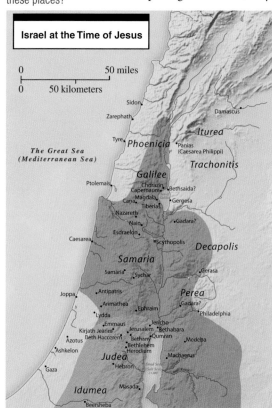

Israel at the Time of Jesus

0   50 miles
0   50 kilometers

as a living Word. If Philip had answered the question from an historical perspective, he would have said that the prophet was speaking about the nation of Israel. However, by the time Philip met the eunuch, the passage from Isaiah, understood as a living Word, had helped the Church to find meaning in Jesus' Passion and death. Therefore, in answer to the question, Philip interprets this passage and others in relation to Jesus. The eunuch is converted and asks for Baptism.

eunuch
An emasculated man. Such men were excluded from the assembly of the Lord (see Deuteronomy 23:1).

Paul's Conversion

Though Saul (also called Paul) is still persecuting Christians, he too has a profound conversion experience while on the road to Damascus. Suddenly, there is a flash of light and a voice says, "Saul, Saul, why are you persecuting me?" (Acts of the Apostles 9:4). Paul asks who this person is, and the voice replies, "I am Jesus, whom you are persecuting" (9:5). Paul is left blind and unable to eat or drink for several days. But Paul learns from this experience that Jesus completely identifies with his followers. The voice did not ask, "Why are you persecuting my followers?" but "Why are you persecuting *me*?"

A disciple of Christ named Ananias has a vision in which he is directed by the Lord to go to Paul. He doesn't want to go because he has heard how Paul has persecuted Christians. The Lord tells Ananias that Paul "is a chosen instrument of mine to carry my name before Gentiles, kings, and Israelites" (Acts of the Apostles 9:15). Ananias then goes to meet Paul, restores his sight, and Paul regains his strength. Paul then ceases to persecute Christians and begins to proclaim Jesus Christ.

Notice that throughout the Acts of the Apostles, Luke emphasizes due delegation of authority and unity. Even a charismatic person like Paul, who received his commission directly from the Risen Christ, acts in unity and cooperation with the Church in Jerusalem.

The Ongoing Conversion of Peter

Paul has now learned that Gentiles are to be invited into covenant love also. It remains for Peter to learn the same. Peter has a dream in which a sheet comes down full of all kinds of animals, clean and unclean according to Jewish Law. A voice tells Peter to "slaughter and eat" (Acts of the Apostles 10:13). Peter, in fidelity to the Law, refuses. The voice says, "What God has made clean, you are not to call profane" (10:15). This dream leaves Peter completely puzzled.

Peter, the Church, and the Holy Spirit

Luke is careful to point out that even Peter could not go off and act independently of the Church in Jerusalem. After baptizing Gentiles, and then returning to Jerusalem, Peter had to explain himself. His fellow circumcised believers accused him: "You entered the house of uncircumcised people and ate with them" (Acts of the Apostles 11:3).

© George Muresan / Shutterstock.com

Peter does not resent or dismiss as unimportant his fellow believers' concern. Were it not for his dream and his experience at Cornelius's house, Peter would have agreed with them. So Peter explains everything carefully. For a second time, we hear about Peter's dream, about the invitation to Cornelius's house, and about what happened after he arrived. Peter asks, "If then God gave them the same gift he gave to us when we came to believe in the Lord Jesus Christ, who was I to be able to hinder God?" (Acts of the Apostles 11:17).

Peter's questioners are completely satisfied with this answer. They too are open to new insights offered to them through the inspiration of the Holy Spirit.

Catholic Wisdom

The Ascension of Jesus

In the Nicene Creed, we proclaim that Jesus sits "at the right hand of the Father" (*Roman Missal*). The right hand is a symbol of power, because for most people the right hand is the dominant and more powerful hand. "The Father's right hand" is a symbol of Christ's glory, honor, divinity, and oneness with the Father, as God and man (see *CCC*, 663). The Ascension marks the entrance of Jesus' humanity into Heaven. Though hidden from our eyes, he will come again in glory.

However, a man named Cornelius, a centurion, also has a vision in which he is directed to summon Peter to his house. Under normal circumstances Peter would not have gone to a Gentile house. However, because of his dream, Peter realizes that he must not call any person profane or unclean (see Acts of the Apostles 10:28). So Peter goes and preaches to those in Cornelius's house. The Holy Spirit comes upon all of them, and Peter realizes that he cannot refuse them Baptism.

Peter, like Philip and Paul, comes to realize that God does not agree with the prejudices taught about others. God loves even eunuchs and Gentiles and offers salvation to every single person. ✝

Article 27 Witness to Christ to the Ends of the Earth (Acts of the Apostles, Chapters 13–28)

The focus of the second half of the Acts of the Apostles is primarily on Paul and his three missionary journeys (see chapters 13–14; 15:40—18:22; 18:23—21:17), all of which begin and end in Antioch. The concluding chapters tell us about Paul's trials in Jerusalem and his years in Rome.

Find Antioch in Syria on this map. Then trace each of Paul's missionary journeys, both departing and returning. (Note the direction of the arrows.)

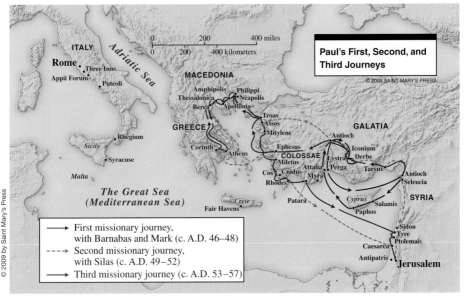

Paul's First, Second, and Third Journeys

© 2009 SAINT MARY'S PRESS

→ First missionary journey, with Barnabas and Mark (c. A.D. 46–48)
---→ Second missionary journey, with Silas (c. A.D. 49–52)
→ Third missionary journey (c. A.D. 53–57)

As Luke continues to give us an account of the spread of Christianity throughout the then-known world, he also continues to stress that the Holy Spirit is leading the Church every step of the way. For instance, Luke tells us that while those in the church in Antioch were worshipping, "the holy

The Sacrament of Holy Orders

In the Acts of the Apostles, we have seen the introduction of two of the ministries of the Church that still exist today, the ministries of deacon and presbyter. The presbyter is that person we now know as a priest. Both deacon and priest are two of the three degrees of ordained ministry in the Church. The first and highest degree is that of bishop. These three ministries—deacon, priest, and bishop—are indispensable to the Church and have been so from the beginning. They provide the foundation for the organic structure of the Church. Indeed one cannot speak of "the Church" without including these three ministries.

The bishop (from the Greek word *episcopos*) receives the fullness of the Sacrament of Holy Orders. This Sacrament makes him part of the college (meaning "assembly" or "group") of bishops and makes him a visible head of the diocese entrusted to him. (Auxiliary bishops are bishops who assist bishops, archbishops, or cardinals.) Bishops, as successors to the Apostles and members of the college of bishops, not only concern themselves with the welfare of their own dioceses but also take on as their apostolic responsibility and mission the welfare of the entire Church, under the authority of the successor of Saint Peter, the Pope.

Spirit said, 'Set apart for me Barnabas and Saul for the work to which I have called them'" (Acts of the Apostles 13:2). Those in the church in Antioch lay hands on Paul and Barnabas, formally commissioning them for their missionary journey.

As Paul and Barnabas travel, they always begin their preaching in the synagogues. Many Jews accept their teaching, but some do not. To those who reject the teaching, Paul and Barnabas say: "It was necessary that the word of God be spoken to you first, but since you reject it . . . we now turn to the Gentiles. For so the Lord has commanded us, 'I have made you a light to the Gentiles, that you may be an instrument of salvation to the ends of the earth'" (Acts of the Apostles 13:46–47).

Paul and Barnabas also formally appoint church leaders, often called **elders** or **presbyters**. Luke tells us that they "appointed presbyters for them in each church and, with prayer and fasting, commended them to the Lord in whom they had put their faith" (Acts of the Apostles 14:23). Due delegation and church unity are concerns of Luke's throughout the Acts of the Apostles.

elder
A person appointed to have authority in governing a local church.

presbyter
A synonym to *elder* in the Acts of the Apostles and an alternative word for *priest* today.

The Council of Jerusalem

When Paul and Barnabas return to Antioch, they report back on all that has happened. There are some in Antioch who insist that in order to be saved, Gentile Christians must obey the Jewish Law and be circumcised. Paul and Barnabas have been welcoming Gentiles and not insisting that they obey the Jewish Law. Rather than just ignore their critics, or divide into two factions, the church in Antioch sends Paul, Barnabas, and some others to Jerusalem to talk this over with the Apostles and elders (see Acts of the Apostles 15:2). The stage is set for the first council held by the Church.

After arriving in Jerusalem, Paul and Barnabas tell the Apostles and presbyters about their experience. Some Pharisees in Jerusalem agree with those who have objected to the Gentiles having been welcomed without having to obey the Law. They say, "It is necessary to circumcise them and direct them to observe the Mosaic law" (Acts of the Apostles 15:5). After listening to a great deal of debate, Peter shares with the group his own experience with Cornelius. In conclusion, Peter says, "We believe that we are saved through the grace of the Lord Jesus, in the same way as they" (15:11). Peter is reminding his listeners that although a Jewish Christian might continue to obey the Law, that Jewish Christian does not believe that it is obedience to the Law that is saving him or her. Those who obey the Law and those who don't are both saved the same way: through the grace of Jesus Christ.

The decision is made that circumcision will not be required of Gentile Christians. A letter is sent by emissary to Antioch. The letter prefaces the decision with: "It is the decision of the holy Spirit and of us not to place on you any burden beyond these necessities" (Acts of the Apostles 15:28). The letter then goes on to elaborate on what restrictions are required, such as not eating meat from animals sacrificed to idols (see 15:29).

The Holy Spirit and the Church

The Holy Spirit is the anointing of Christ upon the Church. Christ, the Head of the Church, continually pours out the Holy Spirit on its members, thus building up, enlivening, and sanctifying the Church, who is the sacrament of the Holy Trinity's communion with the human race. The Church is also the Temple of the Holy Spirit, who is the soul of the Mystical Body of Christ and the source of the Church's life, unity, diversity, gifts, and charisms. The Holy Spirit also leads the Church in her missionary activity. He urges the Church to walk the same paths that Christ walked in evangelizing those who are poor, following the way of poverty, obedience, service, and self-sacrifice, even to death and resurrection with him. For as the apologist Tertullian wrote in the early years of the Church, "The blood of martyrs is the seed of Christians"[4] (CCC, 852).

Peter and Paul's Unity with Christ

As Luke continues to describe Paul's missionary activity, we can't help but notice that Paul's experiences are similar to Peter's, and both of their experiences are similar to Christ's. All are guided by the Holy Spirit, all perform miraculous acts of power, all suffer persecution, and all preach constantly. By stressing these similarities, Luke is teaching his readers the same thing Paul was taught when Jesus asked, "Why are you persecuting me?" Jesus is one with his disciples. Peter and

Paul are continuing the mission of Jesus Christ. Where they are, Christ himself is also present. For this reason, Peter and Paul are sometimes referred to as "other Christs."

As the Acts of the Apostles continues, Luke emphasizes the unity between Paul and Christ as he tells us of Paul's arrest and trials in Jerusalem. One cannot read this account (see Acts of the Apostles, chapters 21–26) without being reminded of Jesus. Both Paul and Jesus are tried before the Sanhedrin, both are tried before a Roman governor, both are tried before a Jewish Herodian king, both are found innocent by Roman authorities, and both are abused and

Pray It!

Come, Holy Spirit

On Pentecost Sunday the entire Church prays the sequence "Come, Holy Spirit" (Veni Sancte Spiritus) after the Second Reading of the Mass. The following translation is not one used in the liturgy, but it can be used for private prayer.

Come, Holy Spirit,
And send out from heaven
Your radiant light.

Come, father of the poor,
Come, giver of gifts,
Come, light of our hearts.

Best consoler,
Sweet guest of the soul,
Sweetness of cool refreshment.

Rest in labor,
Relief in heat,
Consolation in weeping.

O most blessed light,
Fill the center of the hearts
Of your faithful.

Without your divine power,
There is nothing in humans,
Nothing is innocent.

Wash what is soiled,
Water what is dry,
Heal what is wounded.

Bend what is rigid,
Warm what is chilled,
Guide what is astray.

Give to your faithful,
Who trust in you,
The seven sacred gifts.

Give the reward of virtue,
Give the goal of salvation,
Give eternal joy.
Amen. Alleluia.

(Sr. Irene Nowell, translator, "Translation of the Pentecost Sequence")

ridiculed by the crowds. The main difference, of course, is that while Jesus is crucified, Paul, after appealing to the Roman emperor for a hearing (see 25:11), is sent to Rome.

Paul in Rome

The Acts of the Apostles remains silent on what finally happens to Paul. Given Luke's theme, this is as it should be. Luke's Acts of the Apostles is not primarily about Peter and Paul but about how Jesus Christ became Light to the Gentiles. By the end of the Acts of the Apostles, a Christian community, not founded by Paul, is already well established in Rome. The Acts of the Apostles ends with Paul's living peacefully under house arrest, where "he remained for two full years in his lodgings. He received all who came to him, and with complete assurance and without hindrance he proclaimed the kingdom of God and taught about the Lord Jesus Christ" (Acts of the Apostles 28:30–31). The Good News had truly arrived at the cultural center of the then-known world, the great city of Rome. ✝

Part Review

1. What is the Acts of the Apostles often called? Why?

2. What is the effect of the Holy Spirit's coming at Pentecost?

3. What five points are included in the *kerygma?*

4. How does Philip interpret Isaiah for the eunuch?

5. What is the significance of what the Lord says to Paul on the road to Damascus?

6. What is the significance of Peter's dream and his experience with Cornelius?

7. How does Luke continue to emphasize that it is the Holy Spirit who is leading the Church?

8. What is decided at the Council of Jerusalem?

9. How does Luke emphasize the parallels between Peter and Paul and Christ?

The Johannine Writings

Part 1

The Gospel of John

As you will discover, the Gospel of John differs from the synoptic Gospels, and so this introduction differs as well. Enjoy these scriptural readings as you begin your study.

Beginnings

Narrator: Welcome to the Gospel of John. You are invited to new life in Jesus Christ, Word of the Father, upon whom the Holy Spirit rests, as in a new creation. You are invited to hear the Word that gives meaning to all life and to follow the Light that overcomes all darkness. Later, you may want to compare how closely the readings from the Gospel of John follow these readings from the Book of Genesis: Genesis 1:1–2 and Genesis 1:3–5.

Reader:

In the beginning was the Word
> and the Word was with God,
> and the Word was God. (John 1:1)
He was in the beginning with God.
All things came to be through him,
> and without him nothing came to be. (John 1:2–3)

All:

What came to be through him was life,
> and this life was the light of the human race;
the light shines in the darkness,
> and the darkness has not overcome it. (John 1:3–5)

The articles that follow will open this invitation to you and help you to understand the power of the Gospel of John.

The articles in the part address the following topics:

- Article 28: "Comparison and Contrast: John and the Synoptic Gospels" (page 151)

- Article 29: "Allegory in the Seven Signs" (page 156)

- Article 30: "The Paschal Mystery in the Gospel of John" (page 159)

- Article 31: "John's Post-Resurrection Accounts" (page 163)

© Manolis Grigoreas / Private Collection / Malva Gallery / The Bridgeman Art Library

An Overview of the Gospel of John

The Gospel of John	
Inspired author:	unknown, but traditionally attributed to the Apostle John; a member of a Christian community possibly founded by a beloved disciple of Jesus (the Johannine community)
Approximate date of writing:	AD 90–100
Location of writing:	traditionally Ephesus, but may have been Antioch or Alexandria
Audience:	a Jewish Christian community that may have included Gentiles and Samaritans
Image of Jesus:	noble and powerful, one with the Father; fully in control of his destiny, even through his Passion and death to his Resurrection
Genealogy:	none
Themes:	Jesus, the preexistent Word of God; the Risen Christ among us taught through the account of his seven great signs and the I AM statements
Sources:	unknown; most of the material in the Gospel of John is unique to this Gospel
Symbol of Gospel:	the eagle, who by legend flies high enough to look directly at the sun, as Jesus, the Word of God, sees the face of the Father

A Glance at the Gospel of John

John 1:1–18: prologue: a poem about the Word of God

John 1:19—12:50: the Book of Signs: Jesus' miracles and teachings, disputes with "the Jews"

Chapters 13–20: the Book of Glory: the Last Supper; Jesus' suffering, death, and Resurrection

Chapter 21: epilogue: an appearance of the Risen Jesus

Article 28 Comparison and Contrast: John and the Synoptic Gospels

From the moment you start reading the Gospel of John, you will notice how different this Gospel is from the synoptic Gospels. John does not start with Jesus' public ministry, as does Mark, or with an infancy narrative, as do Matthew and Luke. Rather, John begins his Gospel with the same three words that began the Book of Genesis, "In the beginning" (Genesis 1:1). He then continues with a hymn that is set in the heart of eternity, before time began and before the world was created. In this hymn we learn that Jesus is the pre-existent Word who, from the beginning, "was with God" and "was God" (John 1:1). The Word existed before Creation, for "All things came to be through him" (1:3). It is this Word that "became flesh" (1:14) and dwelt among us.

Nathaniel Under the Fig Tree, by James Tissot (1836–1902), portrays an example of Jesus' all-knowing and all-seeing love for each individual. See the Gospel of John.

Catholic Wisdom

The Word of Power

Did God create the universe and then leave it to "tick along" by itself, like a clock? No. God keeps the universe in existence by his Word. The Word of God is a word of power, for the Son "sustains all things by his mighty word" (Hebrews 1:3) and by the Holy Spirit, "the Lord, the giver of life" (Nicene Creed).

metaphor
A figure of speech in which a word or phrase that ordinarily designates one thing is used to designate another, making an implied comparison.

The Disciples Know Who Jesus Is

In addition to beginning his Gospel in a completely different way, John presents the level of understanding reached by Jesus' disciples completely differently. As we noted, in the synoptic Gospels, the narrator and the reader know Jesus' identity all along, but the disciples do not. In John's Gospel, the disciples also know the true identity of Jesus. Even before Jesus' public ministry begins, John the Baptist gives witness to him as "the Lamb of God, who takes away the sin of the world" (1:29). Shortly afterwards, still before Jesus had begun to teach or preach, Andrew tells Peter that Jesus is the Messiah (see 1:41), and Nathaniel declares that Jesus is the "Son of God" (1:49). A spotlight is on Jesus' divinity from beginning to end.

Allegories, Not Parables

In the synoptic Gospels, we noted that although Jesus teaches in many ways, his primary way of teaching the people is through parables. But in John's Gospel, Jesus does not tell a single parable. Instead Jesus gives long theological discourses that start out as dialogues but end up as monologues. Very often Jesus is talking to a person who misunderstands what he is saying. The person takes Jesus' words literally when he intends them metaphorically. For instance, Jesus tells Nicodemus that a person must be born again of water and the Spirit. Nicodemus asks how a person can be born again: "Surely he cannot reenter his mother's womb and be born again, can he?" (John 3:4). Nicodemus' misunderstanding gives Jesus the opportunity to elaborate and to make clear that he is using the language of **metaphor**: He is talking not about physical birth but about spiritual birth, about the new creation that takes place at Baptism.

This pattern of Jesus' speaking metaphorically and being misunderstood is repeated (see the woman at the well in 4:11; the disciples in 4:33). By repeating this pattern, John is teaching his audience to think metaphorically rather than literally.

Like the people in the Gospel, we too might misunderstand at first. We also must learn to think metaphorically. In order to understand John's Gospel, we must develop the ability to see levels of meaning, to understand allegory. This will be effortless for some, and for others it will be difficult. If you find it difficult, don't give up! Once you develop the skill, you will see the allegory. Unless one can learn to think metaphorically, to think allegorically, it will be difficult to understand the intended meaning of much of John's Gospel.

Double Meanings

In addition to John's accounts of Jesus' mighty acts—his signs—having two levels of meaning, so do many of John's words. For instance, John the Baptist immediately identifies Jesus as the Lamb of God. This expression has two meanings. It refers both to the lamb in Exodus whose blood put on the lintels of the Israelites' homes caused the angel of death to pass over those homes (see chapter 12). At the same time, it refers to the lamb in Isaiah (see 53:7, 10) who goes silently before the shearer. (Recall Philip's explaining this passage to the eunuch in the Acts of the Apostles.)

As you read John, see if you can figure out the double meanings in expressions like "lifted up," "living water," and "I AM." The more you are able to discern two levels of meaning, the more you will understand what John wishes to teach us.

© Jane Tyson / iStockphoto.com

John's Seven Signs

The synoptic Gospels depict Jesus' performing many miraculous acts of power. We said when reading Mark that the word used for these acts, *dynameis*, is the root word for our word *dynamite*. In John the remarkable miraculous acts

Jesus performs are not called *dynameis* but *semeion,* meaning "signs." Instead of the many miracles in the synoptics, there are only seven *signs* in John's Gospel. Of these seven, five have much in common with miracles described in the synoptic Gospels, such as the healing of a lame person or a blind person, but two have no parallel in the other Gospels: the wedding feast at Cana and the raising of Lazarus. In addition, there are no exorcisms in John.

John's accounts of Jesus' miracles focus on symbolic meaning rather than on the concrete action itself. The physical miracles—signs—symbolize a deeper truth and reality. When Jesus changes water into wine (see 2:1–11), John foreshadows that Jesus will be the Blood (wine) of the New Covenant. In the account of Jesus' healing of the official's son (see 4:46–54), faith in Jesus leads to wholeness and health. The feeding of the five thousand (see 6:1–14) alludes to Jesus' satisfying our spiritual hunger. The story of Jesus walking on water (see 6:16–21) demonstrates that Jesus has the power to calm our every fear and rid our hearts

Pray It!

The Eternal Word

We celebrate the Incarnation of the Word of God in a special way at Christmas. This prayer refers directly to the Word of God:

Almighty God and Father of light,
a child is born for us and a son is given to us.
Your eternal Word leaped down from heaven
in the silent watches of the night,
and now your Church is filled with wonder
at the nearness of her God.

Open our hearts to receive his life
and increase our vision with the rising of dawn,
that our lives may be filled with his glory and his peace,
Who lives and reigns for ever and ever.
Amen.

(Roman Missal)

The Word of God is incarnate now, and we can pray this prayer on any day, at any time, to ask the Father to open our hearts to receive the life, glory, and peace of Jesus Christ.

of all anxiety. The restoration of sight to the blind man (see 9:1–7) symbolizes spiritual insight into the real identity of Jesus. The blind man has eyes of faith to see the one and only Light—Jesus Christ. Lazarus's resurrection from the dead (see 11:21–44) heralds Christ's power over life and death and shows that Jesus is the path to eternal life. It foreshadows the death and Resurrection of Jesus.

Why is John's Gospel so different? Once more the reason is that John is responding to the needs of his audience. John's Gospel dates to about AD 90. Jesus' expected return on the clouds of Heaven is long overdue. John's audience is asking, Where is the Risen Christ? John's response is, The Risen Christ is here with us now. Open your eyes and see him in the Church and in those signs that we now call the Sacraments. When we learn to understand the allegorical level of meaning in John's accounts, we begin to understand that John's Gospel is not just about Jesus' public ministry. It is also about the presence of the Risen Christ in the lives of his audience and in our lives as well. From beginning to end, John's Gospel teaches us to see the Risen Christ present in our midst. ✝

Sharing God's Life

Why would God have gone to the trouble of becoming incarnate and living among his human creations?

Two great thinkers in the Church have formulated answers to this same question. Saint Athanasius, an early Doctor of the Church, said, "For the Son of God became man so that we might become God." And Saint Thomas Aquinas said, "The only-begotten Son of God, wanting to make us sharers in his divinity, assumed our nature, so that he, made man, might make men gods." These saints certainly did not mean that we would ever become equal to God but that we human beings would share in God's life, love, and glory, both on earth and in eternity.

God wanted to share not only his creation but also his divine life with us through his Son, the Word. When we unite with the Word of God, we unite with God. Through the working of the Holy Spirit and the sharing of the life of the Son of God, we become sons and daughters of God in Christ.

The Wedding at Cana, by Duccio di Buoninsegna, an altarpiece painted from 1308 to 1311 for the Cathedral of Siena, in Siena, Italy. What baptismal and Eucharistic meaning is found in the Gospel account of the wedding at Cana?

© Erich Lessing / Art Resource, NY

Article 29 Allegory in the Seven Signs

John's Gospel is traditionally understood to consist of the prologue (1:1–18), the Book of Signs (1:19—12:50), the Book of Glory (chapters 13–20), and the epilogue (chapter 21). The Book of Signs includes John's account of seven mighty acts by Jesus. As you will recall, an allegory has two levels of meaning: the literal and the intentional, or symbolic. You will not have any difficulty understanding the literal level of the accounts of the seven signs. However, John is teaching something about not only the actual Jesus but also the presence of the Risen Christ in the life of his late first-

Catholic Wisdom

The Sacraments of Christian Initiation

Three Sacraments together (Baptism; Confirmation, which in the early Church was administered with Baptism; and the Eucharist) constitute the Sacraments of Christian Initiation. Baptism begins new life in Christ, Confirmation strengthens it, and the Eucharist provides lifelong nourishment with the Body and Blood of Christ for complete transformation into this new life. The Eastern Churches continue to administer Confirmation immediately after Baptism, followed by reception of the Eucharist; in this tradition, the unity of the three Sacraments of Christian Initiation is highlighted.

century audience. This is the intentional, or symbolic, level of meaning.

You already have the ability to think allegorically. For instance, when studying Mark's Gospel, we talked about the allegorical interpretation of the Parable of the Sower (see Mark 4:13–20). If you had been with someone in the crowd to whom Jesus told this parable, and that person had said, "I want to go and talk to Jesus about fertilizer," you would have known immediately that the person had misunderstood the topic of the account. Whether interpreted as a parable or an allegory, the account is about people's receptivity to God's Word, not about increasing crop yield.

The Seven Signs in the Gospel of John	
Wedding at Cana	John 2:1–12
Cure of Royal Official's Son	John 4:46–54
Cure of Man at Pool of Bethesda	John 5:1–18
Multiplication of the Loaves	John 6:1–15
Walking on the Water	John 6:16–21
Cure of Man Born Blind	John 9:1–41
Raising of Lazarus	John 11:1–44

The First Sign

The allegorical or symbolic level of meaning of John's seven signs is not always self-evident. However, once you know that the accounts are allegorical, you will have less difficulty discerning that second level of meaning. To assist you in this endeavor, let's consider the allegorical level of meaning in Jesus' first sign, the wedding feast at Cana (see John 2:1–11).

In this first account, as in all seven accounts, Jesus stands for the Risen Christ. A wedding or marriage, in both the Old and New Testaments, stands for God's relationship with his people. At the wedding, Jesus' mother, who goes unnamed (this is a signal that Mary functions as a symbol in John's Gospel, a symbol of the Church), tells Jesus that there is no wine.

Jesus' response to his mother is, "Woman, how does your concern affect me? My hour has not yet come" (John 2:4). As you read this response, does it strike you as odd? Does it perhaps seem rude? Why would Jesus call his own

New Eve

A reference to Mary, "mother of all the living," emphasizing her role in the new creation brought about by Christ. It is because Mary is the New Eve that in statues she is often portrayed standing on a snake, which represents the Devil in the Book of Genesis.

mother "woman"? When an author wants you to look for an allegorical level of meaning to his or her story, he or she has to say something at the literal level that doesn't make sense. The reader then searches for an explanation, and, in considering the possibility of an allegorical level of meaning, finds that everything makes perfect sense.

The fact that Jesus addresses his mother as "woman" is an allusion to the Book of Genesis. As we have noted, John alluded to that book as he began his Gospel. Both works begin "In the beginning . . ." Genesis begins with an account of physical Creation. John mentions Creation too but then moves on to an account of a spiritual re-creation. In Genesis, Eve is called Eve because she is the mother of all the living (see Genesis 3:20). In John's Gospel, Mary, who stands for the Church, is the **New Eve** because she is the mother of all the living in the new spiritual order.

The Meaning of the Seven Signs

John's accounts of Jesus' seven signs teach about various aspects of our spiritual journey: The cure of the nobleman's son is about the role of faith. The cure of the man at the pool in Bethesda is about the sacramental power to forgive sin. The miracle of the loaves is about Eucharist, our nourishment for the journey. Jesus' walking on water is about Jesus' constant presence with us through life's storms. The cure of the man born blind is about Christ as our source of *sight*, of truth. The raising of Lazarus is affirming that our ultimate destiny is eternal life.

As you read John, you will notice that all the lessons taught through allegory are also taught through dialogue. For instance, the lesson about

being born again of water and the Spirit is taught through the wedding at Cana and also through the dialogue with Nicodemus. (See John 3:1–15.)

The more you grow in your ability to understand John's allegorical method and his meaning, the more you will grow in your ability to see the Risen Christ present in your own life and in your own spiritual journey from new birth to eternal life.

Jesus' "hour has not yet come" means that the time for Jesus' Passion, death, Resurrection, and Ascension, and his return in glory on the clouds of Heaven, has not yet come. Yet Jesus' saving work is present: He asks the servants to fill empty ablution jars with water that he changes into wine. The empty jars stand for the old way of being in right relationship with God—through the Law. Jesus is initiating a new way of being in right relationship with God—through the New Law. Water and wine stand for Baptism and the Eucharist, two of the Sacraments of Christian Initiation.

At the symbolic level, the account of the wedding feast at Cana is about the first step, the *initial* step, of our spiritual journey in the new spiritual order that Jesus has established. In response to his audience's question, "Where is the Risen Christ?" John is teaching his main point: The Risen Christ is present in his Church and in the Sacraments. ✞

In *Jesus Washing Peter's Feet*, by Ford Madox Brown (1821–1893), notice the looks of shock and dismay on the faces of the Apostles. One holds his head in his hands. Why was this event so shocking, and what does it say to us?

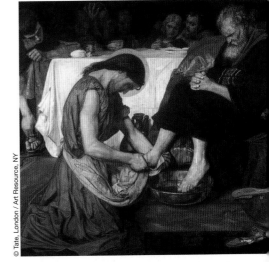

Article 30 The Paschal Mystery in the Gospel of John

John's emphasis on Jesus' divinity, which was evident in his prologue and in the Book of Signs, continues throughout his account of the Paschal Mystery of Christ. In fact, in John's account of Jesus' Passion and death, we never lose sight of the fact that

© Tate, London / Art Resource, NY

Catholic Wisdom

The Word of God: Human and Divine

In the early eighth century, a debate emerged within the Church about whether it was acceptable to venerate sacred images or icons. If no one has seen the face of God, can the human face of Jesus be portrayed in icons and other images? At the Second Council of Nicaea in 787, the Church answered yes, for "who venerates the icon is venerating in it the person of the one depicted"[1] (CCC, 477). When, at the time appointed, the Word and Image of the Father became incarnate, he, without losing his divine nature, assumed a human nature, including a human body that can be reflected in images (see CCC, 476).

Jesus is divine, that Jesus came from the Father and will return to the Father. It is because Jesus' glory continues to shine through his suffering that this section of John's Gospel is called the Book of Glory (see John, chapters 13–20).

The Last Supper

John gives a very different account of Jesus' last meal with the disciples than we read in the synoptic Gospels. In John's Gospel the last meal is not the Passover meal and there is no institution of the Eucharist. That is not to say that John does not emphasize the Eucharist. He definitely does. However, John teaches that the Risen Christ is present in the Eucharist through the *sign* of the multiplication of the loaves (see John 6:1–15) and through the "Bread of Life Discourse" (see 6:22–59). The Last Supper is the occasion for the washing of the feet and Jesus' long "Last Supper Discourse."

In John, Jesus' last meal with his disciples is twenty-four hours before the Passover, on Thursday night. (Thus the Passover itself and the Sabbath fall together on the next day; see John 18:28). This means that Jesus is killed (at noon on Friday) at the same time the Passover lambs are being killed for the Passover meal to be eaten Friday night. Remember, Jesus was identified as "the Lamb of God, who takes away the sin of the world" (1:29) at the beginning of the Gospel.

Live It!

Service with a Smile

When Jesus washed the feet of his disciples, he did something that the lowliest of servants would normally do, in order to show us that no task should be considered beneath us. He also did it as an example of how to serve one another in everyday matters. Such service begins within our own families.

Who "washes feet" in your household? Who does the tasks that no one likes to do—like putting away the dishes, keeping family areas neat, taking out the garbage, cleaning the bathrooms? Are you doing your share, or are you more often being served than serving?

When we pitch in and do these "menial" chores without complaining, we follow Jesus who came not to lord his power over us but to show us how to serve. When we bring an attitude of love and cheerful assistance to the work, we can transform what starts out as a burden into a sign of our care and respect for our family and friends.

By telling us about the washing of the feet rather than the institution of the Eucharist, John is teaching the ramifications of being Eucharistic people. Those who receive the Bread of Life and become the Body of Christ are called to serve, not to be served. Jesus makes the lesson explicit: "If I, therefore, the master and teacher, have washed your feet, you ought to wash one another's feet" (John 13:14).

Jesus is fully conscious of his own preexistence. At that last meal, Jesus prays, "Now glorify me, Father, with you, with the glory that I had with you before the world began" (John 17:5). After this prayer Jesus and his disciples go to the garden, but there is no agony there. Jesus does not pray to be relieved of this cup. In fact, during the arrest Jesus says: "Shall I not drink the cup that the Father gave me?" (18:11). Jesus came to do a job, and he wants to complete it.

I AM
God's name as revealed to Moses at the burning bush; repeated by Jesus in John's Gospel. John uses the I AM statements to teach the divinity of Jesus.

Arrest, Crucifixion, Death

Jesus' divinity is also evident at Jesus' arrest. When the arresting soldiers come, Jesus asks them: "'Whom are you looking for?' They answered him, 'Jesus the Nazorean.' He said to them, 'I AM'"(John 18:4–5). When Jesus says I AM, the arresting soldiers "turned away and fell to the ground" (18:6). Jesus' **I AM** is an allusion to God's revealing his name to Moses at the burning bush (see Exodus 3:14). For just an instant, the arresting soldiers see Jesus' divinity and fall to the ground in awe, just as was declared at the giving of the Law on Mount Sinai: Those who see the Lord "will be struck down" (Exodus 19:21). (Look to "The Great I AM" sidebar on the next page for a more detailed discussion of the I AM statements of Jesus given in this Gospel.)

Jesus' mother and the beloved disciple are with Jesus at the Crucifixion. Again Jesus' mother goes unnamed. Again Jesus calls her "woman." Again she stands for the Church. The beloved disciple also goes unnamed and also functions as a symbol. This figure appears for the first time at Jesus' last meal with his disciples. We will learn more about the beloved disciple in our next article. Here Jesus turns to his mother and says: "'Woman, behold, your son.' Then he said to the disciple, 'Behold, your mother'" (John 19:26–27). In this way the Gospel reveals that the Church is the mother of all of Jesus' beloved disciples. Jesus' death will bring about a new creation, new life, for him and for his disciples, and so

Mary's role in that creation as the New Eve, "mother of all the living" is again emphasized as she stands near the cross (see *CCC*, 511).

Jesus' last words are, "It is finished" (John 19:30). Jesus had completed his work. The soldiers take Jesus' body down from the cross. They break the legs of the other two who were crucified, but they do not break Jesus' legs. This is another allusion to the Passover lamb, whose bones were not to be broken (see Exodus 12:46). Instead they pierce Jesus' side, "and immediately blood and water flowed out" (John 19:34). If you are thinking allegorically, you will immediately see blood and water as symbols for the Eucharist (the Body

The Great I AM

A traditional American hymn includes this refrain:

> Hallelujah, hallelujah,
> Hallelujah, praise the Lamb!
> Hallelujah, hallelujah,
> Glory to the great I AM!

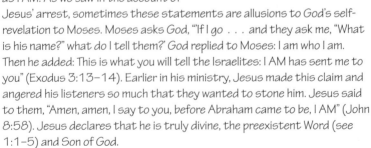

© Elio Ciol/CORBIS

Throughout John's Gospel, John presents Jesus referring to himself as I AM. As we saw in the account of Jesus' arrest, sometimes these statements are allusions to God's self-revelation to Moses. Moses asks God, "'If I go . . . and they ask me, "What is his name?" what do I tell them?' God replied to Moses: I am who I am. Then he added: This is what you will tell the Israelites: I AM has sent me to you" (Exodus 3:13–14). Earlier in his ministry, Jesus made this claim and angered his listeners so much that they wanted to stone him. Jesus said to them, "Amen, amen, I say to you, before Abraham came to be, I AM" (John 8:58). Jesus declares that he is truly divine, the preexistent Word (see 1:1–5) and Son of God.

In addition Jesus makes statements such as these: "I am the bread of life" (John 6:35); "I am the light of the world" (8:12); and "I am the true vine" (15:1). Remember that John's audience is asking, "Where is the Risen Christ?" John associates Jesus with all that was created through the pre-existent Word. For John, all that nurtures and sustains life becomes a sign of the presence of the Risen Christ in our lives.

and Blood of Christ) and Baptism, the same Sacraments of Christian Initiation presented symbolically at the wedding feast at Cana. The Church is born from the Body of Christ. The Church is nourished by the Body and Blood of Christ. The Church *is* the Body of Christ. ☩

Article 31 John's Post-Resurrection Accounts

As you know, John's late first-century audience had lived past the time of the expected return of Jesus on the clouds of Heaven. They are asking, "Where is the Risen Christ?" In his narratives about Jesus' post-Resurrection appearances, John describes person after person who "sees the Lord." John is teaching that Jesus did return. His post-Resurrection appearances were a return, and now Jesus is with his people and will remain with them always.

© Erich Lessing / Art Resource, NY

In *Doubting Thomas* (1621), by Giovanni Guercino (1591–1666), Jesus blesses Thomas because Thomas saw and believed. We are blessed because we do not see yet believe. How can Jesus help you to believe? Ask him for that blessing.

Jesus' Promise to Return

At Jesus' last meal with his disciples, he says: "Peace I leave with you; my peace I give to you. . . . Do not let your hearts be troubled or afraid. You heard me tell you, 'I am going away and I will come back to you'" (John 14:27–28). Later at that same meal, Jesus says: "So you also are now in anguish. But I will see you again, and your hearts will rejoice, and no one will take your joy away from you" (16:22).

These promises of Jesus' return with the gifts of peace and joy are fulfilled at his post-Resurrection appearance to the disciples. John tells us that when the disciples were gathered together, "Jesus came and stood in their midst and said to them, 'Peace be with you.' . . . The disciples rejoiced when they saw the Lord" (John 20:19,20). The disciples are now rejoicing, as Jesus promised they would be when they saw him again.

symbol

An object or action that points to another reality and leads us to look beyond our senses to consider a deeper mystery.

The Beloved Disciple

In the last article, we briefly mentioned the beloved disciple as he stood at the foot of the cross. The beloved disciple goes unnamed, a signal that he functions in John's narrative as a **symbol** pointing to a deeper reality.

The beloved disciple is a symbol of love. It is significant that the beloved disciple and Peter, who represents authority, regularly appear together. The beloved disciple is pictured as being closer to Jesus. He believes first, before anyone else, and he recognizes Jesus first. For instance, after Mary Magdalene tells Peter and the beloved disciple about the empty tomb, they both run to the tomb (see John 20:1–10). The beloved disciple gets there first but respectfully waits for Peter to arrive. Peter enters the tomb first but comes to no conclusion about what he is seeing. The beloved disciple is the second to enter the tomb but is the first to believe and the only one to believe before he has actually seen Jesus in a post-Resurrection appearance. John is teaching that love gets you there first!

The same theme is present when Jesus appears to the disciples at the Sea of Tiberias. All seven disciples see and hear Jesus, but it is the beloved disciple who recognizes him and says to Peter, "It is the Lord" (John 21:7). When Jesus delegates special authority to Peter, in the last chapter of this Gospel, it is only after Peter has declared his love for Jesus three times (see 21:15–19). Once again John is teaching the priority of love in being a true disciple of Jesus Christ. Authority is good and necessary, but love is always essential.

Blessed Are Those Who Have Not Seen

When Jesus appears to Mary Magdalene, she, following Jesus' instructions, returns to the disciples and tells them, "I have seen the Lord" (John 20:18). When Jesus appears to the disciples, they tell Thomas, "We have seen the Lord" (20:25). Thomas, like many in John's audience, hasn't seen the Lord. Thomas declares that he will not believe unless he can actually touch Jesus' wounds. Obviously Jesus was with Thomas (as Jesus is always present with each of us and knows our situation) when Thomas was failing to perceive his presence or to believe in him. We know this because later, when Jesus does appear to Thomas, he offers him the opportunity to touch his hands and his pierced side. Had he not been present with Thomas, Jesus would not have known to make the exact offer that Thomas needed. When Thomas does realize that he is seeing Jesus, he declares, "My Lord and my God!" (20:28). Jesus' words to Thomas are John's words to his late first-century audience: "Blessed are those who have not seen and have believed" (20:29). The same words are addressed to us today. ⚜

The Need for Authority

Some background information about the Johannine community will help us to understand the community's need to balance love with legitimate authority—the authority represented by Peter in the Gospel of John. Scripture scholars think the community that produced both John's Gospel and the letters attributed to John had undergone a very painful experience. First, because they had emphasized Jesus' divinity, they were expelled from the Jewish synagogue (see John 9:22). As long as they belonged to the synagogue, they did not have to participate in emperor worship (the Romans exempted the Jews from this requirement), but once expelled they were no longer exempt and so were vulnerable to persecution for refusing to worship the emperor.

Later some of the members of this Christian community had emphasized Jesus' divinity to the exclusion of his humanity. This caused a schism, or major division, in the community. (We will see evidence of this in the letters of John.) After the schism, the remaining community, who believed in both Jesus' divinity and his humanity, had a new understanding of the importance of duly delegated authority. The lack of recognized authority had contributed to division, to their inability to solve their differences.

Part Review

1. Name five differences between John's Gospel and the synoptic Gospels.

2. What question is John's audience asking? What is John's response?

3. Explain the second, or allegorical, level of meaning in John's account of the wedding feast at Cana.

4. What signal does John give in recounting the wedding at Cana that invites us to look for a deeper meaning?

5. How does John present Mary as the New Eve?

6. What is the main point of the allegorical level of meaning in the seven signs? Give some examples.

7. How does John's account of Jesus' last meal differ from the account in the synoptic Gospels? What is John teaching?

8. What is the significance of the soldier's not breaking Jesus' legs and of the water and blood that flow from Jesus' side?

9. What is John teaching through his post-Resurrection accounts?

10. What is John teaching by introducing the beloved disciple and having him repeatedly paired with Peter?

Part 2

The Book of Revelation

You may have seen this along a city street: Someone is carrying a homemade sign or wearing a sandwich board (one sign on the front and another on the back) warning, "The end is near!" So far, as we know, these "doomsday prophets" have been wrong. But have you ever seen an apology?

On October 9, 1995, this cartoon by Mick Stevens appeared in the *New Yorker* magazine: A "doomsday prophet" is carrying a sign that reads: "Yesterday in this space I predicted that the world would come to an end. It did not, however. I regret any inconvenience this may have caused." All of this is to say that the Book of Revelation, our next topic of study, is *not* about the end of the world! However, many people seem to think this book is an actual description of the warning signs to come before the world as we know it disappears.

This misunderstanding may not be surprising, as the Book of Revelation is written in a literary form unfamiliar to us called apocalyptic literature. This apocalyptic book was written in a code meant to be understood by the persecuted Christians of its time. In the following articles, we break this code and find out the real meaning, the meaning the author intended, of the many symbols and the dramatic language for which this book is famous. In doing so we find that the teachings of the Book of Revelation also apply to our own lives as disciples of Christ.

The articles in this part address the following topics:

Article 32 The Conventions of Apocalyptic Literature

This tapestry is from a series known as The Apocalypse of Angers (1373–1387), woven for Louis I, Duke of Anjou, France. An angel is pointedly dictating to John. See Revelation 1:9–20.

The Book of Revelation, an example of apocalyptic literature, may be the most misunderstood book on the face of the earth. The misunderstanding is that the book predicts events that will occur before the end of the world. Because the world is still here, some consider it possible that the *end-time* is near and that Revelation is speaking about people and events in our own time. This misunderstanding leads some people to surmise that the mysterious 666 is a present-day world leader and that the world is approaching Armageddon, the final battle.

Why do so many people misunderstand the Book of Revelation? One reason is that it is written in a literary form uncommon in our culture. We are familiar with the kind of writing we are reading when we read many of the books in the Bible such as songs (psalms), letters (epistles), and allegories. Our knowledge of these kinds of writing is an invaluable help in correctly understanding what the inspired human authors of biblical books are teaching. We do not have this same advantage when reading apocalyptic literature.

© Erich Lessing / Art Resource, NY

prophet

A person God chooses to speak his message of salvation. In the Bible, primarily a communicator of a divine message of repentance to the Chosen People, not necessarily a person who predicted the future.

Apocalyptic Literature

Apocalyptic literature was well known from the second century BC to the second century AD. It first became popular when the Israelites were suffering severe persecution under Antiochus Epiphanes, around 165 BC. At this time the book of Daniel, the other book of apocalyptic literature in the Bible, was written.

The Book of Revelation was written when Christians were suffering persecution under the Roman emperor Domitian (AD 81–96). All apocalyptic literature was written during times of persecution. Its purpose was not to predict events that would occur before the end of the world but to offer hope to those who were suffering. The hope offered was that the end-time was near, the end of their present persecution.

The Real Meaning of Prophecy

In addition to misunderstanding the conventions and purpose of apocalyptic literature, another reason many people misunderstand the topic addressed in the Book of Revelation is that they misunderstand the purpose of biblical prophecy. They think the function of a biblical prophet was to predict inevitable future events.

In fact, the function of a biblical **prophet** was to call people to fidelity to God's covenant love. Prophets did this in two ways: If people were sinning, the prophet called for repentance and warned of future suffering. However, if people were suffering, the prophet assured them that God would save them. God had promised to protect them, and God always keeps his promises.

It is not a mistake to understand the Book of Revelation as prophetic. As the book begins, John says, "Blessed are those who listen to this prophetic message and heed what is written in it" (Revelation 1:3). As it concludes John says, "Blessed is the one who keeps the prophetic message of this book" (22:7). In addition, John is commissioned as a prophet. He is told that he "must prophesy again about many peoples, nations, tongues, and kings" (10:11).

Revelation is prophetic not because it predicts inevitable events in our future. It is prophetic because it offers hope to those who are suffering.

Conventions of Apocalyptic Literature

Apocalyptic literature has its own conventions. You are already familiar with the idea that various kinds of writing follow specific conventions. For instance, in the first section of this student book, we noted that addressing someone as "Dear" in a letter, whether or not that person is dear to you, is a convention. It is a convention when writing a fairy tale to begin with the phrase "Once upon a time." The minute you read those words, you know that what follows is an imaginative story composed by an author, not an account of an actual event.

It is a convention of apocalyptic literature to begin by claiming that the work contains a hidden revelation (*apocalypse* means "revelation") that was known only to God and that he or an angel gave the revelation to a chosen person in a vision. Revelation begins just this way: "The revelation of Jesus Christ, which God gave to him, to show his servants what must happen soon. He made it known by sending his angel to his servant John, who gives witness to the word of God and to the testimony of Jesus Christ by reporting what he saw" (1:1–2).

The End-Time

Another convention of apocalyptic literature is to have the angel instruct the one who has received the revelation to put it in a sealed book that can be read only at the end-time. For instance, in the Book of Daniel the angel Gabriel tells Daniel that "the words are to be kept secret and sealed until the end time" (12:9). In Revelation, however, John is told *not* to seal the book because "the appointed time is near" (22:10). The *end-time* or *appointed time* to which the author is referring is obviously not the end of the world. If it were, we would not be here today, studying the Book of Revelation; rather, the end-time is the time when the original audience was reading the book, the time when their persecution was about to end. ✝

The Lamb of God on Mount Zion, by Albrecht Dürer (1471–1528), portrays the multitude of 144,000 worshipping the Lamb and singing a song of victory. See Revelation 14:1–3.

© Alfredo Dagli Orti / Art Resource, NY

Article **33** Symbolic Language in the Book of Revelation

The Book of Revelation was written in symbolic language, in code, so that Christians who were being persecuted by the Romans could read and understand it, but those doing the persecuting could not. Imagine that you were a persecuted Christian during the reign of Domitian (AD 81–96). You had expected Christ to come in glory on the clouds of Heaven before now. To make matters worse, some of your relatives have been killed. Based on your own experience, it appears that evil is triumphing over good. Whatever happened to Christ's victory over evil? Why isn't Christ protecting his people?

A fellow Christian slips you a message from the Book of Revelation, one that gives you great hope. In it the author describes himself receiving a vision of God's throne room and asking: "Who are these wearing white robes?" (7:13). He is told: "These are the ones who have survived the time of great distress; they have washed their robes and made them white in the blood of the Lamb" (7:14). This is a passage that you as a first-century Christian would have understood. However, a Roman soldier would not have understood the religious importance of the passage.

Because this particular imagery, Jesus as the Lamb of God, has made its way into our liturgy, we who live in the twenty-first century also understand what it means to say that the martyrs are wearing white because their garments have been washed in the blood of the lamb. It means that because the martyrs joined their suffering to Jesus', they not only died with Christ but they rose with Christ. They are now safe in the heavenly throne room where the victory of good over evil is already complete.

Live It!

A Message of Hope

The Book of Revelation was written for Christians being persecuted and losing hope. When we consider the suffering and pain in the world around us, we too may ask: Why so much suffering? Where is Christ? Where is his love and victory?

The Book of Revelation assures us that Christ's victory has already happened and that his love has conquered suffering and death. We here on earth are trying to "catch up" to the vision of the New Jerusalem presented to us in this book of consolation.

Copy the following passage on each of two index cards. Tape one to your mirror or other place where you will see it often. Save the other for a friend:

> Behold, God's dwelling is with the human race. He will dwell with them and they will be his people and God himself will always be with them [as their God]. He will wipe every tear from their eyes, and there shall be no more death or mourning, wailing or pain, [for] the old order has passed away.
>
> . . . Behold, I make all things new.
>
> (Revelation 21:3–5)

Understanding the Code

Though some of the symbolic language, the code, in the Book of Revelation is familiar to us, much of it is not. However, once we understand the meaning of the symbols, we will be able to understand the author's intent. For example, we may not know what words such as *seven, horns,* and *eyes* stand for. So when we read "Then I saw . . . a Lamb that seemed to have been slain. He had seven horns and seven eyes" (Revelation 5:6), we may simply picture such a creature in our minds and not translate the picture into an idea. But after we understand that *seven* stands for perfection, *horns* stands for strength or power, and *eyes* stands for knowledge, we realize that the author is claiming that the lamb is all powerful and all knowing. Only God is omnipotent and omniscient. The author is teaching that Jesus is God.

A second way the author uses symbolic language (recognizable to Christians but not to their persecutors) to teach that Jesus is God is through allusion to the Book of Daniel. In the first vision, the author describes seeing "one like a son of man. . . . The hair of his head was as white as white wool or as snow, and his eyes were like a fiery flame" (Revelation 1:13–14). In the Book of Daniel, when the author describes God, he says: "His clothing was snow bright, / and the hair on his head as white as wool; / His throne was flames of fire" (7:9). Later a figure like a "son of man" comes to God and receives power from him (7:13). By attributing to the Son of Man all the imagery that was used previously to describe God, the author is teaching that Jesus, the Son of Man, is God.

Revelation is not only offering hope but is encouraging those who are being persecuted to avoid the *second death.* They must be marked with the *sign of the lamb* (Baptism), not the *sign of the beast* (joining in worship of the Roman emperor as though he were God). The second death is judgment after life on earth (see Revelation 21:7–8). Those who avoid martyrdom by worshipping the emperor will be judged guilty and will be thrown into the fiery pit, unlike those who have accepted martyrdom and are now victorious in Heaven. ✝

Two Symbolic Numbers

Two of the most often misunderstood passages in the Book of Revelation involve the numbers 666 and 144,000. Biblical scholars have discovered, through studies of history and ancient numerology, that the number 666 stands for a most evil person and that the number 144,000 stands for the whole Church.

As the author describes a succession of beasts (Roman emperors) he says: "Wisdom is needed here; one who understands can calculate the number of the beast, for it is a number that stands for a person. His number is six hundred and sixty-six" (Revelation 13:18). The number 666 is both a reference to a particular person and a universal symbol of evil.

The Hebrews and Greeks assigned numeric value to letters. The numeric value of the letters in Nero Caesar's name add up to 666. Remember, Nero was emperor during the time when the audience of Mark's Gospel was being persecuted. In addition, 6 was a bad number because it is one less than 7 (the number symbolizing perfection) and half of 12 (the number symbolizing completeness). To express the superlative, the author of Revelation repeats the number 6 three times. Thus the number 666 stands for superlative evil.

In the Book of Revelation, 144,000 people are marked with the "seal of the living God" (see 7:1–4). Some mistakenly think this means that only 144,000 will be saved. However, this number is a symbolic number, with other significant numbers within it, as follows: 12 symbolizes completeness and stands for the Twelve Tribes and the Twelve Apostles; the number 1,000 stands for an incalculable or eternal amount. Thus 12 x 12 [144]) x 1,000 is 144,000. This number stands for the New Israel, the whole Church. In Heaven there is room for everyone.

666

12

7

144,000

Article 34 An Overview of Revelation

When you read the Book of Revelation from beginning to end, as you should read any book you hope to understand, you may well find yourself confused. Instead of a well developed plot that moves steadily along, you find yourself immersed in a series of images that begin to blend into one another. The events that are described when the seven seals are open seem almost indistinguishable from the events that are described when the seven bowls are poured. You will be better able to keep track of what the author is teaching if you have an overview of the book.

This portrayal of the heavenly Jerusalem shows the victorious Jesus, the Lamb of God, from whom the waters of life (Sacraments) are flowing. This art is located in the Church of San Pietro al Monte, in Civate (Lecco), Italy.

© Scala / Art Resource, NY

The Setting: The Heavenly Court

The setting for the Book of Revelation is the heavenly court. Though the author tells us that he is John, and that he is in exile on the island of Patmos because he "proclaimed God's word and gave testimony to Jesus" (1:9), Patmos is not the setting for the book. While on the island, John writes that he has had a series of visions of the heavenly court, the content of which he is now reporting.

The Book of Revelation describes seven visions of the heavenly court. Each vision will precipitate events on earth. From the heavenly court, (1) the seven letters will be sent (see 2:1—3:22); (2) the seven seals will be opened (see

6:1—8:1); (3) the seven trumpets will be blown (see 8:2—11:19); (4) the battle between the devil and the woman will take place (see 12:1—18); (5) the seven bowls will be poured (see 15:1—16:21) and Babylon (a symbol of Rome) will fall (see 17:1—19:10); (6) the Word will go forth to fight the final battles (see 19:11—20:15); and (7) the final victory of good over evil will be revealed (see 21—22:21).

Part of the message of hope in the Book of Revelation rests on the heavenly court as the setting for the book. The Lamb of God is victorious in Heaven and is worshipped by the martyrs. The hoped for and promised victory of good over evil is already accomplished in Heaven. Though the battle has not yet completely played out on earth, its outcome is predetermined. The hope offered is not that Jesus *will* overcome evil but that Jesus *has* overcome evil. One must simply remain faithful to share in his victory.

The Seven Seals

First Seal: a white horse with a victorious rider (conquest) (see Revelation 6:1–2)

Second Seal: a red horse whose rider carries a huge sword (war) (see 6:3–4)

Third Seal: a black horse whose rider carries a scale (famine) (see 6:5–6)

Fourth Seal: a pale green horse whose rider is Death, accompanied by Hades (see 6:7–8)

Fifth Seal: the souls of the martyrs, given white robes (see 6:9–11)

Sixth Seal: a great earthquake, symbolizing judgment (see 6:12–17)

Seventh Seal: "silence in heaven for about half an hour" (8:1), followed by the blowing of the angels' trumpets

Descriptions of Present Suffering

During the second vision (see Revelation 4:1–11), God is pictured holding a sealed scroll. An angel asks, "Who is worthy to open the scroll and break its seals?" (5:2). (Remember, in apocalyptic literature, when seals are open it means the end-time is present.) At first it seems that no one is worthy to open the seals. However, an elder tells John: "The lion of the tribe of Judah, the root of David, has triumphed, enabling him to open the scroll with its seven seals" (5:5). Only Jesus is worthy to open the seals because only Jesus is able to reveal God's plan and to initiate the events that bring his plan to fulfillment.

The Mystery of Evil

One of the more puzzling descriptions in the Book of Revelation is the thousand-year reign (see 20:1–10). In this account an angel throws Satan into the abyss for a thousand years, after which he will be released for a short time. Meanwhile, the **martyrs** reign in Heaven with Christ for a thousand years. Unlike the rest of the dead, the martyrs share in this first resurrection. Others will not rise until the end of the thousand years. After his release the Devil makes one more attempt on the holy city before he is finally defeated forever.

What is John teaching through this strange account? We can draw two conclusions with confidence. The first is that John is continuing his martyrology. The martyrs have a special place in Heaven. The second is that John, like his audience, is grappling with the mystery of the recurring nature of evil. Though evil does recur, it can never prevail. Jesus, who is himself God, has conquered evil.

As each seal is opened, something terrible takes place on earth. Through symbols the author is describing the kinds of suffering his audience is presently enduring. The horsemen (first, second, third, and fourth seals) represent conquest, war, famine, and death. The martyrs under the altar (fifth seal) are told that the people's suffering is not quite over (see Revelation 6:11). At the opening of the sixth seal, a great earthquake erupts. The seventh seal precipitates another vision of the heavenly court, and the blowing of the seven trumpets. Again cataclysmic events are unleashed. With the opening of the seals, one quarter of the earth is affected. With the blowing of the trumpets, one third of the earth is affected. Things will get worse before they get better.

The Fall of Babylon and Final Victory

Although episodes resemble one another a great deal, there is some forward movement in the plot. The images change from describing persecution to describing judgment and then salvation. With the pouring of the seven bowls (see Revelation 16:1–21), Babylon is destroyed (see 16:19—18:24). *Babylon* is code for *Rome* because both empires destroyed the Temple in Jerusalem, Babylon during the Babylonian Exile (587–537 BC) and Rome in AD 70.

The book ends with the final victory of good over evil not only in Heaven but on earth. In his final vision, John is shown the **New Jerusalem**, the bride of the lamb. There is no sun in the New Jerusalem, "for the glory of God gave it light, and its lamp was the Lamb. The nations will walk by its light" (Revelation 21:23–24). When nations walk by the light of Christ, peace will reign on earth as it does in Heaven. ✝

martyr
A person who suffers death because of his or her beliefs. The Church has canonized many martyrs as saints.

New Jerusalem
In the Book of Revelation, a symbol of a renewed society in which God dwells; a symbol of the Church, the "holy city," the assembly of the People of God called together from "the ends of the earth"; also, in other settings, a symbol of Heaven.

Catholic Wisdom

The Secrets of Our Hearts

At the end of time, at the judgment of both the living and the dead, Christ "will reveal the secret disposition of hearts" (*CCC*, 682). Judgment will depend on both our faith and our works, whether we have accepted or rejected God's grace during our lives. In the particular judgment, at our death, Christ will judge each of us immediately, as Saint John of the Cross wrote: "At the evening of life, we shall be judged on our love" (*CCC*, 1022).[2]

Article 35 Eternal Truths of Revelation

salvation
From the Latin *salvare,* meaning "to save," referring to the forgiveness of sins and the restoration of friendship with God, attained for us through the Paschal Mystery—Christ's work of redemption accomplished through his Passion, death, Resurrection, and Ascension. Only at the time of judgment can a person be certain of salvation, which is a gift of God.

The Book of Revelation is written to a specific audience, those suffering persecution under Domitian (AD 81–96), and it does not predict events that will precede the end of the world, so why is it in the canon? Why is this book truly Revelation? By *Revelation* we mean not in the sense of being a work of apocalyptic literature but in the sense of revealing the truths God has chosen to reveal to us for the sake of our **salvation**.

The Book of Revelation has a place in the canon because it teaches a number of universal truths: that Christ is God, our Judge, and our Savior, and that he offers us eternal life. Though these truths appear throughout the Book of Revelation, they are also repeated in the book's epilogue (see 22:6–20). Each of these truths is just as important for us as it was for the original audience.

The Tree of Life, by Gustav Klimt (1862–1918), is an image of the happiness of the heavenly Jerusalem. See Revelation 22:1–5. The tree bears fruit twelve times a year and its leaves are healing. Note the dove in the tree, a symbol of the Holy Spirit.   © CORBIS

Christ Is God

The Book of Revelation emphasizes over and over that Jesus Christ is himself God. We have already seen that Jesus is presented as the Lamb with seven horns and seven eyes and that the imagery applied to God in the Book of Daniel is applied to Jesus, the Son of Man, in the Book of Revelation. In the epilogue John tells of Jesus' saying, "I am the Alpha and the Omega, the first and the last, the beginning and the end" (22:13). Alpha and Omega are the first and last letters of the Greek alphabet.

As the book ends, the author emphasizes that only God should be worshipped. John tells us that when he fell down at the foot of the angel who revealed things to him, the angel said: "Don't! I am a fellow servant of yours and of your brothers the prophets and of those who keep the message of this book. Worship God" (Revelation 22:9). Because John depicts Jesus' being worshipped in the heavenly court, John is teaching that Jesus is God.

Christ Is Judge

The Book of Revelation emphasizes that human beings will be held accountable for their actions. The fate of the martyrs and the fate of the persecutors will not be the same. Jesus will judge each person individually. Jesus says: "Behold, I am coming soon. I bring with me the recompense I will give to each according to his deeds" (Revelation 22:12). That human beings will be held accountable for their actions is good

God's Love Conquers All

The negative images in the Book of Revelation (images of plague, famine, and savage beasts) have caused confusion about the meaning of this book. The point of the Book of Revelation is that, yes, evil exists, and the followers of Christ will experience evil (as in the persecutions suffered by the early Church), but, more important, Christ has conquered evil. The Book of Revelation, while assuring us that each of us will be held accountable for our actions, assures us as well that the persecutors of Christians will also be held accountable and will, in the end, be defeated.

For the Book of Revelation, above all, assures God's people of his love. John says: "God himself will always be with them [as their God]. He will wipe every tear from their eyes, and there shall be no more death or mourning, wailing or pain" (Revelation 21:3–4). Those who know Christ and live in hope also live in love, not fear. The final victory of Christ is portrayed as a wedding feast (see 19:9). The final victory of Christ is a victory of love.

news or bad news depending on one's life choices. In the context of the Book of Revelation, it was good news for the martyrs but bad news for the persecutors.

Christ Is Savior

The Book of Revelation also emphasizes that Jesus is our Savior. We no longer need to be slaves to sin. We have already seen that the martyrs have been saved. They are dressed in white because their garments have been washed in the blood of the Lamb. John refers to this truth in the epilogue when he says, "Blessed are they who wash their robes so as to have the right to the tree of life and enter the city through its gates" (Revelation 22:14). Those who are faithful to Christ will have eternal life because Christ, through his Passion, death, and Resurrection has redeemed the human race.

The *tree of life* is, of course, a reference to the tree that was in the Garden of Eden. Those who have access to the tree of life will live forever.

Eternal Life

By emphasizing that the martyrs are already victorious in Heaven, John teaches that those who die with Christ also rise with Christ. Death is not the end. In biblical language "to die with Christ" has two meanings: It can mean to suffer

Pray It!

Come, Lord Jesus!

Perhaps you've heard the word *Maranatha*. It is a phrase, *Marana tha*, in the language Jesus spoke, Aramaic, meaning, "Come, Lord Jesus!" It is found both at the end of the Book of Revelation and at the end of Paul's First Letter to the Corinthians (see 16:22).

The earliest Christians often used it as a short greeting. It was a way of expressing both faith that Jesus would return and hope that he would return soon.

Today we often use it as a prayer during Advent, but we can pray it at any time, for Jesus still comes to us today, will come to us tomorrow, and will come again at the end of time: "The one who gives this testimony says, 'Yes, I am coming soon.' Amen! Come, Lord Jesus!" (Revelation 22:20).

a martyr's death, but it can also mean to be baptized. The author refers to Baptism when he says: "The Spirit and the bride say, 'Come.' Let the hearer say, 'Come.' Let the one who thirsts come forward, and the one who wants it receive the gift of life-giving water" (Revelation 22:17).

Finally, the author is encouraging those who are suffering to remain faithful: "The righteous must still do right, and the holy still be holy" (Revelation 22:11). What could motivate a person who is being persecuted to persevere in his or her beliefs even if those beliefs lead to death? The motivation that John offers is hope of eternal life based on faith in Jesus Christ, who is himself God and who reigns in Heaven and has redeemed us from our sins. ✝

Part Review

1. Name two major misunderstandings that cause people to misinterpret the Book of Revelation.

2. Name the conventions of apocalyptic literature.

3. Why is the Book of Revelation written in symbolic language?

4. What does the writer of the Book of Revelation mean when he says that the Lamb has seven eyes and seven horns?

5. What is the setting for the Book of Revelation? What is being taught through this setting?

6. How does the Book of Revelation depict suffering, judgment, and salvation?

7. What does the Book of Revelation teach about Jesus Christ?

8. How does the Book of Revelation motivate people to remain faithful?

The Letters of Paul

Part 1

Introduction to the Letters of Paul

Not so many years ago, if you wanted to communicate with someone at a distance, especially if that communication was significant to you in some way, you would write a letter. (Long-distance telephone calls were expensive and therefore rare in most families.)

Letters from faraway loved ones were often saved, tied together with ribbon, and cherished through the years as personal treasures. Although today many people still send birthday cards and other short communications by mail, the art of letter-writing in our culture seems to be in decline. Calling, texting, and e-mailing are so much quicker!

We, the Church, are extremely fortunate to have today the body of letters that were saved and cherished through the centuries by the Church, and eventually, if not tied together with ribbon, were bound together in the New Testament so that today we might learn and live from their divinely inspired words. In this section we examine the categories of letters and the conventions of letter-writing in New Testament times, the differences between the Acts of the Apostles and Paul's letters in describing the same events, and the particular form and characteristics that mark the letters of Saint Paul.

The articles in this part address the following topics:

- Article 36: "Overview of the New Testament Letters" (page 184)
- Article 37: "Paul's Letters Compared to the Acts of the Apostles" (page 189)
- Article 38: "The Form and Characteristics of Paul's Letters" (page 192)

Article 36 Overview of the New Testament Letters

The New Testament includes twenty-one books that are referred to as letters, or epistles. (You might want to refer to the chart on page 19 in section 1 for this list.) These letters are organized by Scripture scholars into various categories. Although thirteen of these letters claim to be Paul's, most Scripture scholars believe that Saint Paul actually wrote only seven of them. Of the twenty-one letters, some are referred to as pastoral letters and some others are called catholic epistles. Some of the letters are named after the receiving community (e.g., the Corinthians), others after the individual receiver (e.g., Timothy), and still others after the purported sender (e.g., James). Some follow the conventions of letter-writing and some do not. Given this great variety, it is helpful, before reading individual letters, to consider an overview of the New Testament letters.

© Jim Hollander/epa/Corbis

The Dead Sea Scrolls, similar to ones used in New Testament times, were written by the Essenes, a Jewish monastic community, and were discovered in 1947 in the Qumran caves, Israel. Featured here is the Book of Isaiah.

Paul, the Last Apostle

You may remember that Paul was a former persecutor of the followers of Christ and a convert to Christianity. (See section 2, part 5, article 26, "Witness to Christ in Judea and Samaria [Acts of the Apostles, Chapters 8–12]" to recall the conversion of Saint Paul.) Paul describes himself as an Apostle, yet one born late, "last of all," (1 Corinthians 15:8), specially chosen by God to take the message of salvation in Christ from its origins in Jerusalem to the wider world of the Gentiles. In order to do this, he made three missionary journeys (and a final last journey to Rome) and founded communities, or churches, along the way. Once a church was established, he moved on, but, as occasion demanded, kept in touch by letter with the people he had evangelized. (See map of Paul's journeys section 2, part 5, article 27, "Witness to Christ to the Ends of the Earth [Acts of the Apostles, Chapters 13–28]".)

If you know someone who must travel frequently, that person has probably told you that travel is not always fun. If this is true in our day, when airports provide every convenience for travelers and planes arrive at destinations in hours rather than days, it was a thousand times more true in the days of Saint Paul. In his Second Letter to the Corinthians, Paul describes his difficulties in travel. In addition, Paul worked as a tent maker to support himself, so as not to depend on the community he was evangelizing (see Acts of the Apostles 18:3). Also there was "the daily pressure upon me of my anxiety for all the churches" (2 Corinthians 11:28)—the churches to whom he wrote his letters.

Why did Paul put himself through all this? Because he had been captured by the love of Christ and wanted to share the Good News that Christ had died and was raised for the salvation of all people. He wanted to share Christ's saving love with the world: "The love of Christ impels us" (2 Corinthians 5:14).

Paul's Letters

The work of Scripture scholars suggests that Paul actually wrote First Thessalonians, First and Second Corinthians, Philippians, Philemon, Galatians, and Romans. You will notice that this is not the order in which the letters appear in the New Testament; there, Romans appears first. The New Testament is arranged by type of recipient and then by length. It divides the thirteen letters attributed to Paul

Live It!

A Real Letter

Throughout his letters Paul makes sure his recipients understand his love and care for them. At the beginning or end of his letters (or both), we find heartfelt greetings of love and concern. And Paul always mentions Jesus Christ, and his love, grace, or peace. How welcome these greetings must have been to those who knew Paul personally!

Today letter-writing is almost a lost art, but a real letter, not just a text message or an e-mail, is still meaningful. When you write a letter, you are giving a gift of yourself, and your letter becomes a tangible keepsake.

Is there someone in your life who would love to receive a letter from you? Maybe a sibling, a friend, or a grandparent? Today write a real letter or note telling that person what is going on in your life and what they mean to you—just a few words, in your own handwriting, to show you care.

pseudonymous
Written by one person
but attributed to
another as a way of
honoring an esteemed
predecessor.

into two groups (letters to church communities and letters to individuals) and within each group lists the letters from longest to shortest. Romans is first because it is the longest letter to a church community.

Letters Attributed to Paul

Even though six additional letters (Ephesians, Colossians, Second Thessalonians, First and Second Timothy, and Titus) claim to have been written by Paul, many Scripture scholars believe these are later letters written by disciples of Paul and attributed to him. To attribute one's work to an admired predecessor was a convention of the time called *pseudonymity,* from the Latin meaning, literally, "false name." Today we know that some writers publish their work under a pseudonym, or a fictitious name. Often the reason for this is that the writer has chosen to hide his or her identity. This differs from the reasons why the writers of some of the New Testament letters attributed their work to Paul. At that time writing a **pseudonymous** letter was a way to honor a mentor and to place one's work in the context of that mentor's work.

Three of the letters attributed to Paul (First and Second Timothy and Titus) are referred to as the pastoral letters because they are addressed to pastors of individual churches and give instructions about pastoral matters within those churches. When we read the pastoral letters and the other pseudonymous letters, we discuss why these letters are not thought to be contemporary with Paul.

Hebrews

The Letter to the Hebrews follows the thirteen letters attributed to Paul. The author of Hebrews is unknown to us. Though Hebrews is named a letter, it is not, in terms of form, a letter at all. In a letter the author would have named himself, the sender, as well as the receiver in the first line. Although Hebrews does not observe the conventions of letter-writing as it begins, it does observe them as it ends. Because of this lack of form, Scripture scholars describe Hebrews as a homily that ends like a letter.

The Catholic Epistles

The last letters in the New Testament are called the catholic epistles. They are James; First and Second Peter; First, Second, and Third John; and Jude. These letters are called catholic because they are addressed to a catholic or universal audience, not to a particular house church. In each case the letter is named after the purported sender.

Although the letters named after James (the "brother of the Lord"), Peter, and Jude (the brother of James) all claim within the letter to be from that person, many Scripture scholars again suggest that the letters are pseudonymous. (Note that *brother* can mean any male relative, such as a cousin. It can also mean close companion or follower. James is a relative of Jesus who is usually called "brother of the Lord.") As we will discover when we read the letters, the issues discussed do not seem to be contemporaneous with the first-generation Church.

As we read the New Testament letters, we must remember to continue to be contextualists, considering the literary form and recognizing that not everything said in a letter is a universal truth; rather, specific applications of universal truths are made to particular social settings. We should continue to consider the beliefs of the time. (For example, as we discussed earlier in this student book, New Testament letters were written before people realized that for one person to be the property of another was beneath the dignity of a human being.) We must remember that we are reading about a pilgrim Church that is growing in its understanding over time. Within the letters we will see a development in people's understandings of Church and of formal Church structures.

Above all, we must also remember that we are reading the inspired Word of God. Thus, as we discussed in section 1, we need to also take into account the role of the Holy Spirit, the role of the Magisterium of the Church, the spiritual sense of Scripture, and Scripture and Tradition forming the one Deposit of Faith, and we should pay attention to what God wants to reveal through the human words of the inspired author. ✝

The Humility of Saint Paul

In his work of evangelization, Paul was always reluctant to boast about his work as an Apostle. In the First Letter to the Corinthians, he writes:

> For I am the least of the apostles, not fit to be called an apostle, because I persecuted the church of God. But by the grace of God I am what I am, and his grace to me has not been ineffective. Indeed, I have toiled harder than all of them; not I, however, but the grace of God [that is] with me. (15:9–10)

But, at one point, he was forced into boasting to the Corinthians of his background and his ministry, his labors and his sufferings, in order to convince the Corinthians of the authenticity of his message. But even at the end of that boast, he concludes, "I will rather boast most gladly of my weaknesses, in order that the power of Christ may dwell with me" (2 Corinthians 12:9).

Paul, the founder of churches, the great Apostle to the Gentiles, set aside his ego in order that Christ might be preached. When the Corinthians tried to form "cliques," proclaiming their loyalty to either Paul or Apollos (another well-known teacher of the faith), Paul put a stop to it, urging them to focus on Christ: "So let no one boast about human beings, for everything belongs to you, Paul or Apollos or Cephas, or the world or life or death, or the present or the future: all belong to you, and you to Christ, and Christ to God" (1 Corinthians 3:21).

Article 37 Paul's Letters Compared to the Acts of the Apostles

We have two main sources of information about Saint Paul and his ministry to the Gentiles: Paul's own letters and the Acts of the Apostles. Sometimes, such as in their descriptions of the Jerusalem Council, these two sources do not entirely agree. This lack of agreement may cause you to ask: "Which one is right?" or, "How can both works be in the canon if they do not agree?" Responding to these questions will not only help us to better understand Paul's letters and the Acts of the Apostles but also will help us to understand the relationship between them.

The Council of Jerusalem

Before we respond to the questions above, let us first note how Paul's Letter to the Galatians and the Acts of the Apostles differ in their descriptions of the Jerusalem Council (see Galatians 2:1–10 and Acts of the Apostles 15:1–35). As you already know from reading the Acts of the Apostles, it was at the Jerusalem Council that, through the guidance of the Holy Spirit, the Church decided that Gentiles who became Christian did not have to become Jewish Christians; they did not have to be circumcised.

Paul, who was writing about AD 54–55, describes his meeting with some of the Apostles as a private meeting during which all agreed not to require circumcision for Gentiles. Paul says:

> I went up [to Jerusalem] in accord with a revelation, and I presented to them the gospel that I preach to the Gentiles—but privately to those of repute. . . . They saw that I had been entrusted with the gospel to the uncircumcised, just as Peter to the circumcised, for the one who worked in Peter for an apostolate to the circumcised worked also in me for the Gentiles, and when they recognized the grace bestowed upon me, James and Cephas [Peter] and John, who were reputed to be pillars, gave me and Barnabas their right hands in partnership, that we should go to the Gentiles and they to the circumcised. (Galatians 2:2,7–9)

Saints Peter and Paul, "the pillars of the Church," are often portrayed together, as they represent the two-pronged mission of the early Church: to the Jews (Peter with keys) and to the Gentiles (Paul with sword).

© Zvonimir Atletic / Shutterstock.com

Deep Background on Paul

© Zvonimir Atletic / Shutterstock.com

The Acts of the Apostles gives us valuable background information about the communities to which Paul is writing. We know from Acts that Paul visited and established churches in all the communities to which he wrote except Rome. For instance, we know from the Acts of the Apostles that Paul visited Thessalonica during his second missionary journey. Some Thessalonians were persuaded by Paul's teaching, but others caused such an uproar that Paul had to leave abruptly (see 17:1–9). This information gives us the setting for Paul's letter. We also know from Acts that Paul established the Church in Corinth during his second missionary journey (see 18:1–28). Paul stayed in Corinth for eighteen months and was followed by another preacher named Apollos, an Alexandrian Jew known for his eloquence. This information gives us some important clues as we seek to understand the sometimes painful relationship Paul had with the Corinthians. For example, see 1 Corinthians 1:10–17, where Paul urges the Corinthians to put aside their differences and to be loyal, not to Apollos or to him, but to Christ.

As you learned from reading the Acts of the Apostles, Luke, who was writing about AD 80, describes the meeting in Jerusalem as a public meeting during which everyone's opinion was heard before a decision was made. Once the decision was made, it was formally written down and promulgated. The decision involved not only the question of circumcision but also questions regarding the observance of dietary laws (see Acts of the Apostles 15:1–35).

Which Account Is Right?

Both of these accounts are right. Each is right in the sense that the inspired human authors convey what God intends to reveal, even if the accounts differ in details. That is why each is in the canon. Paul is right in insisting that Gentiles need not be circumcised. Luke is right in reporting what the Church, under the guidance of the Holy Spirit, decided in these very difficult matters. The fundamental agreement of these two documents consists in this essential truth: The Church is universal and is called to a universal mission to all people.

But if we ask which description is closer to what actually happened historically, the answer is, most probably, Paul's. Paul is writing a letter. Though a letter is not an objective historical report, Paul is close in time to, and has firsthand knowledge of, many of the events captured in his letters. Luke is further away in time from the events he describes and relies more heavily on accounts passed on through oral and written tradition. As you will see when you read Galatians, Paul is angry when he writes this letter because some false teachers had been telling the Galatians that they needed to be circumcised and obey the Jewish Law. Paul is defending his own previous teaching and his own authority as coming straight from God. As part of his self-defense, Paul acknowledges that he checked out his actions with the reputed pillars of the Church in Jerusalem, and they too agreed that what he had taught was correct.

Luke's account in the Acts of the Apostles does not attempt to describe what we would have seen had we been present. Remember, accounts that come through oral tradition do not claim to be exact quotations or to describe social settings with precise detail. Luke has most likely conflated several individual events at which different issues were addressed and described them as being solved on a single occasion.

When we read accounts of the same incident in both Paul's letters and in the Acts of the Apostles, and when those

Catholic Wisdom

Paul and the Cross

It is important to remember that Paul's first encounter with Jesus was as the resurrected Christ. . . . The realization that Christ who was risen was also the Jesus of Nazareth who had been crucified made an explosive impact on Paul's entire way of understanding reality. . . . In the reality of the Cross, the God of Israel and the God of Jesus Christ had defied human logic. . . . The Cross was no longer a sign of death but a pledge of life.

(Donald Senior, "Paul and the Cross")

accounts differ in details, Paul's letters are probably describing those details with more historical accuracy than is Acts. Yet, in their different ways, both Paul's letters and the Acts of the Apostles bring us the Word of God and the truths that God intended to reveal. ✝

Article 38 The Form and Characteristics of Paul's Letters

As you know, although the human biblical authors are inspired, they remain human beings with all the characteristics of human beings. They are people of their time and culture. They express themselves as those in their culture express themselves. They have virtues and faults and teach keen, revealed insights as well as false presumptions. These human characteristics are nowhere more evident than they are in Paul's letters.

As noted earlier, in Paul's day, letters began with a formula that named both the sender and the receiver. This was followed by a thanksgiving that introduced the topic of the letter, that is, the sender's purpose for writing. The body of the letter expanded on this topic. Finally, the letter closed with personal greetings and benedictions.

As you read the New Testament letters, try to remain aware of these conventions. When the conventions are not followed, it is for a reason—a reason we will want to discover.

Note the sword at Saint Paul's side. It is customary for saints to be pictured with the instrument of their martyrdom. As a Roman citizen, Paul was not crucified but beheaded with a sword—a less painful death.

© Geoffrey Clements/CORBIS

Paul appropriated, or used for his own purposes, this traditional form in his letters. For instance, First Corinthians begins: "Paul, called to be an apostle of Christ Jesus by the will of God, and Sosthenes our brother, to the church of God that is in Corinth" (1:1–2). After this traditional beginning, Paul gives thanks: "I give thanks to my God always on your account for the grace of God bestowed on you in Christ Jesus, that in him you were enriched in every way" (1:4–5).

Paul then launches into the subject matter of the particular letter. As he ends, Paul sends greetings: "The churches of Asia send you greetings. Aquila and Prisca together with the church at their house send you many greetings in the Lord" (1 Corinthians 16:19). Paul then ends with a blessing: "The grace of the Lord Jesus be with you. My love to all of you in Christ Jesus" (16:23–24).

Note that both the beginnings and endings of Paul's letters often include thanksgivings, with mention of the Lord Jesus Christ (see *Catechism of the Catholic Church [CCC]*, 2638.) Here again we find Paul's focus on Jesus: for Paul, making the love of Jesus Christ known to the world was the focus of his life and of his every letter.

Following this form is so typical of Paul that when a letter fails to follow the form, questions are raised about whether Paul actually wrote the letter. For instance, in letters written to churches Paul had visited, he typically sends many personal greetings. In the Letter to the Ephesians, he does not. This is one of the reasons scholars suggest that this letter is pseudonymous.

Paul: God's Human Instrument

One of the interesting things about reading a person's letters is that you learn not only about the topics the writer discusses but also about the writer. Paul reveals a great deal about his personality in his letters.

In Second Corinthians we learn that Paul can be deeply hurt and is not embarrassed to say so. Paul describes having

Pray It!

Live Your Prayer

In his First Letter to the Thessalonians, Paul ends with advice about both life and prayer. He urges them: "Admonish the idle, cheer the fainthearted, support the weak, be patient with all. See that no one returns evil for evil; rather, always seek what is good [both] for each other and for all. Rejoice always. Pray without ceasing. In all circumstances give thanks, for this is the will of God for you in Christ Jesus" (5:14–18).

Rejoice always? In all circumstances gives thanks? These are attitudes of prayer, and if we can rejoice and thank God in all circumstances, we will be "praying always," especially if we are supporting the weak and are patient with all.

Try following Saint Paul's advice. The next time you face a negative situation, rejoice and thank God, knowing that he is with you. Ask for his help in seeking the right path toward peace.

written the Corinthians a painful letter: "For out of much affliction and anguish of heart I wrote to you with many tears, not that you might be pained but that you might know the abundant love I have for you" (2:4).

Paul can also be extremely angry and does not hesitate to express that anger. Paul is angry with the Galatians for listening to false teachers who are insisting that they be circumcised. For Jews, then and now, circumcision is a sign of acceptance of God's covenant; but, as we have learned, the Council of Jerusalem decided that it would not be required of Gentile Christians. Paul says: "O stupid Galatians! Who has bewitched you, before whose eyes Jesus Christ was publicly portrayed as crucified? . . . Are you so stupid? After beginning with the Spirit, are you now ending with the flesh?" (Galatians 3:1,3).

Paul loves with the same deep passion and is quick to express that love. He tells the Philippians: "It is right that I should think this way about all of you, because I hold you in my heart, you who are all partners with me in grace. . . . For God is my witness, how I long for all of you with the affection of Christ Jesus" (Philippians 1:7,8).

Despite Paul's confidence that what he is teaching is true, and despite his adamancy, Paul is, on occasion, self-reflective. He has a deep sense of sinfulness, and shares these private thoughts with others. In his Letter to the Romans, Paul says: "We know that the law is spiritual; but I am carnal, sold into slavery to sin. What I do, I do not understand. For I do not do what I want, but I do what I hate. . . . Miserable one that I am! Who will deliver me from this mortal body? Thanks be to God through Jesus Christ our Lord" (7:14–15,24–25).

Paul, like every human being, has some presumptions that are not born of experience. For instance, Paul expected Jesus to return in glory during his lifetime. That this turned out not to be the case in no way negates the truth of the resurrection of the dead. When writing to the Thessalonians, concerned about those who died while waiting for Jesus' return, Paul describes Christ's coming and assures them, saying, "Indeed, we tell you this, on the word of the Lord, that we who are alive, who are left until the coming of the Lord, will surely not precede [in resurrection] those who have fallen asleep" (1 Thessalonians 4:15).

It is because the inspired biblical authors are human, still limited by human life and presumptions, that we must be contextualists. Under the authority of the Magisterium, and through the inspiration of the Holy Spirit, we are guided as we seek to grow in our understanding of God's Revelation. We can then fulfill the mandate of the *Dogmatic Constitution on Divine Revelation* (*Dei Verbum*, 1965):

> Seeing that, in sacred scripture, God speaks through human beings in human fashion, it follows that the interpreters of sacred scripture, if they are to ascertain what God has wished to communicate to us, should carefully search out the meaning which the sacred writers really had in mind, that meaning which God had thought well to manifest through the medium of their words. (12) ✝

Paul's Rhetorical Devices

Rhetoric is the skillful use of language in speech or writing. Paul received an excellent education, and we know this because we recognize his skillful use of language. His use of rhetorical devices common in his day reflects both his education and his culture. One example of Paul's use of a rhetorical device is his argument through *diatribe*. To argue through diatribe is to make an assertion, pose a question, respond to your own question, then pose another question, and so on.

Paul uses this method of argumentation when probing the mystery of God's judgment on sinners and his saving power. How can we believe both that God judges us according to our behavior and that he has redeemed us even though we are sinners? How can God be both judge and redeemer? In addressing this paradox, Paul asks: "What are we to say? Is there injustice on the part of God? Of course not!" (Romans 9:14). This pattern continues until all possible questions have been raised and considered.

Part Review

1. Which letters are thought to have been written by Paul?

2. What is a pseudonymous letter? Which letters are attributed to Paul? To whom are the other pseudonymous letters attributed?

3. What were the conventions of letter-writing in Paul's day?

4. How do the Acts of the Apostles and Galatians differ in their descriptions of the Jerusalem Council? How can we account for these differences?

5. In what sense are both accounts right?

6. What does Paul reveal about his personality in his letters?

7. How do Paul's letters reflect that he is a person of his time and culture?

Part 2

The Letters to the Corinthians

The city of Corinth was an important urban center, and its residents were accustomed to a materialistic and competitive atmosphere. Though the Corinthians embraced Paul's message, they had questions and concerns about their new faith.

Paul's opening greeting in First Corinthians, though warm and welcoming, also hints at some of the issues Paul will discuss:

> I give thanks to my God always on your account for the grace of God bestowed on you in Christ Jesus, that in him you were enriched in every way, with all discourse and all knowledge, as the testimony to Christ was confirmed among you, so that you are not lacking in any spiritual gift as you wait for the revelation of our Lord Jesus Christ. He will keep you firm to the end, irreproachable on the day of our Lord Jesus [Christ]. God is faithful, and by him you were called to fellowship with his Son, Jesus Christ our Lord. (1:4–9)

Paul is concerned that the Corinthians are putting aside the "testimony to Christ" that he gave them, and, in the practice of their version of Christianity, are succumbing to erroneous ideas and practices that have given rise to the problems Paul recounts.

In First Corinthians, Paul deals with factions and divisions in the community, considers questions about behavior and marriage, and gives direction on women's roles in the churches. He also considers important questions about the Eucharist and about the Resurrection of Christ. In Second Corinthians, Paul defends his own ministry. As we will see, his defense has implications for our own Christian discipleship.

The articles in this part address the following topics:

- Article 39: "First Corinthians: Responding to Community Problems" (page 198)

- Article 40: "The Eucharist and Resurrection in First Corinthians" (page 204)

- Article 41: "Second Corinthians" (page 207)

Article 39 First Corinthians: Responding to Community Problems

First Corinthians was written while Paul was on his third missionary journey (see Acts of the Apostles 19:1–20, 1 Corinthians 16:8). In this letter, written in Ephesus in about AD 56, Paul responds to reports from people associated with a woman named Chloe, who informed him of the disunity and immorality taking hold among the Corinthians, and also to a letter he had received from the Corinthians asking him a number of questions (see 1 Corinthians 7:1). Paul also deals with factions and divisions in the community, considers questions about behavior and marriage, rejects the ideas of a group known as the spirit people, gives direction on women's roles in the churches, and counsels on the relationship between a man and a woman in marriage.

Factions and Divisions

Beginning at Antioch in Syria, trace Paul's third journey all the way to Corinth and back to Jerusalem.

The city of Corinth was a seaport and a city that today we might call a melting pot of various peoples. Gentiles, Jews,

© 2009 by Saint Mary's Press

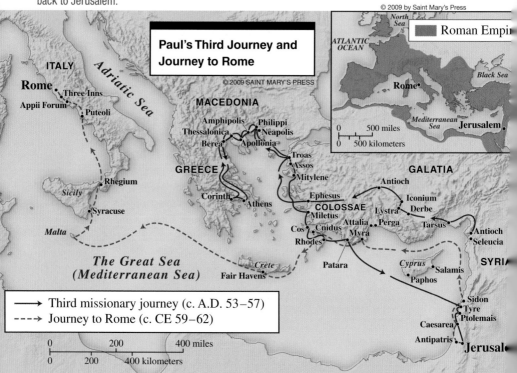

Paul's Third Journey and Journey to Rome

© 2009 SAINT MARY'S PRESS

→ Third missionary journey (c. A.D. 53–57)

- - → Journey to Rome (c. CE 59–62)

the rich, and the poor were all drawn to Corinth for the same reasons that people are drawn to big cities today—for work, certainly, and for a certain cultural mix that can be found in a large urban area.

In the First Letter to the Corinthians, Paul confronts divisions that had sprung up in the Corinthian church: The Corinthians had been identifying themselves by their favorite evangelist (Paul, Apollos, or Cephas) over and above their common identity and unity as Christians. Paul quickly brings them back, not to the human wisdom of any individual preacher, but to the wisdom of the cross of Christ: "We proclaim Christ crucified . . . to those who are called, Jews and Greeks alike, Christ the power of God and the wisdom of God" (1 Corinthians 1:23–24). In regard to ministry, Paul affirms, "What is Apollos, after all, and what is Paul? Ministers through whom you became believers. . . . I planted, Apollos watered, but God caused the growth" (3:5–6). Paul reminds them that, in the end, no matter who brought them to faith in Christ, what matters most of all is that they belong to Christ (see 3:23).

Questions of Behavior

Among this diverse group of people, some formerly pagan, some formerly observant Jews, there arose questions regarding certain issues of sexual morality. What is the Christian attitude toward incest, lawsuits in civil (i.e., pagan) courts, promiscuity in sexual matters? Paul's answers link morality to an understanding of the meaning of being united with Christ.

On the question of incest, the Corinthians may have mistakenly assumed that their Christian freedom meant that previous strictures about marriage (both in the Mosaic Law and in Gentile custom) no longer held for them. Paul definitely reminds them that marriage to a father's wife (which was forbidden under Mosaic Law) is not tolerated even among the Gentiles, so certainly should not be tolerated among the followers of Christ. Using imagery from the Jewish Passover, Paul urges them to throw out the "old yeast" (the influence of sin) and become a fresh batch of dough, making unleavened bread filled with "sincerity and truth" (1 Corinthians 5:8).

Regarding lawsuits against other Christians, Paul is shocked that the Corinthians would set their case before the pagan courts of justice: "Can it be that there is not one among you wise enough to be able to settle a case between brothers? But rather brother goes to court against brother, and that before unbelievers?" (1 Corinthians 6:5–6). The fact that they would bring lawsuits against one another shows that they have failed as Christians. Paul insists that they should let themselves be cheated rather than bring a lawsuit against another Christian.

As for sexual morality, Paul warns the Corinthians to not allow themselves to be dominated by anything. It may seem from 6:13 that the Corinthians are comparing sexual desires to food: to paraphrase, "Christians may eat any kind of food, and that is normal for the body; sexual activity fulfills a need, just like food." However, Paul reminds them that their bodies are members of Christ: "Whoever is joined to the Lord becomes one spirit with him" (6:17). Paul explains that sexual activity is therefore a gift of oneself to another in Christ, and that the members of Christ's body cannot be involved in sexual activity that does not recognize or honor this gift. Sexual activity is not meant simply to fill a need, and sexual activity without a marital commitment is a sin against one's own body, which is the temple of the Holy Spirit: "Do you not know . . . that you are not your own? For you have been purchased at a price. Therefore glorify God in your body" (6:19–20).

Questions about Marriage and about Women

No person who grew up in the United States can read First Corinthians without having some questions about Paul's attitude toward marriage and toward women. Does Paul think it best not to marry (see 7:27–28)? Does Paul think that even in marriage it would be better for a man not to touch a woman (see 7:1)? Let us take a closer look at the First Letter to the Corinthians as we explore these questions.

Marriage and Celibacy

As always, to understand an inspired author's intent, we must put what that author has to say in the contexts in which it appears in the Bible. Two of the contexts for Paul's First Letter to the Corinthians are Paul's presumption that the end-time would be soon and his argument against the ideas of some adversaries concerning the proper Christian understanding of the relationship between spirit and body.

As you will learn when we study First Thessalonians, Paul makes it evident that he expected the second coming during his lifetime. Paul again reveals this presumption in First Corinthians when he says, "For the world in its present form is passing away" (7:31). It is within this context that Paul advises people to stay as they are: If they are married, they should stay married; if they are single, they should stay single. Paul gives this advice in response to a question about whether virgins should marry. He says he has no commandment from the Lord on this matter. However, he also offers what he thinks best, "because of the present distress" (7:26). Paul makes it clear that people don't sin based on whether they marry. But, he argues, why make a long-term commitment now, when the "present form is passing away"?

In the Church today, some feel called in faith to remain unmarried for this same reason: This world is "passing away" and preparation for God's Kingdom, in service to God and to his people, takes precedence over all else. Together with vows of poverty and obedience, these men and women take vows of chastity, usually as members of a religious community. These three vows are called the evangelical counsels because they are advised in the New Testament writings but not demanded of everyone in this absolute way.

Sexuality within Marriage

Does Paul think that even in marriage it is better for a man not to touch a woman (see 1 Corinthians 7:1–2)? He does not. This is an idea held by a loosely defined group, referred to as the spirit people by contemporary Scripture scholars. Paul adamantly disagrees with the ideas of this group. In the words of biblical scholar Jerome Murphy-O'Connor about the spirit people: "The nature of God was more important to them than loving one's neighbor" ("Paul's Second Letter to the Corinthians," *Update Your Faith,* December 2004). The spirit people emphasized the spirit and the mind so much that they saw no value in the body. This devaluing of the body resulted in thinking, on the one hand, that sexual sins were not all that serious. On the other hand, because they thought that only the spirit mattered, they concluded that sexual relations within marriage were not all that important.

The Sacrament of Matrimony

The Sacrament of Matrimony is a covenant modeled on that between Christ and the Church, in which a baptized man and a baptized woman make a permanent commitment to one another and form an intimate and exclusive union of life and love. This covenant was created by God, with its own special laws. Marriage has two special purposes: the good of the couple as well as the generation and education of children. Christ himself raised Marriage to the dignity of a Sacrament, as it signifies the union of Christ and the Church.

This means that the love Christ has for us, the Church—a love so great that he gave his life for us—is the love that, by the grace of this Sacrament, the husband and wife offer to each other. The grace of the Sacrament of Matrimony brings the human love of the spouses to the perfection of the love of Christ. This Sacrament also strengthens their indissoluble unity, and makes them holy as they help each other through life and toward eternity.

This thinking caused some of Paul's converts to write him and ask him a question.

Paul is responding to that question when he writes: "Now in regard to the matters about which you wrote" (1 Corinthians 7:1). Then he quotes a statement from their letter: "'It is a good thing for a man not to touch a woman'" (7:1). Paul then proceeds to argue against such an idea. Paul thinks both a husband and a wife have authority over the other's body (see 7:4). Neither should deny the other (see 7:5).

Roles of Men and Women in Marriage

What are Paul's views on marriage and the relationship between the man and the woman in marriage? These too can be easily misunderstood. As Paul introduces his instructions regarding women wearing veils, he says, "But I want you to know that Christ is the head of every man, and a husband the head of his wife, and God the head of Christ" (1 Corinthians 11:3). Does this passage support the subjugation of wives? When we hear the word *head,* we tend to think "boss." Yet if God is the Head of Christ, the word *head* can't imply subjugation.

When Paul uses the word *head,* he does not mean "boss," but rather "source." The Greek word that Paul uses for *head (kephale)* is never used to mean "authority" or "superiority" (see *New Jerome Biblical Commentary*, page 808, number 53). We use the word *head* in this way when we talk about the head of a river. In saying that the husband is head of his wife, Paul is referring to the story of Adam and Eve, in which the woman is created from man. Paul makes his allusion more clear when he says, "For man did not come from woman, but woman from man" (1 Corinthians 11:8). It is clear that Paul does not mean his statement to support one sex dominating another when he adds: "Woman is not independent of man or man of woman in the Lord. For just as woman came from man, so man is born of woman; but all things are from God" (11:11–12). ✝

Article 40 The Eucharist and Resurrection in First Corinthians

In First Corinthians, Paul emphasizes two truths central to Christian identity: the presence of Christ in the Eucharist and the resurrection of the body. The context for Paul's teaching on the Eucharist is his dismay that the Corinthians are ignoring the poor in their midst at Eucharistic gatherings. The context for Paul's teaching on the resurrection of the body is his having learned that some Corinthians are denying the resurrection of the dead and therefore the Resurrection of Christ himself.

The Eucharist

In First Corinthians we find our earliest account in the Scriptures of the institution of the Eucharist. Paul tells the Corinthians that what he taught them about the Eucharist he had received from the Lord:

> That the Lord Jesus, on the night he was handed over, took bread, and after he had given thanks, broke it and said, "This is my body that is for you. Do this in remembrance of me." In the same way also the cup, after supper, saying, "This cup is the new covenant in my blood. Do this, as often as you drink it, in remembrance of me." For as often as you eat this bread and drink the cup, you proclaim the death of the Lord until he comes. (11:23–26)

Paul's point in reminding the Corinthians of this teaching is that those who receive the Body and Blood of Christ become one Body in Christ. The Corinthians are one body in Christ, but when they gather for the Eucharist, they don't act like it. Paul asks, "Do you show contempt for the church of God and make those who have nothing feel ashamed?" (1 Corinthians 11:22) Paul is outraged that the Corinthians are ignoring the needs of their fellow Christians, and at a Eucharistic meal, of all places!

Paul then warns the Corinthians, "For anyone who eats and drinks without discerning the body, eats and drinks judgment on himself" (1 Corinthians 11:29). To "discern the body" at Eucharist is not only to recognize the gift Jesus has given us in Eucharist, his own Body and Blood, but to recognize the unity of those who receive that Body and who become the **Body of Christ**.

The Resurrection of the Body

When he addresses the subject of resurrection—both the Resurrection of Christ and the resurrection of the dead—Paul once more begins by reminding the Corinthians what he previously taught them:

Body of Christ
A term that when capitalized designates Jesus' Body in the Eucharist, or the entire Church, which is also referred to as the Mystical Body of Christ.

© Antonio V. Oquias / Shutterstock.com

Stained-glass art of the Last Supper from a Catholic church in the Philippines. Paul's understanding of the Eucharist is not just "Jesus and me" but "Jesus and everyone." How can you "take in" the whole Body of Christ?

Live It!

The Spiritual Gifts

As part of his teaching on the unity of Christ's Body, the Church, Paul compares the Body of Christ to a human body. Paul says: "As a body is one though it has many parts, and all the parts of the body, though many, are one body, so also Christ. For in one Spirit we were all baptized into one body, whether Jews or Greeks, slaves or free persons, and we were all given to drink of one Spirit" (1 Corinthians 12:12–13).

As parts of one body, the Church, we have different gifts, gifts that are meant to be of service to the whole body. Every part of the body is needed. "The eye cannot say to the hand, 'I do not need you'" (1 Corinthians 12:21). Though there are many gifts, the greatest gift is love. When we help and encourage one another, when we care for those who are poor, sick, or hungry, we are accepting and using the gift of love (see 1 Corinthians, chapter 13). How can you accept and use your gifts today?

Now I am reminding you, brothers, of the gospel I preached to you. . . . For I handed on to you as of first importance what I also received: that Christ died for our sins in accordance with the scriptures; that he was buried; that he was raised on the third day in accordance with the scriptures; that he appeared to Cephas, then to the Twelve. (1 Corinthians 15:1,3–5)

The reason Paul is reteaching this truth is that some of the Corinthians are denying the resurrection of the body. Paul says: "But if Christ is preached as raised from the dead,

The Body of Christ

When discussing both the Eucharist and the resurrection of the dead and the Resurrection of Christ, Paul uses the word *body* to mean something in addition to flesh and blood. When discussing the Eucharist, he uses *body* to describe not only Jesus' Body and Blood present in Eucharist but also the unity and identity of Christ's Church, the Body of Christ.

When discussing the resurrection of the dead, Paul uses *body* to name not just flesh and blood but a whole person, as we do when we say the word *somebody*. An embodied person is a unique individual who is able to be in relationship with other unique individuals. Paul is assuring the Corinthians that they, as loving people in community with others, will continue to be alive after death. They will experience the resurrection of the body, just as Jesus did (see 1 Corinthians 15:49).

how can some among you say there is no resurrection of the dead?" (1 Corinthians 15:12). Paul insists that a belief in the resurrection of the dead is core to our faith: "For if the dead are not raised, neither has Christ been raised, and if Christ has not been raised, your faith is vain; you are still in your sins" (15:16–17). Paul explains that denial of the resurrection of the body leads to a denial of Christ's Resurrection. To deny Christ's Resurrection is to deny the saving effects of Christ's Passion, death, and Resurrection. If this were the case, the Corinthians would have not been saved and would still be living in sin.

Paul employs diatribe as he continues to pose questions: "But someone may say, 'How are the dead raised? With what kind of body will they come back?'" (1 Corinthians 15:35). Paul then makes it clear that the body that rises is not the flesh and blood body that dies: "Flesh and blood cannot inherit the kingdom of God" (15:50). Rather, what dies is "a natural body; it is raised a spiritual body" (15:44). Paul completes his thought by concluding, "Death is swallowed up in victory" (15:54) and "Thanks be to God who gives us the victory through our Lord Jesus Christ" (15:57). ✝

Article 41 Second Corinthians

When you read Second Corinthians, you will notice several things that will raise questions in your mind. First, something painful seems to have happened between Paul and the Corinthians. Paul explains to the Corinthians why he did not come to see them as he had intended. He assures the Corinthians that he did not change his plans lightly. Paul says: "But I call upon God as witness, on my life, that it is to spare you that I have not yet gone to Corinth. . . . For I decided not to come to you again in painful circumstances" (2 Corinthians 1:23, 2:1). Of course, both Paul and the Corinthians know what the painful circumstances are, so Paul has no need to give a full explanation. We do not know all the details and so are left to wonder exactly what happened.

These are ruins of the ancient city of Corinth. During Saint Paul's time, Corinth was a thriving and densely populated seaport.

Second Corinthians: More Than One Letter?

A second question that reading the text will raise in your mind is why Paul's accounts seem on occasion to be interrupted. For instance, why does the subject change so abruptly between 2 Corinthians 2:13 and 2:14? The subject raised, Paul's going to Macedonia in order to find Titus, isn't picked up again until chapter 7. This is a noticeable lack of continuity.

Why does the tone of the letter change so radically? In the first chapters, Paul talks a great deal about reconciliation. Starting with chapter 10, Paul seems to be more agitated and feels a great need to defend himself. He says, "And even if I should boast a little too much of our authority, which the Lord gave for building you up and not for tearing you down, I shall not be put to shame" (2 Corinthians 10:8). In addition, Paul has some harsh words about his adversaries: "For such people are false apostles, deceitful workers, who masquerade as apostles of Christ. And no wonder, for even Satan masquerades as an angel of light" (11:13–14).

Further, why do there seem to be two separate pleas for contributions to the **Jerusalem collection**? (see 2 Corinthians

Pray It!

What Is Love?

This is Saint Paul's "still more excellent way" (1 Corinthians 12:30) to live. Consider making it a guide for your life:

If I speak in human and angelic tongues but do not have love, I am a resounding gong or a clashing cymbal. . . . If I have all faith so as to move mountains, but do not have love, I am nothing. If I give away everything I own, and if I hand my body over so that I may boast but do not have love, I gain nothing.

Love is patient, love is kind. It is not jealous, [love] is not pompous, it is not inflated, it is not rude, it does not seek its own interests, it is not quick-tempered, it does not brood over injury, it does not rejoice over wrongdoing but rejoices with the truth. It bears all things, believes all things, hopes all things, endures all things.

. . . So faith, hope, love remain, these three; but the greatest of these is love.

(1 Corinthians 13:1–7,13)

8:1–9,15; 9:1; this was a collection for the church in Jerusalem that Paul had agreed to previously and mentioned in Galatians 2:6–10).

Based on these examples, many Scripture scholars surmise that Second Corinthians is a compilation of several letters written on different occasions. Yet, even with its repetition of topics and rapid changes of subject and tone, this letter is valued by the Church for its many insights into the life and teachings of the Apostle Paul.

Paul's Defense of His Ministry

Perhaps because of his painful relationship with the Corinthians, Paul offers some profound thoughts in defense of his own **ministry** and on what every person's ministry should be. The core of ministry is to conform oneself to Christ. In this context Paul himself comes to terms with two important aspects of ministry: the call to be ministers of reconciliation and the call to accept and find meaning in suffering.

Reconciliation

Paul recognizes that Jesus reconciled the human race to God—the Father, Son, and Holy Spirit. Therefore a person who ministers in Christ's name must be a minister of reconciliation. Paul says: "For the love of Christ impels us, once we have come to the conviction that one died for all; therefore, all have died. He indeed died for all, so that those who live might no longer live for themselves but for him who for their sake died and was raised" (2 Corinthians 5:14–15).

Paul is now living for Christ and carrying on Christ's mission of reconciliation. Paul says:

> So whoever is in Christ is a new creation: the old things have passed away; behold, new things have come. And all this is from God, who has reconciled us to himself through Christ and given us the ministry of reconciliation, namely, God was reconciling the world to himself in Christ, not counting their trespasses against them and entrusting to us the message of reconciliation. (2 Corinthians 5:17–19)

Given this context, one can understand just how deeply Paul longed to be reconciled with the Corinthians. As mentioned at the beginning of this article, Paul alludes to

Jerusalem collection

The collection for the poor in Jerusalem that Paul thought was extremely important and agreed to support.

ministry

Based on a word for "service," a way of caring for and serving others and helping the Church fulfill her mission. *Ministry* refers to the work of sanctification performed by those in Holy Orders through the preaching of God's Word and the celebration of the Sacraments. It also refers to the work of the laity in living out their baptismal call to mission through lay ministries, such as that of lector or catechist.

"painful circumstances" (2 Corinthians 2:1) in his relationship with the Corinthians, and he has had to correct them in his first letter: "For out of much affliction and anguish of heart I wrote to you with many tears, not that you might be pained but that you might know the abundant love I have for you" (2:4). Paul begs the Corinthians to be reconciled to God: "We implore you on behalf of Christ, be reconciled to God" (5:20). Paul, as Christ's ambassador or "middle man," wants to lead the people he loves to Christ. Once a person is reconciled to God, reconciliation with others—including Paul himself—will follow.

Suffering

It is by conforming himself to Christ that Paul was able to find meaning in his suffering. Paul says: "We are afflicted in every way, but not constrained; perplexed, but not driven to despair; persecuted, but not abandoned; struck down, but not destroyed; always carrying about in the body the dying of Jesus , so that the life of Jesus may also be manifested in our body" (2 Corinthians 4:8–10). Paul believes that just as Jesus' suffering had redemptive power, so, once joined to Christ's, does his suffering have redemptive power: Paul says: "If we are afflicted, it is for your encouragement and salvation" (1:6).

Yet in his sufferings, Paul never loses his trust in God: "He rescued us from such great danger of death, and he will continue to rescue us; in him we have put our hope [that] he will also rescue us again." (2 Corinthians 1:10).

Despite the difficulties between himself and the Corinthians, Paul is confident that he can also trust in them, as he continues, "As you help us with prayer, so that thanks may be

Catholic Wisdom

Inner Conversion

In a homily for Ash Wednesday, Pope Benedict XVI spoke on 2 Corinthians 5:20:

We beseech you on behalf of Christ, be reconciled to God. . . . Paul experienced in an extraordinary way the power of God's grace, the grace of the Paschal Mystery which gives life to Lent itself. He presents himself to us as an "ambassador" of the Lord. Who better than he, therefore, can help us to progress productively on this journey of inner conversion?

given by many on our behalf for the gift granted through the prayers of many" (2 Corinthians 1:11). ✝

Paul's Thorn in the Flesh

Still another way in which Paul found meaning and purpose by conforming his life to Christ's was in accepting his own weaknesses. After Paul defends himself by reminding the Corinthians of the revelations he has received, he adds, "Therefore, that I might not become too elated, a thorn in the flesh was given to me, an angel of Satan, to beat me, to keep me from being too elated" (2 Corinthians 12:7). We do not know what this "thorn," this particular problem or weakness, was. Paul begged God to relieve him of this problem, but God did not do that.

Instead, God told Paul, "My grace is sufficient for you, for power is made perfect in weakness" (2 Corinthians 12:9). Paul now accepts his weaknesses "in order that the power of Christ may dwell with me" (12:9). Paul is "content with weaknesses, insults, hardships, persecution, and constrains, for the sake of Christ" (12:10).

No one is perfect. Each one of us has our own "thorn in the flesh." Each one of us is weak in one way or another. Each one of us can depend on the grace of God to support us in our weakness and to help us through the difficult times we experience. Whatever our problems, we can find help through parents and friends, teachers, counselors, and in quiet prayer with God, who created us and loves us.

Part Review

1. Name two contexts that must be considered when reading First Corinthians.

2. How does knowledge of these contexts affect your understanding of what Paul has to say about marriage?

3. What are the Corinthians doing when they gather for Eucharist?

4. What two meanings does the "body" of Christ have in Paul?

5. What does Paul teach about the resurrection of the body? In what context does he teach this?

6. What is Paul teaching by comparing the Church to a human body?

7. What evidence is there that Second Corinthians is a compilation of several letters?

8. Name three ways that Paul, in his ministry, conforms himself to Christ.

Part 3

Romans and Galatians

When Paul wrote to the Romans, he was writing to people he had never met. He had never visited Rome, and he did not found the church there, as he had founded the churches of Corinth, Galatia, and Philippi. Yet the Letter to the Romans has several striking characteristics: Of all the Pauline letters, it is the longest. In its length and breadth, it covers the basic beliefs of Christianity to which Paul urges the Romans to hold fast: that we can be saved only through faith in Jesus Christ, and that, though free from the Law of Israel, we are all the more bound in conscience to the New Law of Love. This Law of Love has its roots, of course, in the love Christ has for us, and of this love Paul writes so eloquently: "What will separate us from the love of Christ? . . . For I am convinced that neither death, nor life . . . nor any other creature will be able to separate us from the love of God in Christ Jesus our Lord" (Romans 8:35,38–39).

The territory of Galatia was around Ankara, modern Turkey. In this letter Paul insists that the Christian message he had previously taught the Galatians is the true faith: that Christ's death on the cross and his Resurrection from the dead won our salvation, and there is no need to add observances of the Jewish Law (circumcision and other regulations) to the core teaching of faith in Christ and love of one another.

The articles in this part address the following topics:

- Article 42: "Justification by Faith in Romans and Galatians" (page 214)

- Article 43: "Christians, Law, and Conscience" (page 218)

- Article 44: "Love of Others" (page 222)

© Zvonimir Atletic / Shutterstock.com

Article 42 Justification by Faith in Romans and Galatians

In both Romans and Galatians, Paul teaches a fundamental truth: justification comes through faith in Jesus Christ, not through obedience to the Law. In Galatians, the earlier of the two letters, Paul is angry as he teaches that one does not earn salvation through obedience to the Law. In Romans the tone is much different. Paul is writing to a community whom he has yet to meet. The same truth is taught without the angry tone. In both Galatians and Romans, Paul draws on the Old Testament to persuade his readers that they are now free from the Law. They have been saved through Jesus Christ.

The Social Context for Galatians

The reason Paul is upset when he writes to the Galatians is that he has heard that some people are teaching them a message different from the message that he taught them. Paul's letter is his response

Pray It!

Prayer in the Holy Spirit

In Romans, Paul describes the work of the Holy Spirit within us, even when we have difficulty in prayer: "The Spirit too comes to the aid of our weakness; for we do not know how to pray as we ought, but the Spirit itself intercedes with inexpressible groanings. And the one who searches hearts knows what is the intention of the Spirit, because it intercedes for the holy ones according to God's will" (8:26–27).

Sometimes, in difficulty or temptation, short prayers are best. Here are a few to keep in mind:

- Lord, have mercy!
- "Abba, Father!" (Romans 8:15)
- O God, come to my aid!
- Come, Lord Jesus!
- Christ be with me!
- Come, Holy Spirit!

You might like to make up your own short prayer to strengthen your faith and to pray in time of need.

How Are We Justified?

Justification, or the righteousness of God, comes to us from the Holy Spirit. Because the Holy Spirit unites us by faith and Baptism to the Passion and Resurrection of Christ, we are made sharers in the divine life. We are not justified by our own actions. Justification is a gift from God.

Justification has two aspects: turning toward God and turning away from sin. When we do this, we can then accept God's forgiveness and be restored to his righteousness. Yet this turning toward God is itself a grace from God. Justification includes the forgiveness of sin, being made holy by God, and the inner renewal (conversion) of our inner self.

Through his Passion, Christ merited justification for us, which is granted to us at Baptism. Justification makes us more like God in his righteousness. The ultimate goal of our justification is the glory of God the Father and his Son, Jesus Christ, and eternal happiness in Heaven with the Holy Trinity. Justification is "the most excellent work of God's mercy" (*CCC, 2020*).

and reminder to the Galatians of the truth. He says, "But there are some who are disturbing you and wish to pervert the gospel of Christ" (Galatians 1:7). The *perversion* is that the Galatians, who are Gentile Christians, are being taught that they must be circumcised in order to be saved. In other words, Gentiles who have become Christian must also obey the Jewish Law in order to be in right relationship with God.

By the time Paul was writing Galatians (AD 54–55), this question had already been resolved. Paul knew from a revelation (see Galatians 2:2) that Gentiles did not have to obey the Jewish Law. They were saved through faith in Jesus Christ, not through observance of the Law. In addition, Paul had gone to Jerusalem to check on this very question with the leaders of the Church, and all had agreed that Gentiles did not have to be circumcised (see 2:1–10). Paul couldn't believe that the Galatians were being so foolish as to listen to these false teachers. It is this social setting that gives Paul the opportunity to teach the Good News of Jesus Christ once more: "For in Christ Jesus, neither circumcision nor uncircumcision counts for anything, but only faith working through love" (5:6).

justification

God's action of bringing a sinful human being into right relationship with him. It involves removal of sin and the gift of God's sanctifying grace to renew holiness.

Torah

A Hebrew word meaning "law," referring to the first five books of the Old Testament.

The Social Setting of Romans

The Letter to the Romans is unique among Paul's writings in that Paul did not found the church in Rome, and he did not have the deep and complicated relationship with the Romans that he had with the Corinthians, Galatians, and Philippians. Paul is writing in hopes that he will be able to visit the church in Rome in the near future (Romans 1:13). Paul tells the Romans that he is eager to preach the Gospel to them in Rome (1:15).

Paul then gets right to the core of the matter. He says: "For I am not ashamed of the gospel. It is the power of God for the salvation of everyone who believes: for Jew first, and then Greek" (Romans 1:16). In the rest of the letter, Paul explores this theological core in depth (see Romans, chapters 1–5), and then discusses its ethical implications (see chapters 6–16).

Explanation by Analogy

In both Galatians and Romans, Paul explains the concept of justification through faith rather than works by using the account of Abraham in the Book of Genesis as an analogy. It is interesting that Paul would turn to one of the books of the Law, or **Torah**, in order to seek insight regarding the question of whether specific laws were still binding. The Old Testament communicated God's Revelation in Paul's life, as it

Live It!

Faith and Works

In 1999 representatives of both the Catholic Church and the Lutheran World Federation came together, and, as a result of previous extensive dialogue, clarified and agreed on the meaning of *justification by faith*. This agreement is an important step forward in ecumenical relations between Lutherans and Catholics.

The agreement states, "Together we confess: By grace alone, in faith in Christ's saving work and not because of any merit on our part, we are accepted by God and receive the Holy Spirit, who renews our hearts while equipping and calling us to good works" (Lutheran World Federation and the Catholic Church, "Joint Declaration on the Doctrine of Justification," 15).

Resolve today, in the spirit of this declaration, to live your faith in Jesus from the heart. Be alert to ways the Holy Spirit may call you to reach out to others in love and in good works.

does in ours. In addition, Paul uses the account of Abraham as a living Word to speak on a subject different from that being addressed by the original authors. In using the Bible in this way, Paul is following the custom of his day. We know from reading the Gospels that not only Jesus but also Jesus' adversaries quoted the Scriptures constantly as they taught and debated.

Paul points out: "If Abraham was justified on the basis of his works, he has reason to boast; but this was not so in the sight of God. For what does the scripture say? 'Abraham believed God, and it was credited to him as righteousness'" (Romans 4:2–3). Abraham obviously did not obey the Law; the Law did not exist when Abraham lived (1850 BC). Paul insists: "It was not through the law that the promise was made to Abraham and his descendants that he would inherit the world, but through the righteousness that comes from faith" (4:13).

Just as Abraham was justified through faith, not through the Law, so are both Jews and Gentiles. All "are justified freely by his grace through the redemption in Christ Jesus" (Romans 3:24). ✝

Our Father in Faith

At the Eucharist, in "Eucharistic Prayer I," we hear Abraham identified as "our father in faith" *(Roman Missal)*. Abraham is the father of the Chosen People, the Jews, and our father too, in faith, because he believed God's promise to make of him a great nation and a great blessing (see Genesis 12:1–4). Abraham's faith was later tested by God's request that he sacrifice his son, Isaac, through whom this very promise would be fulfilled (see Genesis 22:1–19). As we know, God did not, in the end, require this sacrifice but promised to reward Abraham's faith. Abraham thus became a model of faith for the Chosen People and for us.

But what is faith? First, it is a supernatural gift from God. Belief in God is not something we arrive at totally on our own. To believe, we need the help and grace of the Holy Spirit. Second, faith involves our whole person. Faith in God means we "adhere" (or stick) to God with our whole being. As God reveals himself to us through his words and actions, we say yes to him, not just intellectually but with our entire will. Faith is necessary for salvation and is "a foretaste of the knowledge that will make us blessed in the life to come" (Saint Thomas Aquinas, *Comp. theol,* 1, 2, in *CCC,* 184).

Born for Freedom

In addition to using an Old Testament account as an analogy to explain a New Testament insight, Paul uses an Old Testament account as an allegory to explain the same insight: Christians are not bound by the Law. In Galatians, Paul uses the account of Abraham and his two sons, "one by the slave woman [Hagar] and the other by the freeborn woman [Sarah]" (4:22) to explain his teaching. Hagar's son was Ishmael; Sarah's son was Isaac. Paul declares: "The son of the slave woman was born naturally, the son of the freeborn through a promise. Now this is an allegory. These women represent two covenants" (4:23–24).

Paul's point is that the Galatians are children of the promise made to Abraham: "Now you, brothers, like Isaac, are children of the promise" (Galatians 4:28). The Galatians, the Romans, and we are all free of the Law because we are saved not by obedience to the Law but by faith in Jesus Christ.

Article 43 Christians, Law, and Conscience

As you already know, Paul teaches the Galatians and the Romans that they are free of the Law. At the same time, in his Letter to the Romans, Paul insists that Christians be "subordinate to the higher authorities" (13:1). Christians must obey Roman law both to avoid punishment and "because of conscience" (13:5).

Are these statements compatible with each other? Why are Christians free from the Jewish Law but not free from civil laws? What if a law is unjust so that it is against one's conscience to obey it? To understand what Paul is teaching, we have to put his words in the social context in which he wrote them. We also have to consider what Paul meant by *law* and *conscience*.

Freedom from the Law

In the last article, we explored the context in which Paul taught that Christians are free of the Law. In this context, the *Law* to which Paul is referring includes the instructions that the Jews followed regarding such things as circumcision and clean and unclean food. The question of obedience to the Jewish Law regarding these two issues was an extremely controversial topic in Paul's day. Jews who had become Christian, and who still kept the Jewish Law, found it difficult to share a meal with Gentile Christians who felt no obligation at all to obey the Law.

© zhang bo / iStockphoto.com

The next time you face a decision, take some quiet time to ask yourself three questions: What do my family and friends advise? What do I think I should do? God, what do you want me to do? God's answer will bring peace.

Paul, a Jew, taught that Gentiles were not bound by the Jewish Law. (We will see the tension caused by this teaching in both Galatians and Romans.) Paul insists that Gentile Christians need not be circumcised or obey the eating regulations in order to be in right relationship with God. Obedience to these regulations does not earn one salvation. Salvation has been accomplished by Jesus Christ. Both Jew and Gentile have been "reconciled to God through the death of his Son" (Romans 5:10).

Love Fulfills the Law

Freedom from the Jewish Law does not at all mean freedom to do whatever one pleases. In Galatians, Paul says, "For you were called for freedom. . . . But do not use this freedom as an opportunity for the flesh; rather, serve one another through love" (5:13). Like Jesus, Paul teaches that "the one who loves another has fulfilled the law" (Romans 13:8). Here Paul is referring to the Commandments in the Law, or Torah. No one is free from the requirement to obey the Commandments. Paul tells the Romans: "The commandments, 'You shall not commit adultery; you shall not kill; you shall not steal; you shall not covet,' and whatever other commandment there may be, are summed up in this saying, . . . 'You shall love your neighbor as yourself'" (13:9).

The Demands of Love

People who are raised in different cultures form different consciences in regard to specific acts. For instance, in Paul's day, people who had been raised in the Jewish culture and who had obeyed the eating laws every day of their lives would find it against their conscience to eat pork. People who had been raised in a Gentile culture would understand perfectly why Paul insisted that Christians need not obey the Jewish laws concerning clean and unclean food.

This confusion over dietary restrictions was evidently present in Rome. What should be done? Could Gentile and Jewish Christians not eat together? Paul tells those who think it is fine to eat food that a Jew would consider unclean that they should refrain from acting on their freedom if in doing so they would scandalize a fellow Christian. Just as love fulfills the whole Law, so love trumps, or outranks, freedom from the Law. Paul says, "If your brother is being hurt by what you eat, your conduct is no longer in accord with love" (Romans 14:15). Out of love for neighbor and respect for the neighbor's conscience, people should not exercise their freedom from the Law if their actions would cause pain to another. Can you think of a situation in which this rule would apply today?

Obedience to Civil Law

When Paul teaches the Romans that they must be subordinate to civil authority, Paul is assuming that **civil law**, the law pertaining to the state, is just and that it promotes peace. Paul says: "Do you wish to have no fear of authority? Then do what is good and you will receive approval from it, for it is a servant of God for your good" (Romans 13:3–4).

Paul teaches that all authority, including civil authority, is from God: "Let every person be subordinate to the higher authorities, for there is no authority except from God, and those that exist have been established by God" (Romans 13:1). To disobey civil authority is thus to disobey God. Therefore Paul instructs the Romans to "pay to all their dues, taxes to whom taxes are due, toll to whom toll is due, respect to whom respect is due, honor to whom honor is due" (13:7). To obey civil law, when civil law is just, is to respect others and to promote the common good.

Conscience

Paul does not address the question of what one should do if it is against one's conscience to obey civil law, nor does he address **civil disobedience** (disobeying a law that is unjust or immoral). That is not the social context for his letter. However, Paul does discuss **conscience**. What does he mean by the word?

The first time Paul speaks of conscience in Romans, he is speaking about the Gentiles who, of course, did not inherit the Law. Nevertheless many Gentiles lived in accordance with the Law. Paul says their actions showed that "the demands of the law are written in their hearts, while their conscience also bears witness and their conflicting thoughts accuse or even defend them" (Romans 2:15). (In other words, at times their conscience places guilt or blame on them; at other times it excuses, or defends, them.)

Conscience, in Paul's culture, was understood to be not so much an inner interior voice that might urge people to act contrary to the accepted norms of their society; rather, it was an internalization of moral values, an interior standard, based on the norms of the society in which people were raised. When deciding right and wrong, the question would

civil law
Law pertaining to the state and its citizens as distinct from the Church.

civil disobedience
Deliberate refusal to obey an immoral demand from civil authority or an immoral civil law.

conscience
The "interior voice," guided by human reason and Divine Law, that leads us to understand ourselves as responsible for our actions, and prompts us to do good and avoid evil. To make good judgments, one needs to have a well-formed conscience.

not be, "What do I personally think is right?" but, "What have I been taught about accepted behavior in my society?"

As we know, Paul, like Jesus, based decisions of conscience on love (see Romans 13:9), not on cultural norms. His admonition to obey civil authority is based on a presumption that civil law is ordered to establish justice and peace in society. Therefore people should obey it, not just out of fear of punishment but also "because of conscience" (13:5). It is the right and loving thing to do. ✝

Conscience

God has given each of us a spiritual soul, with intellect and free will, and so we are, from our very conception, oriented toward God and set on the path toward eternal happiness. We are helped on our journey by the guidance of our conscience. The law within our conscience, the moral law, obliges us to "do what is good and avoid what is evil" (cf. *Gaudium et Spes*, 16) (*CCC*, 1713). What is conscience? It is a judgment by our reasoning powers by which we recognize the moral quality (the goodness or badness) of a concrete act. To make moral judgments, a conscience must be well formed. Each of us must make efforts to educate and form our conscience to make upright, truthful moral judgments, according to reason and conforming to the true good that God, our Creator, wants for his creation. This does not mean that conscience is always correct in its judgments. In matters of morality, it can make a right judgment (in accordance with reason and following the Divine Law) or a wrong judgment (going against these two necessary criteria). However, we are obliged to follow the certain judgment of our conscience, even if at times it may be wrong due to ignorance or error. Such errors in judgment are not free of guilt, however, if they result from a failure to learn as much as we possibly can about moral living. Our conscience must be formed by the Word of God, the light for our path, which we incorporate into our lives through faith and prayer and then act upon in love.

Article
44 Love of Others

At the core of the Gospel, as Paul preaches it in Galatians and Romans, is the Good News that God loved us and saved us even while we were sinners. We did not earn salvation.

We received it as a gift. In response to this gift, we are called to love God and to love our neighbor.

Although Paul emphasizes these truths over and over, some passages in Romans are often taken out of context and used to incite prejudice, rather than love, toward others. Of course, when we treat others with prejudice, we ourselves are sinning. To guard against this, we examine some often misinterpreted passages as they relate to the Jews and to those whom today we call homosexuals.

The Jews

Although Paul was the Apostle to the Gentiles, he himself was a Jew. Paul believed that the Jews too would be saved. Why? For the same reason Gentiles are saved: because of God's righteousness and his saving power. Paul introduces this topic as he begins his Letter to the Romans. He says: "For I am not ashamed of the gospel. It is the power of God for the salvation of everyone who believes: for Jew first, and then Greek" (1:16). But what about a Jew who does not believe?

This question gains urgency because Paul later says, "If you confess with your mouth that Jesus is Lord and believe in your heart that God raised him from the dead, you will be saved" (Romans 10:9). Does this mean that Jews who do not confess Jesus cannot be saved? The passage is often used to assert just that. However, when we read Paul's statement in the context of Romans, we cannot support such a conclusion.

As Paul continues to mull over what to him is a terribly painful mystery, the fact that some of his fellow Jews are rejecting the Good News of Jesus Christ, he professes his belief that the Jews too will be saved. He says: "I do not want you to be unaware of this mystery, brothers . . . a hardening has come upon Israel in part, until the full number of the Gentiles comes in, and thus all Israel will be saved. . . . In respect to election, they are beloved because

© Nancy Louie / iStockphoto.com

On the occasion of a *bar mitzvah*, a boy (or a girl at her *bat mitzvah*) reads aloud a passage of Scripture in Hebrew. The phrase *bar* (or *bat*) *mitzvah* means "son (or daughter) of the commandment."

Sincerely Seeking God

The Second Vatican Council's *Dogmatic Constitution on the Church* (*Lumen Gentium*, 1964) explains that salvation is not limited to people who profess to be Christians: "Those also can attain to salvation who through no fault of their own do not know the Gospel of Christ or His Church, yet sincerely seek God and moved by grace strive by their deeds to do His will as it is known to them through the dictates of conscience" (16). As Pope Paul VI stated, "Other religions . . . try to counter the restlessness of the human heart. . . . The Catholic Church rejects nothing that is true and holy in these religions" *(Declaration on the Relation of the Church to Non-Christian Religions* [Nostra Aetate, 1965], 2). Christ's saving power, through his cross and Resurrection, is "the fountain from which every grace flows" (4) for the salvation of all.

© AMIT DAVE/Reuters/Corbis

of the patriarchs. For the gifts and the call of God are irrevocable" (Romans 11:25–29).

When read in context, it is evident from Paul's statements that the Jews will be saved because God is faithful to his gift and to his call. Paul's teaching, that if you confess Jesus with your lips you will be saved, does not mean that if, through lack of understanding and in good conscience, you fail to confess Jesus with your lips you cannot be saved. The statement cannot be used to pass any kind of negative judgment on the Jews or any others who do not profess faith in Jesus.

Homosexuals

In his Letter to the Romans, Paul argues that all have sinned, both Jew and Gentile, and all need to be saved. Gentiles have sinned by not recognizing and worshipping the Creator, but instead worshipping images of their own making: "While claiming to be wise, they became fools and exchanged the glory of the immortal God for the likeness of an image of mortal man or of birds or of four-legged animals or of snakes" (Romans 1:22–23). People participating in lust-filled same-sex activity is also mentioned (see 1:26–27) as another example of what happens when people refuse to acknowledge God as God and Creator and instead worship created things. Some people interpret these verses to mean that Paul is condemning homosexual persons. But this is a serious misinterpretation of Paul's words.

Paul then goes on to describe other sins that the Gentiles have committed: "They are gossips and scandalmongers and they hate God. They are insolent, haughty, boastful, ingenious in their wickedness, and rebellious toward their parents" (Romans 1:29–30). This description is about Gentiles in general, not about those described in Romans 1:26–27. It is an abuse of Paul's words to use them to affirm prejudice against people of homosexual orientation or to presume that homosexuals are greater sinners than are their fellow human beings. ✝

Catholic Wisdom

Always Our Children

In 1997 the United States Conference of Catholic Bishops (USCCB) issued a pastoral message to support parents of adolescents or adult children who are homosexual. The bishops urged parents to (1) accept their child with love, as God does, without endorsing a homosexual lifestyle, (2) encourage their child to lead, with the help of God's grace, a chaste life (for all sexual activity outside of marriage between a man and a woman is sinful), and (3) to focus on the person of their child, not the sexual orientation: "God loves every person as a unique individual. . . . God does not love someone any less simply because he or she is homosexual. God's love is always and everywhere offered to those who are open to receiving it" ("Always Our Children," 1997).

Part Review

1. What is the core teaching in both Galatians and Romans?

2. How does Paul use the example of Abraham to explain his teaching in both Galatians and Romans?

3. In the Letter to the Romans, what three meanings are referred to by the word *law*?

4. What is meant by *conscience?* According to Paul, is freedom from the Law or love of neighbor more important? Explain.

5. What passage in Romans is sometimes used in a prejudicial way toward Jews? Explain why this is not a legitimate interpretation of the passage.

6. A passage in Romans (1:29–32) is sometimes used in a prejudicial way toward people whose orientation is homosexual. Explain why this is not a legitimate interpretation of the passage.

Part 4

Other Pauline Letters

In this part we discuss the three remaining letters of the seven letters thought to have been written by Paul himself: First Thessalonians, Philippians, and Philemon. All three letters are written to communities Paul knew well. Although Philemon is named after an individual person, it too includes in its greetings a home church.

Paul's earliest letter, First Thessalonians, is the earliest writing in the New Testament. The letter instructs the Thessalonians about the basics of the Christian life and responds to their questions about those who have died. In this letter Paul discusses what is popularly called the rapture.

Paul's letter to the church in Philippi was written from a prison cell, to a community Paul clearly loved: "I give thanks to my God at every remembrance of you, praying always with joy in my every prayer for all of you. . . . I am confident of this, that the one who began a good work in you will continue to complete it until the day of Christ Jesus. . . . I hold you in my heart" (Philippians 1:3–7). Philippi was located in what is now northern Greece, and Paul's letter is thought to have been written about AD 55–57. In Philippians, Paul explains why he rejoices even in his suffering. He also includes a hymn that leaves no doubt about his teaching of Christ's divinity.

Philemon is such a short letter that it has no chapters, only verses. In this letter we see Paul at his persuasive best, making a request of Philemon, a slave owner who is also a friend. But what is Paul actually requesting?

The articles in this part address the following topics:

Article 45 First Thessalonians

First Thessalonians is the earliest writing in the New Testament canon. Paul started the church in Thessalonica, a port city in northern Greece, on his second missionary journey (see Acts of the Apostles 17:1–9). Paul had to leave Thessalonica abruptly, due to riots started by those who disagreed with his teaching. Paul wanted to return to Thessalonica himself. However, because he was unable to do so, he sent Timothy to go in his place. The occasion for writing First Thessalonians is that Timothy had returned with a good report regarding the church in Thessalonica, as well as some questions from the Thessalonians. It is these questions that Paul addresses in his letter written from Corinth in AD 51 (see 1 Thessalonians 3:6, Acts of the Apostles 18:5).

First Thessalonians deals with two main questions: how to live a life pleasing to God and whether Christians who have died before the second coming have missed out on rising with Christ.

Beginning with Antioch in Syria, trace Paul's first and second journeys. To which of these places did Paul later write letters?

© 2009 by Saint Mary's Press

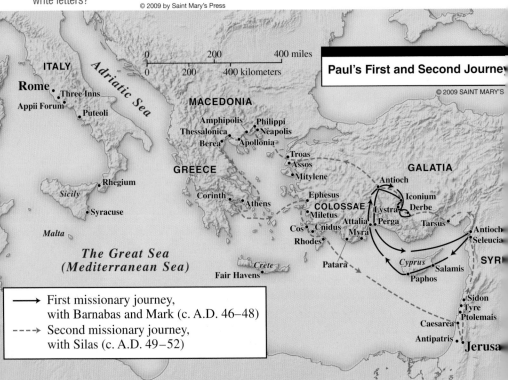

Paul's First and Second Journeys

© 2009 SAINT MARY'S

→ First missionary journey, with Barnabas and Mark (c. A.D. 46–48)

---→ Second missionary journey, with Silas (c. A.D. 49–52)

A Life Pleasing to God

When studying Romans we read a list of sins that Paul claimed the Gentiles had committed. Some of these same sins are addressed in First Thessalonians: worshipping false gods and sexual immorality. Paul congratulates the Thessalonians on turning from false gods to worshipping the one true God: "You turned to God from idols to serve the living and true God and to await his Son from heaven, whom he raised from [the] dead" (1 Thessalonians 1:9–10).

Paul reminds the Thessalonians that God calls them to live a life of holiness and to refrain from immorality. In sexual matters the Thessalonians are told to acquire a wife "in holiness and honor, not in lustful passion as do the Gentiles who do not know God; not to take advantage of or exploit a brother in this matter" (1 Thessalonians 4:4–6). One's sexuality, like every other aspect of life, is to be an expression of love, not a selfish, lustful, or irresponsible act.

In addition to living in holiness rather than impurity, Paul instructs the Thessalonians to "aspire to live a tranquil life, to mind your own affairs, and to work with your [own] hands" (1 Thessalonians 4:11). They are to avoid being dependent on anyone.

Live It!

Mind Your Own Affairs

It is obvious that Paul loves the Thessalonians very much. He says, "You are our glory and joy" (1 Thessalonians 2:20). He encourages them to love one another without being busybodies or gossips. He writes, "We urge you . . . to aspire to live a tranquil life, to mind your own affairs" (4:10–11).

If minding their own affairs was difficult for the Thessalonians, who had no phones or online social networking but communicated by the spoken word, it is even more difficult to mind our own affairs today. How much pain and sadness has been caused by thoughtless gossip, false rumors, and even true reports spread through modern methods of communication, such as text messages, e-mails, and online social networking sites like Facebook? (To spread something damaging to someone's reputation, *even if it is true*, is a sin called detraction. You are detracting from that individual's good name. Of course, reporting wrongdoing to parents, teachers, or authorities in an effort to bring justice when you have knowledge of a crime is not detraction.) No matter what mode of communication you are using—handwritten, spoken, or electronic—it is best to follow the old rule: If you can't say something good about someone, don't say anything at all.

Those Who Have Died

Evidently one of the questions Timothy brought to Paul from the Thessalonians was a concern about the fate of newly converted Christians who had died before the return of the Son of Man on the clouds of Heaven. They wanted to know whether, when Christ comes, those who have died will rise with him. You may remember that this was an issue raised by the Corinthians as well (see section 4, part 2, article 40, "The Eucharist and Resurrection in First Corinthians").

Paul begins to address this question by comforting those who are in grief: "We do not want you to be unaware, brothers, about those who have fallen asleep, so that you may not grieve like the rest, who have no hope" (1 Thessalonians 4:13). Paul then assures the Thessalonians that those who have died with Christ will also rise with Christ: "For if we believe that Jesus died and rose, so too will God, through Jesus, bring with him those who have fallen asleep" (4:14).

As Paul assures the Thessalonians that their departed loved ones have not missed out on the promise of rising with Christ, he reveals a presumption of his time that was not confirmed by events: Paul expected the glorious return of the Son of Man during his lifetime. He says, "Indeed . . . we who are alive, who are left until the coming of the Lord, will surely not precede those who have fallen asleep" (1 Thessalonians 4:15).

Using apocalyptic imagery, with which we are familiar from our study of the Book of Revelation, Paul assures the Thessalonians that "the Lord himself, with a word of command, with the voice of an archangel and with the trumpet of God, will come down from heaven, and the dead in Christ will rise first. Then we who are alive, who are left, will be

Catholic Wisdom

Flying Lies

Saint Philip Neri (1515–1595) was a wise confessor. One day a woman came to him and confessed, "I have been spreading lies about someone." Saint Philip said, "Have you ever shaken the feathers out of a feather pillow? What happens?" The woman replied, "The feathers fly all over!" Saint Philip replied, "How hard would it be to get those feathers back into the pillow? That is how hard it will be to take back all those lies."

caught up together with them in the clouds to meet the Lord in the air" (1 Thessalonians 4:16–17).

We might well wonder, given the facts that Paul reveals a mistaken presumption in this account, and because he uses traditional apocalyptic imagery, what precisely the truth is that he is teaching. Paul is teaching that those who have died before the second coming will rise with Christ and will receive eternal life. Paul wants the Thessalonians to console one another with this Good News. ✝

The Rapture

© Louis-Paul St-Onge / iStockphoto.com

The word *rapture* comes from the passage in First Thessalonians in which Paul says that those who have already died will be the first to rise with Christ and that "we who are alive, who are left, will be caught up together with them in the clouds to meet the Lord in the air" (4:17). *Rapture* is derived from the Latin word *rapiemur*, which in this English translation appears as *caught up*.

The popular idea of the rapture that appears in novels seems to be a combination of Paul's words in First Thessalonians and the passage in Matthew that describes the coming of the Son of Man: "Two men will be out in the field; one will be taken, and one will be left. Two women will be grinding at the mill; one will be taken, and one will be left" (24:40–41). The popular idea of rapture includes many non-Scriptural elements and is not part of God's Revelation.

Paul did not want the Thessalonians to worry about the timing of the second coming. He advises the Thessalonians to put on "the breastplate of faith and love and the helmet that is hope for salvation" (1 Thessalonians 5:8). Children of the light have no reason to fear the coming of the Lord.

Article 46 Philippians

When you read Paul's Letter to the Philippians, you will notice that Philippians, like Second Corinthians, has obvious interruptions in tone and content. For instance, at 3:1 Paul seems to be concluding when he says, "Finally, my brothers, rejoice in the Lord." But in the next verse Paul says: "Beware of the dogs! Beware of the evil-workers! Beware of the mutilation!" (3:2). As with Second Corinthians, such obvious seams are evidence that Philippians is a composite of several letters. Some scholars think Philippians includes three letters, written between AD 55 and 57, that were later combined into one.

Find these places on this map: Jerusalem, Antioch in Syria, Colossae, Ephesus, Philippi, Thessalonica, Corinth.

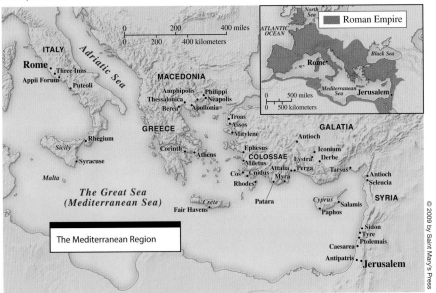

The Mediterranean Region

© 2009 by Saint Mary's Press

Rejoice Even When Suffering

The longest of the three letters is referred to as Paul's joyful letter (see Philippians 1:1—3:1; 4:4–7,21–23). Even though Paul writes this letter from prison, he is full of joy: "But, even if I am poured out as a **libation** upon the sacrificial service of your faith, I rejoice and share my joy with all of you" (2:17).

One reason Paul is so joyful is that he believes his imprisonment and his suffering are advancing the preaching of the Gospel. He says:

> I want you to know, brothers, that my situation has turned out rather to advance the gospel, so that my imprisonment has

become well known in Christ throughout the whole **praetorium** and to all the rest, and so that the majority of the brothers, having taken encouragement in the Lord from my imprisonment, dare more than ever to proclaim the word fearlessly. (Philippians 1:12–14, emphasis added)

libation
The pouring out of a precious liquid as an offering to the Lord.

praetorium
The palace of the governor of a Roman province.

Paul also views suffering, his own and that of the Philippians, as a way of being joined to Christ. Paul tells the Philippians: "For to you has been granted, for the sake of Christ, not only to believe in him but also to suffer for him" (Philippians 1:29).

Paul has so united himself to Christ that he no longer cares whether he lives or dies. His only hope is that "Christ will be magnified in my body, whether by life or by death. For to me life is Christ, and death is gain" (Philippians 1:20–21). Paul longs to "depart this life and be with Christ" (1:23), but he is willing to go on living if that would be better for the Philippians: "Yet that I remain [in] the flesh is more necessary for your benefit" (1:24).

It is in a passage from one of the inserted letters (see Philippians 3:1—4:3, 4:8–9) that Paul sums up his attitude toward suffering. For Paul, the supreme good is to know Christ. Paul has given up everything in order "to know him and the power of his resurrection and [the] sharing of his sufferings by being conformed to his death" (3:10). Paul's hope is to "attain the resurrection from the dead" (3:11). Full of love for Christ, love for the Philippians, and hope in the resurrection, Paul can rejoice in all circumstances.

Pray It!

Garbage In, Garbage Out

Most of us have heard this phrase, sometimes referred to by the acronym GIGO. It comes from computer technology, meaning that if you put incomplete or deficient data into a computer, you will get incomplete or deficient results. The same is true with our minds and hearts. We need to fill them with good thoughts to get good results in our lives. Saint Paul knew this and wrote to the Philippians: "Whatever is true, whatever is honorable, whatever is just, whatever is pure, whatever is lovely, whatever is gracious, if there is any excellence and if there is anything worthy of praise, think about these things. . . . Then the God of peace will be with you" (Philippians 4:8–9). As a start to filling your mind with good thoughts, you might like to memorize these verses and recall them often!

Jesus Christ Is Lord

When we studied the Gospel of John, we took careful note of the hymn with which John starts his Gospel. Philippians includes a hymn near its beginning also (see 2:6–11). This hymn emphasizes Jesus' divinity. Paul includes this hymn in the course of encouraging the Philippians to serve one another, not with self-interest, but with love. Paul wants the Philippians to "have the same attitude" (2:5) as did Christ.

As the hymn begins, it describes Jesus as being "in the form of God" but not regarding "equality with God something to be grasped" (Philippians 2:6). Some Scripture scholars interpret the phrase "in the form of God" as a reference to Jesus' preexistence. Remember, John's hymn begins:

> In the beginning was the Word,
> > and the Word was with God
> > and the Word was God.
> > > (John 1:1)

Other Scripture scholars consider the words of Philippians to be a reference to Genesis in which human beings are made in the image of God (see Genesis 1:27). The man and woman in the garden did think that equality with God should be grasped (see 3:5–7). Jesus did not, as the hymn proclaims:

> Rather, he emptied himself,
> taking the form of a slave,
> coming in human likeness.
> > (Philippians 2:7)

However, as the song continues, there is no doubt it is emphasizing Jesus' divinity. Jesus is to be worshipped as only God should be worshipped:

> At the name of Jesus
> every knee should bend,
> of those in heaven and on earth and under the earth,
> and every tongue confess that
> Jesus Christ is Lord.
> > (Philippians 2:10–11)

This is an allusion to Isaiah in which the Lord says, "To me every knee shall bend; / by me every tongue shall swear" (45:23). To teach that Jesus should be worshipped is to teach that Jesus has "equality with God."

The title Lord is an indication of Jesus' divinity and divine sovereignty. To confess Jesus as Lord is to believe in his divinity. ✝

Death on a Cross

Although Scripture scholars believe that Paul did not compose the hymn that he includes in Philippians, they also surmise that he did add a few words to emphasize his teaching. Those words are "even death on a cross" (Philippians 2:8).

It is hard for us to imagine just how shameful Jesus' manner of death was in his own culture. Crucifixion was reserved for the worst of criminals. The manner of Jesus' death was so shameful that it often went unmentioned. Paul, however, emphasizes that Jesus died on a cross. He wants the Philippians not only to understand Jesus' total humility in accepting such a death but also to model themselves on Jesus.

Article
47 Philemon

Because you have grown up in a culture that recognizes that slavery is wrong, you may find Paul's letter to Philemon surprising. Paul grew up in a culture in which slavery was an accepted part of the social order, and he did not challenge that social order. He recognized the rights of slave owners rather than the rights of slaves; however, Paul did teach that being a Christian changes the way a master treats his slave.

Roman slaves are pictured here feeding wood into furnaces to warm bathwater. The Romans made slaves of people they conquered. For Paul's metaphorical use of Roman slavery to explain freedom in Christ, see Galatians 4:1–7.

© National Geographic Society/ Corbis

Setting and Purpose

The exact date of Paul's Letter to Philemon is unknown. Paul was in prison at the time he wrote the letter (see Philemon 10), but because Paul was imprisoned many times, this information does not help us to date the letter. It could have been written anytime from AD 54 to 56 if from Ephesus, or from AD 61 to 63 if from Rome. Though the letter is primarily to Philemon, it is addressed to two other individuals and to "the church in your house" (see verses 1–2). That Paul's letter is addressed to the larger group is one of many ways Paul puts pressure on Philemon to do as Paul requests.

What does Paul want? The question is not easily answered, as Paul asks for one thing but hints at another. The most obvious purpose for Paul's letter is to ask Philemon to welcome back his runaway slave, Onesimus, without punishing him. Onesimus has become a Christian, as is Philemon, and has been working with Paul. Paul wants Philemon to welcome Onesimus "no longer as a slave but more than a slave, a brother, beloved especially to me, but even more so to you, as a man and in the Lord. So if you regard me as a partner, welcome him as you would me" (Philemon, verses 16–17). In addition, Paul wants to pay any penalty that might be imposed on Onesimus for running away: "And if he has done you any injustice or owes anything, charge it to me. . . . I will pay" (verses 18–19).

Here Paul is acting on a belief that he clearly expresses in Galatians: "For all of you who were baptized into Christ have clothed yourselves with Christ. There is neither Jew nor Greek, there is neither slave nor free person, there is not male and female; for you are all one in Christ Jesus" (3:27–28). For Paul, Baptism doesn't change the social order. A slave is still a slave. But it does change the way a person in power treats those who are accountable to him. The slave owner must treat his slave with the dignity the slave deserves as a fellow Christian and as a beloved child of God. This is the major underlying message of the Letter to Philemon.

Paul's Methods of Persuasion

In addition to addressing his letter to the church, Paul uses some other methods of persuasion. One is flattery. He compliments Philemon on his faith and on how generous he has been in the past: "I hear of the love and the faith you have in the Lord Jesus and for all the holy ones. . . . For I have experienced much joy and encouragement from your love, because the hearts of the holy ones have been refreshed by you, brother" (Philemon, verses 5,7).

Then Paul reminds Philemon that he could order Philemon to do as he asks, but prefers to have Philemon act voluntarily: "Although I have the full right in Christ to order you to do what is proper, I rather urge you out of love . . . so that the good you do might not be forced but voluntary" (Philemon, verses 8–9,14). As though this weren't enough, Paul then reminds Philemon that he is in Paul's debt: "May I not tell you that you owe me your very self. Yes, brother, may I profit from you in the Lord" (verses 19–20).

After becoming Christian, Onesimus returns to Philemon and asks to be released to work with Paul.

© Standard Publishing / Goodsalt.com

Paul's Hinted Request

Though on the surface Paul asks Philemon to welcome Onesimus as a brother in Christ, he also hints that his real request is that Philemon send Onesimus back to aid Paul in his ministry. Paul says that though he is sending Onesimus back to Philemon, he would "have liked to retain him for myself, so that he might serve me on your behalf in my imprisonment for the gospel, but I did not want to do anything without your consent" (Philemon, verses 13–14).

Later, as if to remind Philemon of this preference, Paul says, "With trust in your compliance I write to you, knowing that you will do even more than I say" (Philemon, verse 21). Though Paul does not directly ask Philemon to free Onesimus and send him back to work with him, he certainly hints this is both his hope and his expectation. ✝

Pope Benedict XVI on Difficult Biblical Passages

This excerpt from Pope Benedict's Apostolic Exhortation *Verbum Domini* helps to put difficult passages like Paul's acceptance of slavery into perspective:

> Here it must be remembered first and foremost that *biblical revelation is deeply rooted in history*. God's plan is manifested *progressively* and it is accomplished slowly, *in successive stages* and despite human resistance. God chose a people and patiently worked to guide and educate them. Revelation is suited to the cultural and moral level of distant times and thus describes facts and customs, such as cheating and trickery, and acts of violence and massacre, without explicitly denouncing the immorality of such things. This can be explained by the historical context, yet it can cause the modern reader to be taken aback, especially if he or she fails to take account of the many "dark" deeds carried out down the centuries, and also in our own day. In the Old Testament, the preaching of the prophets vigorously challenged every kind of injustice and violence, whether collective or individual, and thus became God's way of training his people in preparation for the Gospel. So it would be a mistake to neglect those passages of Scripture that strike us as problematic. Rather, we should be aware that the correct interpretation of these passages requires a degree of expertise, acquired through a training that interprets the texts in their historical-literary context and within the Christian perspective. (42)

Part Review

1. What does Paul teach the Thessalonians in answer to the question, How do we lead a life pleasing to God?

2. What does Paul teach the Thessalonians in answer to the question, Will those who have already died rise with Christ? What presumption of Paul's is evident in his answer?

3. According to Philippians, why is Paul able to rejoice in his suffering?

4. What does the hymn in Philippians emphasize about Jesus Christ?

5. What does Paul explicitly ask of Philemon? What does he hint that he wants from him?

6. What is the major underlying message of the Letter to Philemon?

Later Letters

Part 1

Letters Attributed to Paul

As we discussed in our overview of New Testament letters, not all the letters attributed to Paul are believed to have been written by him. In this section we discuss six such letters: Ephesians, Colossians, First and Second Thessalonians, First and Second Timothy, and Titus. All six letters are thought, by some scholars, to date to after Paul's life, from AD 80 to 100.

In Ephesians, the author uses the word *church* in a different way than Paul often used it. In Ephesians *Church* refers not to a group of people gathered in Christ's name in someone's home, but to a cosmic entity: a *One, Holy, Catholic,* and *Apostolic* Church. Reading Ephesians allows us to explore the meaning of each of those words.

The Letter to the Colossians is written to a community that is being falsely taught that worship of Jesus is good, but not good enough, and that one must worship other spirits as well. To respond to this teaching, the author centers on Jesus' identity.

The Second Letter to the Thessalonians responds to a question as well: Has the day of the Lord arrived? The author uses apocalyptic imagery to teach and assure that, although the day of the Lord has not yet arrived, Jesus Christ has already conquered evil.

The First and Second Letters to Timothy and the Letter to Titus are called pastoral letters because they are addressed to pastors who are being encouraged to teach correct doctrine and to maintain church order by appointing stable leaders. Though the letters are attributed to Paul and purportedly addressed to companions of Paul (Timothy and Titus), all three are thought to be pseudonymous.

The articles in this part address the following topics:

Article 48 Ephesians

When you are at Mass, you stand with the congregation and say the Nicene Creed. Part of that Creed states: "I believe in one, holy, catholic and apostolic Church" (*Roman Missal*). Reading the letter to the Ephesians offers us an opportunity to think about the meaning of those words. In this letter, "Paul" (the letter is believed by some to be attributed to Paul, not written by Paul) instructs the Ephesians regarding the identity and mission of the Church and then gives them instructions as to how to lead a life worthy of that call.

The Church Is Catholic

I believe in one God,

the Father almighty,

maker of heaven and earth . . . .

I believe in Jesus Christ,

the Only Begotten Son of God . . . .

© Bill Wittman / www.wpwittman.com

The author of Ephesians does not use the word *church* to refer to a group of Christians meeting in someone's home, as Paul so often does; rather, the author understands the Church to be universal (*catholic* means "universal"), even cosmic. As the author begins, he says that God "chose us in him, before the foundation of the world" (Ephesians 1:4). Continuing, he says that God "has made known to us the mystery of his will in accord with his favor that he set forth in him [Christ] as a plan for the fullness of

Catholic Wisdom

Faith: Individual and Communal

When we say, "I believe," we say this as an individual, for belief is a fully conscious and free human act, appropriate to the dignity of the human person. Yet it is also an ecclesial act, meaning that the Church's faith goes before, gives life to, supports, and nourishes the faith of each individual member of the Body of Christ.

times, to sum up all things in Christ, in heaven and on earth"
(1:9–10). God's salvific plan in and though Jesus Christ is
not for a chosen few but is for all of creation. It is for Jew and
Gentile alike. It is not for one or two generations but for all
people of all times. The universal Church transcends time
and space. The Church is for all, everywhere.

The author, in Paul's name, explains that God's cosmic
plan for the salvation of all through time and space was
revealed to him. It is now his job to make God's will known
to all. He is "to bring to light [for all] what is the plan of
the mystery hidden from ages past in God who created all
things, so that the manifold wisdom of God might now be
make known through the church" (Ephesians 3:9–10). It is
the universal Church's mission to reveal God's plan through
time and space.

The Church Is Holy

That the Church is holy is also stated immediately as the letter begins: God "has blessed us in Christ with every spiritual
blessing in the heavens, as he chose us in him . . . to be
holy and without blemish before him" (Ephesians 1:3–4).
The Gentile Ephesians, without the Law, used to live in sin,
but now they do not: "God . . . brought us to life with
Christ (by grace you have been saved), raised us up with
him" (2:4–6). Having been saved by Christ, the Gentile
Christian Ephesians are now "fellow citizens with the holy
ones and members of the household of God" (2:19). The
term *holy ones* in this passage refers to the Jewish Christians
in Ephesus. Jew and Gentile are now united in Christ.

The Church, made holy by Christ, is to be a temple
where God dwells: "Through [Christ] the whole structure is
held together and grows into a temple sacred in the Lord; in
him you also are being built together into a dwelling place of
God in the Spirit" (Ephesians 2:21–22).

The Church Is Apostolic

In writing Ephesians and attributing it to the Apostle Paul,
the author affirms that what he teaches in this letter is the
truth that was revealed to the Apostles. He also explicitly
states that the source for his teaching is the apostolic witness:
"When you read this you can understand my insight into the

household code
Instructions as to how members of a Christian household should treat one another, similar to but improving upon pagan Greco-Roman codes of conduct for families.

mystery of Christ, which was not made known to human beings in other generations as it has now been revealed to his holy apostles and prophets by the Spirit" (Ephesians 3:4–5). The fact that the author speaks of the Apostles as the *foundation* upon which the Church is built (see 2:20), as though they were of a previous generation, is one of the reasons many Scripture scholars believe this letter to be pseudonymous.

The Church Is One

The unity of the Church rests in Christ. Ephesians presents the Church as the one body of Christ, with Christ as its head: "Living the truth in love, we should grow in every way into him who is the head, Christ, from whom the whole body . . . brings about the body's growth and builds itself up in love" (4:15–16).

The Ephesians are to live in love so as to preserve the unity of the one, holy, and catholic Church: to "live in a

The Four Marks of the Church

The Church is One, Holy, Catholic, and Apostolic. She is characterized by oneness or unity, as described in chapter 4 of Ephesians : "one body and one Spirit . . . one Lord, one faith, one baptism" (verses 4–5). We, the Church, given life by the one Holy Spirit, are "called to the one hope" of our call (verse 4) and we look to the day when our hope is fulfilled and all will be one in God.

The Church is holy, not because her members are holy in their own right, but because her author and source is the Most Holy God; Christ, her bride-groom, gave himself up for her, to make her holy; and the Spirit of holiness gives her life. The Church is "the sinless one made up of sinners" (*CCC*, 867), and her holiness is evident in the saints and in Mary, the Mother of God.

The Church is catholic in two senses. She is catholic because Christ is present in her and has given her the fullness of the means of salvation and also because she reaches throughout the world to all people. In her catho-licity, she is sent out to all, speaks to all, and encompasses all times. The Church is sent out as a missionary for Christ to all the world.

The Church is apostolic because she is built on the Twelve Apostles. She is indestructible and is supported infallibly in the truth, because Christ himself governs her through Peter and the other Apostles, who are present in their successors, the Pope and the college of bishops.

The Household Code

As the author of the Letter to the Ephesians encourages them to live a life worthy of the call they have received, he includes a **household code**. A household code gives instructions as to how the members of a Christian household should treat one another. Two lines, which have historically been abused when taken out of context, are: "Wives should be subordinate to their husbands as to the Lord" and "Slaves, be obedient to your human masters with fear and trembling, in sincerity of heart, as to Christ" (Ephesians 5:22, 6:5). (Recall that wives and slaves were property in the culture to whom the author is writing.)

As we have discussed earlier (see section 1), those who want to use these lines to give permission for one child of God to treat another child of God as though that person were his property are ignoring the line with which the passage starts: "Be subordinate to one another out of reverence for Christ" (Ephesians 5:21). In particular, husbands are directed to "love your wives, even as Christ loved the church and handed himself over for her" (5:25), meaning that as Christ handed himself over to death, so should a husband be ready to lay down his life for his wife.

This passage would have been a challenge to the social order in its original setting. Those in power, husbands and masters, are instructed to treat those in their care, over whom society has given them authority, not as servants or property but as Christ himself would treat them.

manner worthy of the call you have received . . . striving to preserve the unity of the spirit through the bond of peace: one body and one Spirit . . . one Lord, one faith, one baptism; one God and Father of all" (Ephesians 4:1–6). ✝

Article 49 Colossians

Although Colossians comes after Ephesians in the canon (because Colossians is shorter), some Scripture scholars think Colossians was written first, about AD 80.

It appears that the Letter to the Colossians was written to a particular community: a church in Colossae, a city in Asia Minor. Unlike the Letter to the Ephesians, the Letter to the Colossians responds to particular problems the Colossians were experiencing. Because Ephesians does not respond to particular problems and lacks personal greetings, and because some early texts don't include the phrase "in Ephesus," scholars surmise that it was originally a circular letter, a letter that was passed along to a number of different communities. Despite this difference in original audiences, the two letters share an understanding that the Gospel is for the whole world.

The two letters also share an understanding that the Gospel was previously hidden but is now revealed; that God saved the Gentiles, while they were still sinners, through the Passion, death, and Resurrection of Jesus Christ; that Christ is head of the Church, which is his Body; and that the Church is one. Both exhort their readers to live in peace and love, and both have a household code. They are also both attributed to Paul.

The Holy Trinity, by Hildegard of Bingen, a twelfth-century nun. The two circles symbolize the Father and the Holy Spirit. The Word of God, Christ, the only Person of the Trinity who became incarnate, is pictured in human form.

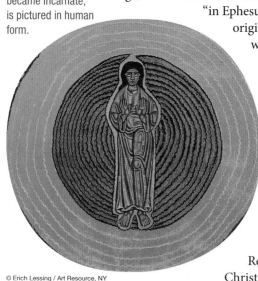

© Erich Lessing / Art Resource, NY

Problems in Colossae

The problem to which the author responds is not the same problem Paul addressed a generation earlier when he argued against the necessity for Gentiles to be circumcised and subject to the Jewish Law (see Galatians 5:1–6). It seems that someone is teaching the Colossians that worship of Jesus is not enough: They should also worship other "elemental powers." The author warns the Colossians: "See to it that no one captivate you with an empty, seductive philosophy according to human tradition, according to the elemental powers of the world and not according to Christ" (Colossians 2:8). Why is worship of "powers" not necessary? Because, in Christ "dwells the whole fullness of the deity . . . [Christ] is the head of every principality and power" (2:9–10).

The author warns the Colossians not to let anyone "pass judgment on you in matters of food and drink or with regard to a festival or new moon or sabbath" (Colossians 2:16).

Then, mimicking the false teachings of those who hold such beliefs, the author says: "Do not handle! Do not taste! Do not touch!" (Colossians 2:21). Because the Colossians have "died with Christ to the elemental powers of the world" (2:20), they should not submit to such meaningless regulations.

Pray It!

A Prayer for Growth in God

The first chapter of the Letter to the Colossians includes a beautiful prayer for growth in the knowledge of God and his will. Pray it for yourself (changing "you" to "I" or "me") and for others, as the writer of Colossians prayed it for the early Christians:

> May you (I) "be filled with the knowledge of his [God's] will through all spiritual wisdom and understanding to live in a manner worthy of the Lord, so as to be fully pleasing, in every good work bearing fruit and growing in the knowledge of God, strengthened with every power, in accord with his glorious might, for all endurance and patience, with joy giving thanks to the Father, who has made you fit to share in the inheritance of the holy ones in light. He delivered us from the power of darkness and transferred us to the kingdom of his beloved Son, in whom we have redemption, the forgiveness of sins."

(Colossians 1:9–14)

firstborn

In relation to Christ, *firstborn* is a reference to Jesus' divinity. Jesus is firstborn of creation and firstborn of the dead, that is, the first to be raised from the dead.

This letter reinforces all that the Colossians have been taught about life in Christ, so that the community might discern the falsehoods presented to them under the guise of truth.

The Identity of Jesus Christ

At the core of the controversy is the identity of Jesus Christ: Is Jesus just one of many powerful spirits, or has all authority been given to Jesus? To lay a foundation from which to respond to this question, the author, in the first chapter, includes a liturgical hymn that celebrates Christ's divinity (see Colossians 1:15–20). Though Scripture scholars believe that the author of the letter is not the author of the hymn, the hymn nevertheless responds directly to the false ideas being taught in Colossae. It begins by referring to Jesus' preexistence: "He is the image of the invisible God, / the **firstborn** of all creation" (1:15). All things in Heaven and on earth were created through him, "whether thrones

The Meaning of Our Suffering

In the person of Paul, the author of Colossians says something that many people find puzzling. He says: "Now I rejoice in my sufferings for your sake, and in my flesh I am filling up what is lacking in the afflictions of Christ on behalf of his body, which is the church" (1:24). Being contextualists who have already read Paul, we are well equipped to understand what the author intends to say.

Obviously the point is not that anything is lacking in the suffering of Christ. (The hymn we have just read makes that abundantly clear.) Here, the author, like Paul, finds meaning in his suffering by joining his suffering to Christ's. As part of the Body of Christ, the author believes that his suffering too can be united to Christ's for the good of the Church. That is why he can say, "For this I labor and struggle, in accord with the exercise of [Christ's] power working within me" (Colossians 1:29).

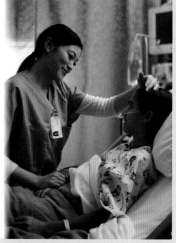

© Rubberball/Corbis

or dominions or principalities or powers" (1:16). Because everything that exists was created through Christ and for Christ, there is certainly no reason to think that Christ lacks something that other spirits have. There is no reason to worship other spirits.

Christ is also the firstborn of the dead. Later the author reminds the Colossians that they were buried with Christ in Baptism and "were also raised with him through faith in the power of God, who raised him from the dead" (Colossians 2:12). Christ has reconciled all things "by the blood of his cross" (1:20), and because he has already accomplished this reconciliation, there is no need at all for the Colossians to fall prey to the various practices of asceticism that are being foisted upon them by the false teachers. Because the Colossians, through Baptism, have been raised with Christ, they should "seek what is above, where Christ is seated at the right hand of God" (3:1), and no longer listen to the false teachers. ✝

This stained-glass window can be found in Saint George's Cathedral, in London. The Risen Christ bears his glorious wounds (on his hands), one hand holding the banner of victory and the other hand raised in blessing.

Article 50 Second Thessalonians

Do you think of Jesus as one who "will kill with the breath of his mouth" (2 Thessalonians 2:8), as the author of Second Thessalonians says? Do you think of God as one who will send a "deceiving power so that they may believe the lie" (2:11)? After all, we have read over and over that the core of the Gospel message is that God loves and saves even sinners. What could these passages from Second Thessalonians mean? To find an answer, we will have to recall what we learned about apocalyptic literature when we discussed the Book of Revelation.

As you remember, apocalyptic literature was written for people suffering persecution in order to assure them that, in the end, good will conquer evil. In a Christian context, the message is that God has not lost power over the unfolding of history; that Jesus, who reigns in Heaven, has already

© The Crosiers / Gene Plaisted, OSC

Tough Love

The author of Second Thessalonians reminds his readers that "when we were with you, we instructed you that if anyone was unwilling to work, neither should that one eat" (3:10). Evidently some of the Thessalonians are refusing to work, are acting in a disorderly way, and, at the same time, are expecting others, out of the goodness of their hearts, to provide them with food. Perhaps they are not working because they think the day of the Lord has already arrived, or will come very soon, so the work is unnecessary.

© Mika/Corbis

The author has no patience for such behavior. If people won't work, let them go hungry. This is not to exclude such a person from the community. To soften this instruction the author adds, "Do not regard him as an enemy but admonish him as a brother" (3:15). Even when people are misbehaving, or misguided, the priority of love of neighbor still prevails.

conquered sin and death; and that it is only a matter of time until Jesus' definitive victory over evil becomes visible on earth. In the Second Letter to the Thessalonians, we examine the setting, the author, and then the apocalyptic imagery to discover the meaning of this letter.

Setting

The Second Letter to the Thessalonians is written to people suffering persecution. This is mentioned as the letter begins: "Accordingly, we ourselves boast of you in the churches of God regarding your endurance and faith in all your persecutions and the afflictions you endure" (1:4).

The people are concerned about the end-time. They are wondering if the day of the Lord has already come. The author assures them that it has not: "We ask you, brothers, with regard to the coming of our Lord Jesus Christ and our assembling with him, not to be shaken out of your minds suddenly, or to be alarmed either by a "spirit," or by an oral statement, or by a letter allegedly from us to the effect that the day of the Lord is at hand" (2 Thessalonians 2:1–2).

The recipients of the letter, the Thessalonians, live in Thessalonica, the port city in northern Greece, as did the recipients of First Thessalonians. Remember, that letter too was written in response to a question about the end-time: Will those who have already died also rise with Christ? Paul assured them they would.

Author

Although the letter claims to be from Paul (see 2 Thessalonians 1:1), it may be pseudonymous. If pseudonymous, the letter dates from AD 80 to 100. The author writes to encourage the suffering Thessalonians to remain faithful to what they were taught: "Therefore, brothers, stand firm and hold fast to the traditions that you were taught, either by an oral statement or by a letter of ours" (2 Thessalonians 2:15).

Live It!

Your Fair Share

Nobody likes a moocher, but we all have had experiences with someone like this. This is the kind of person who never has his or her homework done and wants to look at yours; who asks you for favors all the time but never wants to help you out; who never offers to treat you to a soda, when you have paid for his or her soda over and over again.

The writer of Second Thessalonians has some strong words for those kinds of people: "If anyone was unwilling to work, neither should that one eat" (2 Thessalonians 3:10). The principle is: Contribute your fair share—with family, with friends, and in the community.

We are always encouraged to help those in real need. But being a faithful Christian does not mean allowing someone to take advantage of you. If someone consistently fails to do his or her part, gently but firmly set some boundaries. Some people are simply unaware of how their actions affect others, and honesty is part of what friendship is all about.

lawless one

A symbol of evil, comparable to 666 in the Book of Revelation and to the antichrist in the First Letter of John.

Apocalyptic Imagery

Knowing the concerns and fears of the Thessalonians, we can now explain what the author is teaching by picturing Jesus as one who "will kill with the breath of his mouth" and God as one who would "send a deceiving power." Through the first image, the author is teaching that Jesus will overcome evil. Through the second image, the author is teaching that God has not lost ultimate authority over the course of events. Both of these passages appear in a highly symbolic description of good overcoming evil, of Christ's annihilating the "**lawless one**."

In response to the question about the day of the Lord, the author assures the Thessalonians that before the day of the Lord comes there will be an ultimate manifestation of evil: The "lawless one" will finally be revealed. This lawless one "opposes and exalts himself above every so-called god and object of worship, so as to seat himself in the temple of God, claiming that he is a god" (2 Thessalonians 2:4). It is this lawless one, "the one whose coming springs from the power of Satan in every mighty deed and in signs and wonders that lie, and in every wicked deceit" (2:9–10), whom Jesus will utterly destroy. The lawless one will be rendered powerless when Jesus comes.

Part of the hope offered to the persecuted in apocalyptic literature is assurance that those who are doing the persecuting will be justly condemned. It is as part of this message that the author says that God sent a "deceiving power" so that "all who have not believed the truth but have approved wrongdoing may be condemned" (2 Thessalonians 2:12). God is still ultimately in charge, and those who have done evil will be justly punished. The people's suffering will soon be over, and the persecutors will be held accountable for their actions. For the persecuted that is indeed good news. ✝

Article
51 The Pastoral Letters

The pastoral letters address various Church issues and are named for the pastors to whom they are addressed. All three letters (First and Second Timothy and Titus) are thought by most scholars to have been written by a single author to churches in Asia Minor about the turn of the first century AD. They reflect developed roles in the Church that are not contemporary with Paul. Their concern is not about evangelization but about making sure those who have received true doctrine will not be misled by false teachers—a concern that arose primarily after Paul's death.

The First Letter to Timothy

© Erich Lessing / Art Resource, NY

The author of First Timothy is very concerned that false teachers will have a detrimental effect on the Church to which he is writing. He encourages the recipient, Timothy, to "instruct certain people not to teach false doctrines" (1 Timothy 1:3). One way to assure that false doctrines are not taught is to establish formal leadership roles in the community. These formally designated leaders can speak on behalf of the community.

This fresco of a young man reading a scroll is from Herculaneum, in Italy, a town destroyed by volcanic lava from Mount Vesuvius in AD 79. It reminds us of the young Timothy reading Scripture. See 2 Timothy 3:14–16.

Church Leadership

Though First Timothy describes a number of formal Church roles—bishop, deacon, widow, and presbyter—it says very little about the responsibilities of each role. (In the early Church, the order of widows was a formal order of service.) The author's main concern is the character of the person who fulfills that role. A bishop should be "irreproachable, married only once, temperate, self-controlled, decent, hospitable, able to teach" (1 Timothy 3:2).

Deacons should be "dignified, not deceitful, not addicted to drink, not greedy for sordid gain. . . . If there is nothing serious against them, let them serve as deacons" (1 Timothy 3:8–10). He adds, "Deacons may be married only once and must manage their children and their households well" (3:12).

The letter also gives instructions to and about widows. At the time that this letter was written, women whose husbands had died were particularly vulnerable, as they would have lost not only a husband but a means of support. The author encourages families to care for their widowed

Women in the Church

When Pope Benedict XVI was in charge of the Vatican office for the Doctrine of the Faith, he issued a letter stressing the importance of feminine values. It called for respect for women in society, in the family, and in the world of work. Quoting from Pope Saint John Paul II's apostolic letter *Mulieris Dignitatem*, this letter restated: "*Man is a person, man and woman equally so*, since both were created in the image and likeness of the personal God" ("Letter to the Bishops of the Catholic Church on the Collaboration of Men and Women in the Church and in the World," 8). Thus the Church encourages an active collaboration between the sexes in all areas of human life, and offers Mary, the Mother of God, as an example of faithfulness not only for women but for every baptized Christian.

members. Those widows without family members to care for them should pray for the Christian community, and the community in turn should care for their needs (see 1 Timothy 5:5–8,16). A widow who is "enrolled" in service to the Church must be "not less than sixty years old, married only once, with a reputation for good works, namely, that she has raised children, practiced hospitality, washed the feet of the holy ones, helped those in distress, involved herself in every good work" (5:9–10). The author advises younger widows to marry again, rather than to be idlers and gossipers (see 5:13).

The presbyters "who preside well deserve double honor, especially those who toil in preaching and teaching" (1 Timothy 5:17). The author instructs the community to support the presbyters, for "a worker deserves his pay" (5:18). He directs that accusations against presbyters be supported by two or three witnesses, and also instructs Timothy not to be too eager to accept someone as a presbyter: "Do not lay hands too readily on anyone" (5:22). Potential presbyters must be evaluated carefully (see 5:24–25).

A Word to the Wealthy

The First Letter to Timothy ends with some advice for the wealthy. The author reminds Timothy and his community:

We brought nothing into the world, just as we shall not be able to take anything out of it. If we have food and clothing, we shall be content with that. Those who want to be rich are falling into temptation. . . . For the love of money is the root of all evils, and some people in their desire for it have strayed from the faith and have pierced themselves with many pains. (1 Timothy 6:7–19)

After some personal advice to Timothy, the author continues:

Tell the rich in the present age not to be proud and not to rely on so uncertain a thing as wealth but rather on God, who richly provides us with all things for our enjoyment. Tell them to do good, to be rich in good works, to be generous, ready to share, thus accumulating as treasure a good foundation for the future, so as to win the life that is true life. (1 Timothy 6:17–19)

These instructions to the rich are also related to the author's concern about false teaching, for, as he says, some people, in seeking riches, have strayed from the faith. Wealth has also been associated with the women who were told to be self-controlled and silent (see 1 Timothy 2:11–12), for the previous verse instructs them not to wear signs of wealth (braided hair, gold ornaments, pearls, expensive clothes;

Catholic Wisdom

A Christmas Message

A passage from the Letter to Titus is always read at the Mass at Dawn (the second Mass) on Christmas Day. On that beautiful day we hear:

Beloved:

When the kindness and generous love
    of God our savior appeared. . . .
he saved us through the bath of rebirth
    and renewal by the holy Spirit,
whom he richly poured out on us
    through Jesus Christ our savior,
so that we might be justified by his grace
    and become heirs in hope of eternal life.
                    (Titus 3:4–7)
        (*Lectionary for Mass*, page 109)

see 2:9). It may be these wealthy women, who, having the leisure to travel from house to house, are spreading the false teachings that the author is hoping to correct. In any case, the interpretation of these passages regarding the wealthy women must certainly take into account the contexts of literary form and social setting: The author is writing a letter to a particular community and has in mind specific wealthy women who are causing trouble in the community.

Second Letter to Timothy and Letter to Titus

The Letter to Titus is thought to have been written before First and Second Timothy. Both Second Timothy and Titus deal with the same issues, but Second Timothy deals with them in more depth. Second Timothy adopts the literary device of a farewell discourse or a last will and testament. Paul is pictured at the end of his life, holding himself up as a model, warning of trouble ahead, and encouraging Timothy to be faithful to the teachings he has received. The emphasis on teaching correct doctrine pervades the letter (see 2 Timothy 1:13–14; 2:2; 4:1–2).

Titus also emphasizes the importance of teaching correct doctrine (see 2:1). In order to assure that true doctrine is taught, faithful leaders must be chosen (see 1:9). Titus also includes a household code, similar to the ones we see in Colossians and Ephesians. However, in this household code, wives and slaves are told to be obedient, but those in power, husbands and slave owners, are not given any instruction. The author appears to want to avoid persecution; he does not want the behavior of Christians to threaten the stability of Greco-Roman society. ✝

God's Word for His People

Second Timothy includes one of the most beautiful and true passages about Scripture found in the New Testament. In the context of exhorting Timothy to remain faithful to what he has learned, the author reminds him that he has known Scripture since his infancy. Scripture is capable of giving him "wisdom for salvation through faith in Christ Jesus" (2 Timothy 3:15). This passage continues: "All scripture is inspired by God and is useful for teaching, for refutation, for correction, and for training in righteousness, so that one who belongs to God may be competent, equipped for every good work" (3:16–17).

By the time Second Timothy was written, about the turn of the first century AD, what we call the Old Testament canon was, for the most part, accepted and understood to be God's Word for his people. However, the New Testament canon developed later, so these words of praise for Scripture describe the Old Testament. These words are equally true for the New Testament, and we Christians should take this advice to heart. We treasure both the Old and New Testaments because both communicate God's Revelation.

Part Review

1. What does it mean to say that the Church is one, holy, catholic, and apostolic?

2. What is the core teaching of the household code in Ephesians?

3. What teachings do Colossians and Ephesians share?

4. What does Colossians teach about the identity of Jesus Christ? In response to what problem is this being taught?

5. To what question does the author of Second Thessalonians respond?

6. Explain the images of God and Jesus that appear in Second Thessalonians in the context of apocalyptic literature.

7. Why are First and Second Timothy and Titus called pastoral letters?

8. What topics discussed in the letters reflect a time later than Paul?

9. In First Timothy, what is the author's main concern in describing early Church leadership roles?

Part 2

The Letter to the Hebrews

Although the Letter to the Hebrews ends like a letter, it does not begin like a letter. If Hebrews did begin like a letter, it would tell us either the name of the author or the person to whom authorship is attributed. As it is, we know nothing about the author other than what we can glean from the letter itself.

The author of Hebrews is thought to be a Hellenistic Jewish Christian. That means he has been influenced by the Greek culture (thereby familiar with the philosophy of his day), is extremely familiar with Jewish customs and beliefs, and has wholeheartedly embraced Christianity.

The audience to whom he is writing, the Hebrews, are Jewish Christians who have suffered persecution (see Hebrews 10:32–34), but not to the point of martyrdom (see 12:4). The author fears that some are on the verge of becoming apostates (those who once believed but have renounced faith), and they are no longer meeting together (see 10:25). Such an audience could have been in Jerusalem or Rome between AD 60 and 90.

The letter consists of reasoned arguments and exhortations, interspersed with each other. In the first article we discuss the reasoned arguments. They present Jesus in both his divine and human natures, as a high priest forever, as a perfect sacrifice, and as the mediator of a new covenant. In the second article we discuss the exhortations: The Hebrews should keep their eyes on Jesus and remain faithful in order to enter the heavenly Jerusalem.

The articles in this part address the following topics:

- Article 52: "Christ the High Priest" (page 260)
- Article 53: "Exhortations to Faithfulness" (page 263)

^{Article} 52 Christ the High Priest

The Letter to the Hebrews is difficult for most Christians to understand because we do not have sufficient acquaintance with Israelite practices. The unknown author presumes that his readers know such things as the way sacrifice was offered in the Tabernacle and the way the Day of Atonement was celebrated. He also assumes that his readers are familiar with many Old Testament passages. Based on knowledge of these things, the author, with the "reasoned arguments" mentioned in the introduction, argues by analogy that Jesus is a high priest forever in the order of Melchizedek and that Jesus is the perfect sacrifice that need never be repeated. However, before introducing these themes, the author establishes Jesus' humanity and divinity.

© Scala / Art Resource, NY

In this cross from Armenia (Karapet of Altamar, fifteenth century), Jesus is shown as the Risen High Priest, surrounded by trumpeting angels. His mother, Mary, is below the cross, with the Apostle John and even a candlebearer.

Jesus, True God and True Man

Hebrews emphasizes that Jesus is true God and true man. As the letter begins, the author refers to Jesus' preexistence and to the fact that all that has been created has been created through him: "In times past, God spoke in partial and various ways to our ancestors through the prophets; in these last days, he spoke to us through a son, whom he made heir of all things and through whom he created the universe" (Hebrews 1:1–2). This son is the "very imprint" (1:3) of God's being. After accomplishing "purification from sins / he took his seat at the right hand of the Majesty on high, / as far superior to the angels / as the name he has inherited is more excellent than theirs" (Hebrews 1:3–4).

Having affirmed Jesus' divine nature, Hebrews then goes on to affirm Jesus' human nature: "He had to become like his brothers in every way, that he might be a merciful and faithful high priest before God to expiate the sins of the people. Because he himself was tested through what he suffered, he is able to help those who are being tested" (Hebrews 2:17–18). Jesus was like his brothers; he shared in "blood and flesh" (2:14), he truly suffered, and he truly died. It is because he is both God and man that Jesus was able to be both the merciful High Priest and the perfect sacrifice who expiated the sins of the people.

A High Priest Forever

The author of Hebrews sees in the story of Melchizedek a *type* or a foreshadowing of Jesus. The Book of Genesis says only this about Melchizedek: "Melchizedek, king of Salem, brought out bread and wine, and being a priest of God Most High, he blessed Abram with these words:

> "Blessed be Abram by God Most High,
>   the creator of heaven and earth;
> And blessed be God Most High,
>   who delivered your foes into your hand."
> Then Abram gave him a tenth of everything.
>   (14:19–20)

Because Genesis says nothing about Melchizedek before or after his meeting with Abraham, the author of Hebrews says, "Without father, mother, or ancestry, without beginning of days or end of life, thus made to resemble the Son of God, he remains a priest forever" (7:3).

Catholic Wisdom

Jesus, A Priest Forever

Jesus is a priest forever, for it is he himself who offers the Eucharist: "It is Christ himself, the eternal high priest of the New Covenant, who, acting through the ministry of the priests, offers the Eucharistic sacrifice. And it is the same Christ, really present under the species of bread and wine, who is the offering of the Eucharistic sacrifice" (CCC, 1410).

The Hebrews can be confident that they have been forgiven and that they too will join Christ, a high priest forever, in that heavenly sanctuary.

The audience of the Letter to the Hebrews would have been familiar with the Levitical priesthood, for it was at the core of Jewish worship. In order to show the superiority of the priesthood of Jesus, the author of Hebrews compares the Levitical priesthood to the priesthood of Jesus.

The priests, all born in the tribe of Levi, took turns serving in the Temple, and their priesthood ended at their death. Hebrews says, "Those priests were many because they were prevented by death from remaining in office" (7:23). But Jesus, like Melchizedek, is an eternal high priest, a priest forever. His priesthood did not end at his death, because he rose from the dead and is exalted in Heaven. His priesthood is an eternal priesthood: "Therefore, he is always able to save

The New Covenant

The author of Hebrews tells us that because Jesus is High Priest forever and the perfect sacrifice, Jesus is the mediator of the New Covenant. He reminds his readers that the first covenant with Moses was ritualized with a blood ceremony. Moses took "the blood . . . and sprinkled both the book itself and all the people saying, 'This is the "blood of the covenant which God has enjoined upon you"'" (9:19–20).

Christ, unlike the Levitical high priest, did not enter the inner sanctuary of the Tabernacle to offer sacrifice; Christ entered Heaven so "that he might now appear before God on our behalf" (Hebrews 9:24). In becoming the mediator of the New Covenant, Christ fulfilled the words of Jeremiah, the prophet:

© Pascal Deloche/Godong/Corbis

> "This is the covenant I will establish with
>   them after those days," says the
>   Lord:
> "I will put my laws in their hearts,
>   and I will write them upon their
>   minds. . . .
> Their sins and their evildoing
>   I will remember no more."
>   (10:16–17)

those who approach God through him, since he lives forever to make intercession for them" (7:25).

The Perfect Sacrifice

Jesus, as the faithful high priest, offered the perfect sacrifice: himself. The sacrifices that the high priests offered in the **Holy of Holies**, the inner chamber of the Tabernacle (the inner sanctuary of the Temple, the first Tabernacle being the portable sacred tent that Moses built), needed to be repeated every year on the Day of Atonement. In describing this ritual, Hebrews says: "The high priest alone goes into the inner one [tabernacle] once a year, not without blood that he offers for himself and for the sins of the people" (9:7). In contrast to the high priest, Christ "entered once for all into the sanctuary, not with the blood of goats and calves but with his own blood, thus obtaining eternal redemption" (9:12). Jesus' sacrifice need never be repeated, "For by one offering he has made perfect forever those who are being consecrated" (10:14). ✝

Holy of Holies
The most holy place in the Tabernacle, which at one time contained the Ark of the Covenant. Only the High Priest could enter, and he only once a year.

This stained-glass art from the First Covenant Church, in Saint Paul, Minnesota, shows Christ the King. Christ is a king (note the crown) but also a shepherd, for he carries a shepherd's staff. Jesus is a compassionate king.

Article 53 Exhortations to Faithfulness

Hebrews is often described as a homily that ends like a letter. A homily brings Scripture to bear on the life of the community. Hebrews teaches that Scripture is a living Word both by example and by explicit statement. Hebrews says: "Indeed, the word of God is living and effective, sharper than any two-edged sword, penetrating even between soul and spirit, joints and marrow, and able to discern reflections and thoughts of the heart" (4:12). The author of Hebrews uses Scripture to penetrate the minds and hearts of his readers, encouraging them to persevere in faithfulness and hope until they reach the heavenly sanctuary.

© The Crosiers / Gene Plaisted, OSC

Harden Not Your Hearts

After picturing Jesus enthroned in Heaven, the author exhorts the Hebrews not to "ignore so great a salvation" (Hebrews 2:3). They have every reason to believe that what was "announced originally through the Lord," was then "confirmed . . . by those who had heard," and then confirmed again by "acts of power, and distribution of the gifts of the holy Spirit" among the community (2:3–4). How could the Hebrews ignore what they have been taught about Jesus Christ if it had been confirmed by their own experience?

The author is concerned that the Hebrews are not accepting the Good News they have received. He warns them to "take care . . . that none of you may have an evil and unfaithful heart, so as to forsake the living God. Encourage yourselves daily while it is still 'today,' so that none of you may grow hardened by the deceit of sin" (Hebrews 3:12–13). Then, quoting the Old Testament (Psalm 95:7–8) as he does frequently, he pleads: "Oh, that today you would hear his voice; / 'Harden not your hearts'" (3:8,15).

Pray It!

New Life in Christ

At the anointing after Baptism, the priest prays for the newly baptized:

> The God of power and Father of our Lord Jesus Christ
> has freed you from sin
> and brought you to new life
> through water and the Holy Spirit.
> He now anoints you with the chrism of salvation,
> so that, united with his people,
> you may remain for ever a member of Christ
> who is Priest, Prophet, and King."
> (Rite of Baptism for Children, 98)

Let this prayer remind you of your new life in Christ. If you allow them, the prayers and actions of the liturgy will bring you a deeper understanding of the work of Christ in your life, for he works in the liturgy by the power of the Holy Spirit. His Body, the Church, is herself a sacrament, or sign, through which the Holy Spirit brings us salvation. In the liturgy on earth, we participate, with the entire Church, in the heavenly liturgy.

Milk or Solid Food?

After teaching that Jesus is the faithful and compassionate High Priest, the author accuses the Hebrews of being "sluggish" in their faith: "You have become sluggish in hearing. Although you should be teachers by this time, you need to have someone teach you again the basic elements of the utterances of God. You need milk, [and] not solid food" (Hebrews 5:11–2). He then names the basic areas of teaching (the "milk") that they should now understand and build on: "repentance from dead works and faith in God, instruction about baptisms and laying on of hands, resurrection of the dead and eternal judgment" (6:1–2). However, rather than review these subjects, the author forges on toward the "solid food" of a mature Christian: "Let us leave behind the basic teaching about Christ and advance to maturity, without laying the foundation all over again" (6:1). Apparently the Hebrews have become complacent, content with what they already know, and not eager to advance in their relationship with Christ. The author of Hebrews wants to stretch them beyond the basics and help them to discover the depths of faith in Jesus, and what those depths can offer them.

Live It!

The Living Word of God for You

God speaks to us through the words of Sacred Scripture. If you read Scripture prayerfully, you will find help and guidance in a kind of dialogue between you and God. For example, in reading a familiar passage, you may suddenly be struck by a new meaning or insight that is totally relevant to your life at the moment.

One good way to grow in your understanding of what God wants to reveal to you through Scripture is to read the Word of God on a regular basis, even if for only a few minutes a day. Try it this week. Here are some passages from the Letter to the Hebrews you might read in prayer:

- Hebrews 4:14–16
- Hebrews 4:4–11
- Hebrews 10:5–7
- Hebrews 10:11–18
- Hebrews 12:1–3
- Hebrews 13:1–8
- Hebrews 13:20–21

apostate

A person who was a believer but has abandoned his or her faith.

Keep Your Eyes on Jesus

After teaching that Jesus is a priest forever, the mediator of the New Covenant, and the perfect sacrifice, the author explains why the Hebrews should have confidence, sincerity of heart, and trust:

> Since through the blood of Jesus we have confidence of entrance into the sanctuary by the new and living way he opened for us through the veil, that is, his flesh, and since we have "a great priest over the house of God," let us approach with a sincere heart and in absolute trust, with our hearts sprinkled clean from an evil conscience and our bodies washed in pure water. Let us hold unwaveringly to our confession that gives us hope, for he who made the promise is trustworthy. (Hebrews 10:19–23)

By saying that the Hebrews should have confidence of "entrance into the sanctuary," the author is saying that the Hebrews should have confidence that they will rise with Christ, that they will join him in the heavenly throne room. He encourages the Hebrews to "persevere in running the race that lies before us while keeping our eyes fixed on Jesus, the leader and perfecter of faith" (Hebrews 12:1–2).

The author once more reminds the Hebrews that Jesus reached his exalted state through suffering: "For the sake of the joy that lay before him he endured the cross, despising its shame, and has taken his seat at the right of the throne of God" (Hebrews 12:2). The Hebrews are also suffering. They should once more keep their eyes on Jesus and accept suffering as he did: "Endure your trials as 'discipline'; God treats

Catholic Wisdom

Asking Forgiveness

All sins committed after Baptism can be forgiven in the Sacrament of Penance and Reconciliation, also called the Sacrament of Conversion, Confession, or Reconciliation. The early Church Fathers called this Sacrament "the second plank [of salvation] after the shipwreck which is the loss of grace"[1] (CCC, 1446), with Baptism being the first plank. In the Sacrament of Penance and Reconciliation, the forgiveness of Christ is offered to us through the absolution of the priest (or bishop). The Church has been given this power by Christ.

you as sons. For what 'son' is there whom his father does not discipline?" (12:7).

With a final reminder to "let mutual love continue" (Hebrews 13:1), to not be carried away by false teaching, with a request for prayers, and with a traditional blessing and greeting, the author brings to an end what he calls his "message of encouragement" (13:22). ✝

You Have Come to Jesus

The author of Hebrews is exhorting people not to become **apostates**. In doing this he gives a frightening description of the fate of apostates and a beautiful description of the fate of the faithful. Hebrews says that it is "impossible in the case of those who have once been enlightened . . . and then have fallen away, to bring them to repentance again, since they are recrucifying the Son of God for themselves and holding him up to contempt" (6:4, 6). They are like ground that produces thorns and thistles and is "finally burned" (6:8).

The Hebrews who remain faithful are told that they "have approached Mount Zion and the city of the living God, the heavenly Jerusalem, and countless angels in festal gathering . . . and the spirits of the just made perfect, and Jesus, the mediator of a new covenant" (Hebrews 12:22,23–24). The Hebrews' goal should be communion with God in this heavenly city.

© Julian Kumar/Godong/Corbis

Part Review

1. How does the author of Hebrews emphasize both Jesus' divine and human natures?

2. Why is Jesus a high priest forever?

3. Why does Jesus' sacrificial offering never need to be repeated?

4. What does the author of the Hebrews mean by "milk" and "solid food"? What is he encouraging the community to do?

5. What hope does Hebrews offer to those who are faithful? What imagery is used to express this hope?

6. Name two ways that the Hebrews, by keeping their eyes on Jesus, can remain faithful.

Part 3

The Catholic Epistles

The catholic epistles include the Letter of James; the First and Second Letters of Peter; the Letter of Jude; and the First, Second, and Third Letters of John. These letters are called *catholic* because they are, for the most part, addressed to a universal audience (remember, *catholic* means "universal") rather than to a specific community.

Unlike Paul's letters, which are named after the communities that received them, the catholic epistles are named after the purported senders. In each of the letters, the author is responding to a problem or a challenge that has arisen: in James, to a misunderstanding of Paul's teaching that we are justified by faith, not works; in First Peter, to the suffering encountered by Christians in Roman society; in Second Peter, to the idea that the second coming will never happen; and, in First and Second John, to the idea that Jesus was not human. (The Third Letter of John is a request for hospitality for missionaries.) In every letter people are encouraged to live in love and fidelity to the Revelation they have received through Jesus Christ.

The articles in this part address the following topics:

54 The Letter of James

Article

The letter entitled James claims to be from "James" and to be addressed to "the twelve tribes in the dispersion" (James 1:1). This information leads to three questions: Who is James? Did James write the letter, or is it pseudonymous? Who is the audience? Remember, knowing the audience is important because being familiar with the audience and its concerns helps us to understand the meaning of the letter. This letter emphasizes how one should live as a faithful Christian, a universally appropriate theme.

Author and Audience

The James named in the letter is thought to refer to James ("the brother of the Lord") who was the head of the church in Jerusalem (see Acts of the Apostles 15:13–21). The letter reflects an established Church structure with formally appointed teachers and presbyters—roles that date to later than James's lifetime (he was martyred in the early AD 60s), so the letter is thought to be pseudonymous. In addition, the letter is written in polished Greek, and, when it quotes Scripture, it quotes the **Septuagint**, the Greek translation of the Old Testament. It is unlikely that James, of Jewish heritage and the head of the Church in Jerusalem, would have quoted the Greek Septuagint.

The "twelve tribes in the **dispersion**" might refer to any Israelites who do not live in the holy land. However, because Gentile Christians thought of themselves, along with Jewish Christians, as the New Israel, the greeting does not necessarily exclude Gentile Christians. The location of the audience is simply unknown.

Septuagint

A Greek translation of the Old Testament begun about 250 BC. The Septuagint includes the forty-six books of the Old Testament. It is often referred to by the Roman number LXX, which means seventy, in honor of the legendary seventy rabbis who translated the Hebrew text into Greek in supposedly seventy days.

Dispersion (Diaspora)

Refers to the Israelites' living outside of Palestine after the Babylonian Exile; *Diaspora* means "dispersion" or "the scattered ones."

© Alinari / Art Resource, NY

Saint James the Less, most likely not the author of the Letter of James, is pictured with the symbol of his martyrdom—a fuller's staff, used for wringing out wet clothes. A blow on the head is said to have caused his death.

The Importance of Works

The epistle attributed to James emphasizes the importance of good works. James says: "What good is it, my brothers, if someone says he has faith but does not have works? Can that faith save him? . . . So also faith of itself, if it does not have works, is dead" (2:14,17). Because we have already read Paul's insistence in Galatians and Romans that one is justified through faith, not through works prescribed by the Law, James's teaching calls for an explanation. What kind of "works" is James referring to? To answer this question, let us first review what Paul meant by "works."

In his letters, Paul is responding to the question, Must Gentiles be circumcised? His answer is no. Both Jews and Gentiles are justified by faith in Jesus Christ, not by adherence to rituals prescribed by the Law ("works"). But Paul never suggests that behavior does not matter. After all, a core message of the Gospel, reflected by Paul in his letters, is that we must love one another.

James emphasizes the same message. In fact, it is likely that James is correcting a misunderstanding of Paul's teaching. To insist that one is justified through faith, not works, is not to imply that one's actions are irrelevant. James is reminding his audience that, in addition to faith, the works of love are also necessary.

James continues to argue against a misunderstanding of Paul's teaching: "Do you want proof . . . that faith without

Live It!

Faith in Action

If you were on trial for being a Christian, would there be enough evidence to convict you? Most Christians agree that faith and works of love go hand in hand, as we learn from the Letter of James (see 2:14–17).

So what evidence of your faith shows in your works of love and compassion? After Sunday Mass, how do you share your faith, your love, and your compassion with others during the week? Look for someone who needs a friend, or for volunteer opportunities in your parish or at school. Does your daily prayer and regular confession have ripple effects in the way you treat your family and friends?

Living as a Christian—in deed and in truth, not in name only—takes effort. It means giving your time, talent, and treasure, not just on special occasions, but every day of your life.

works is useless? Was not Abraham our father justified by works when he offered his son Isaac upon the altar? You see that faith was active along with his works, and faith was completed by the works" (2:20–22). James does not disagree with Paul's point in Galatians and Romans that Abraham had faith. He simply notes that Abraham's faith was accompanied by works. So must the faith of James's audience be

The Sacrament of Anointing of the Sick

We see not only the roots of Catholic social justice teachings in James but also the roots of our Sacrament of Anointing of the Sick. James says: "Is anyone among you sick? He should summon the presbyters of the church, and they should pray over him and anoint [him] with oil in the name of the Lord, and the prayer of faith will save the sick person, and the Lord will raise him up. If he has committed any sins, he will be forgiven" (5:14–15).

In these verses James teaches that when a person is sick, he or she should call a presbyter. That person, on behalf of the Church, is to anoint and pray for the one who is sick. One effect of this action is that the person's sins will be forgiven. These elements are still present when the Church celebrates the Sacrament of Anointing of the Sick. This Sacrament has one special purpose: the bestowing of special grace on a Christian suffering from a grave illness or old age.

accompanied by works of love: "For just as a body without a spirit is dead, so also faith without works is dead" (James 2:26).

Social Justice

We can see the roots of the Church's strong social justice teachings in James. When describing faith without works, James says: "If a brother or sister has nothing to wear and has no food for the day, and one of you says to them, 'Go in peace, keep warm, and eat well,' but you do not give them the necessities of the body, what good is it?" (2:15–16). Remember, Paul also taught that a Christian cannot ignore the needs of a neighbor. To do so is to fail to recognize Christ in one's neighbor (see 1 Corinthians 11:23–33).

James then warns his readers against coveting the material things of this earth: "Do you not know that to be a lover of the world means enmity with God?" (James 4:4). He particularly warns the rich: "Behold, the wages you withheld from the workers who harvested your fields are crying aloud, and the cries of the harvesters have reached the ears of the Lord of hosts. You have lived on earth in luxury and pleasure; you have fattened your hearts for the day of slaughter" (5:4–5). Those who have "made it" in this world have a special responsibility toward those who, despite their hard work, are barely surviving.

In addition to treating others justly, James admonishes his readers to rid themselves of jealousy and selfish ambition, to refrain from judging one another, and to persevere in prayer. If James's readers draw near to God, God will draw near to them (see James 4:8). ✝

Article 55 The Letters of First and Second Peter, and Jude

Although First and Second Peter and Jude have much in common, no two are thought to have been written by the same author. In addition, all three letters are thought to be pseudonymous. Evidence within the letters dates their composition to well after the death of Peter, who was martyred around AD 64, and after the probable death of Jude, who was a relative of Jesus and James (see Mark 6:3, Matthew 13:55).

© The Crosiers / Gene Plaisted, OSC

Saint Jude, known as "the brother (cousin) of the Lord," holds an icon of Jesus. A flame (symbol of the Holy Spirit) appears above Jude's head to recall his presence with the Apostles at Pentecost, and he also holds a club.

The First Letter of Peter

The First Letter of Peter probably dates to AD 70–90. Although the letter is attributed to Peter, the author quotes the Greek Septuagint, not the Hebrew Old Testament, which is what Peter would have quoted. In addition, at the end of the letter, the author says: "The chosen one at Babylon sends you greeting" (1 Peter 5:13). It was after AD 70, after Rome had destroyed the Temple in Jerusalem, that *Babylon* was used to refer to *Rome*. *Babylon* stands for *Rome* because it was the Babylonians who previously had destroyed the Temple at the time of the Babylonian Exile (587–537 BC).

The Second Letter of Peter

The Second Letter of Peter is later than the First Letter of Peter. By the time Second Peter was written, Paul's letters had been collected and were considered Scripture (see 2 Peter 3:15–16). This alone places the letter at least as late as the end of the first century AD. In addition, the Apostles

and the first generation of Christians are referred to as
ancestors who have died (see 3:4). The letter could have been
written anywhere from 100 to 125.

The Letter of Jude

Jude too refers to the Apostles as having been in a previous
generation: "But you, beloved, remember the words spoken
beforehand by the apostles of our Lord Jesus Christ" (Jude
17). Jude also appears to have been a source for Second Peter
(see Jude 5–16, 2 Peter 2:1—3:3), meaning Jude was written
earlier than Second Peter, probably between AD 90 and 100.

Catholic Audiences

The audiences for all three letters are general, not specific.
The First Letter of Peter is addressed to "the chosen so-
journers of the dispersion" in five provinces in Asia Minor
(1 Peter 1:1). The author of Second Peter, as a literary device,
presents himself as the same person who wrote First Peter:
"This is now, beloved, the second letter I am writing to you"
(2 Peter 3:1). Each letter is thought to have been written
from Rome to primarily Gentile Christians in Asia Minor.
Jude, on the other hand, is thought to have been written
from Palestine. We know nothing about the recipients other
than that they were being exposed to false teachers.

Exhortations to Fidelity

The authors of First and Second Peter and Jude all urge their
readers to remain faithful: First Peter in the face of suffering;
Second Peter in the face of false teachers who are denying
the second coming and, therefore, judgment; and Jude in the
face of false teachings, the content of which go unnamed.

First Peter

The audience to which First Peter is addressed is obviously suffering. Their suffering is mentioned several times
throughout the letter (see 1:6–7; 3:9,16–18). The author
appears to be advising Christians to avoid further suffering
by accommodating their behavior to the norms of Roman
society: slaves are to be obedient to their masters even if the
masters are cruel; wives are to be obedient to their husbands;
everyone is to obey the king and other civil authorities.

"Be subject to every human institution for the Lord's sake, whether it be to the king as supreme or to governors as sent by him" (2:13–14). Christians are never to return evil for evil but are to join their sufferings to Christ's: "Rejoice to the extent that you share in the sufferings of Christ, so that when his glory is revealed you may also rejoice exultantly" (4:13).

Second Peter

The false teachers against whom Second Peter argues are teaching that the delayed second coming will not occur. Therefore there will be no judgment and so no reason to live the virtuous life of a Christian. The author adopts the literary device of a last will and testament. Peter is pictured near death, holding himself up as a good example, and urging his readers to remain faithful too. They are to "grow in grace and in the knowledge of our Lord and savior Jesus Christ" (2 Peter 3:18).

Jude

Jude also encourages fidelity in the face of false teachings. As part of his argument, Jude emphasizes that God has severely

God Is Patient

The Second Letter of Peter, which was the last of the New Testament books to be written, responds to questions about the second coming that have been raised by false teachers. The questions are these: Will there be a second coming, and, if so, what is causing the delay? As you know, Jesus' contemporaries expected Jesus to return on the clouds of Heaven during their lifetime.

The author of Second Peter insists that the second coming and judgment will occur: "The Lord does not delay his promise, as some regard 'delay'" (3:9). Rather, "With the Lord one day is like a thousand years and a thousand years like one day" (3:8). The second coming has not yet occurred because the Lord "is patient . . . , not wishing that any should perish but that all should come to repentance" (3:9). It is because God is loving and wants all to accept salvation that the second coming has not yet happened.

punished sinners in the past. Some of his examples are from our Old Testament, but some are from apocryphal writings: The Assumption of Moses and the Book of Enoch. The author of the Second Letter of Peter, who appropriates this section of Jude, limits his examples to canonical texts. This is evidence that Second Peter was written after the canon had begun to take shape. ✝

Article 56 The Letters of John

The community for whom the Gospel of John was written was the same community that was the source of the First, Second, and Third Letters of John. The Johannine community was originally made up of Christian Jews who lived in Palestine. However, because they insisted on the divinity of Jesus, they were expelled from the synagogue, leaving them vulnerable to persecution (see John 9:22).

The community then moved to Ephesus. It was there that most of John's Gospel was written, about AD 90. However, the community soon suffered a schism. Some members emphasized Jesus' divinity to the point of denying his humanity. This group eventually left the community. It was after this painful event that the letters of John were written, about AD 100.

Catholic Wisdom

The House of Mary in Ephesus

The Letters of John originate from the Christian community at Ephesus in modern-day Turkey. According to early tradition, Mary, the mother of Jesus, lived out her last years in that city. A small rock chapel just outside the city, consisting of a bedroom and a kitchen, has been honored as the House of the Virgin by at least three modern popes—Paul VI, Saint John Paul II, and Benedict XVI. On August 15 (the Feast of the Assumption), Catholic, Orthodox, and Muslim clerics all conduct a service at the site.

expiation
The act of atoning for sin or wrongdoing.

The Temple of Diana at Ephesus, by Ruggero Giovannini (1922–1983). In the first century AD, Ephesus was the second-largest city in the world. It declined when its harbor was slowly strangled by silt from the Cayster River.

The First Letter of John

You have undoubtedly heard of the antichrist. We first encounter the word *antichrists* in First John. In this letter the word is not used to refer to the identity of someone in contemporary society who is evil, who will be exposed, and who will precede the end-times; rather, the antichrists are the dissenters in the Johannine community who have recently left. Because First John was written in reaction to these antichrists, we can learn what they preached by reading First John's counterarguments.

The dissenters denied the humanity of Jesus Christ. For this reason, First John emphasizes Jesus' human nature. The First Letter of John states: "Every spirit that acknowledges Jesus Christ come in the flesh belongs to God, and every spirit that does not acknowledge Jesus does not belong to God" (4:2–3). That Jesus had a human nature is again emphasized later in the letter: "This is the one who came through water and blood, Jesus Christ, not by water alone, but by water and blood" (5:6). Jesus is a flesh and blood man, who is himself God.

By denying Jesus' humanity, the antichrists discounted the saving effects of Jesus' Passion and death. In response, John emphasizes that Jesus "is **expiation** for our sins, and not for our sins only but for those of the whole world" (1 John 2:2, emphasis added). This truth is repeated later in the letter: "In this is love: not that we have loved God, but that he loved us and sent his Son as expiation for our sins" (4:10).

A second ramification of denying that Jesus was truly man is undercutting the importance of Jesus as a model and teacher for how Christians should act. Jesus is our model, and we learn from him how we should live. Like the Letter of James, First John emphasizes our duty to love one another: "If anyone says, 'I love God,' but hates his brother, he is a liar; for whoever does not love a brother whom he has seen cannot love God whom he has not seen" (4:20), and, "If someone who has worldly means sees a brother in need and refuses him compassion, how can the love of God remain in him? Children, let us love not in word or speech but in deed and truth" (3:17–18).

The author of First John is so appalled that the schismatics have left the community that he accuses them of having committed a deadly sin. First, he says, "Their desertion shows that none of them was of our number" (1 John 2:19). He evidently does not want his community to reach out to the antichrists, even in prayer: "There is such a thing as deadly sin, about which I do not say that you should pray" (5:16). The author is trying to protect his community from the influence of these antichrists.

The Protective Love of Community

In First John the author insists that God is love and that God's commandment is that we must love one another: "God is love, and whoever remains in love remains in God and God in him" (4:16). At the same time, First John does not advise the community to reach out to the dissidents, or even to pray for them (see 5:16). Are these two teachings compatible with each other?

From Second and Third John, we know that the author is an elder or presbyter who has responsibility for the welfare of the community. He has seen that the community was deeply harmed by the false teachings of the dissidents. He does not want them further harmed. It is out of love for the community for which he has responsibility, and out of love for the truth, that the Elder tries to protect his community from further harm.

© Christopher Futcher / iStockphoto.com

The Second Letter of John

Many of the same themes we discussed in First John reappear in Second John. The antichrist has denied Jesus' humanity: "Many deceivers have gone out into the world, those who do not acknowledge Jesus Christ as coming in the flesh; such is the deceitful one and the antichrist" (2 John 7). As with First John, the letter urges people to remain faithful and to love one another: "Let us love one another. For this is love, that we walk according to his commandments" (2 John 5–6). The readers are warned not to welcome the dissidents into their community (see verse 11). Once again the author tries to protect the community from false teachers.

The Third Letter of John

The Third Letter of John is a very short letter of recommendation from the same author, identified in both Second and Third John as the Elder, asking Gaius to offer hospitality to Demetrius, something the leader of a nearby church, Diotrephes, has refused to do (see 3 John 9–10.) It appears that authority lines were not yet clear in the community. Rather than exert his authority over Diotrephes, the Elder (author) simply works around him by writing directly to Gaius. ☩

Pray It!

A Litany from the Letters of John

A litany is a prayer with an invocation and a response. Try praying this in a group setting.

Response: God of light, hear our prayer.
May we have fellowship with God and walk in light,
May we have fellowship with one another and walk in light,
May we know God and keep his commandments,
May we show by our love that the darkness is passing away and the true light is already shining,
May we remain in the light by loving one another.

Response: God of love, hear our prayer.
May we rejoice in knowing that we are children of God,
As God's children, may we love one another,
As Christ laid down his life for us, may we lay down our lives for our brothers and sisters,
May we love not in word or speech but in deed and truth,
May we trust in God, who is greater than our hearts, for forgiveness and peace.

Review

1. Would Paul disagree with James's statement that "faith without works is dead" (James 2:26)? Explain.

2. What Catholic social justice teachings and what teaching regarding a Sacrament appear in James?

3. What evidence within First and Second Peter and Jude argues for their pseudonymity?

4. What are the social contexts for First and Second Peter and Jude?

5. In response to these contexts, what is each author teaching?

6. What happened in the Johannine community after John's Gospel and before the Letters of John were written?

7. What did the antichrists teach? What do First and Second John teach in response to these antichrists?

Glossary

A

allegory: A literary form in which something is said to be like something else, in an attempt to communicate a hidden or symbolic meaning. *(page 78)*

Amen: A Hebrew word that expresses agreement. When used at the beginning of a teaching, as Jesus uses it, the word adds authority to what follows. *(page 106)*

analogy of faith: The coherence of individual doctrines with the whole of Revelation. In other words, as each doctrine is connected with Revelation, each doctrine is also connected with all other doctrines. *(page 36)*

apocalyptic literature: A literary form that uses highly dramatic and symbolic language to offer hope to a people in crisis. *(page 27)*

apocrypha: Writings about Jesus or the Christian message not accepted as part of the canon of Scripture. *(page 64)*

apostate: A person who was a believer but has abandoned his or her faith. *(page 267)*

B

Beatitudes: The teachings of Jesus that begin the Sermon on the Mount and that summarize the New Law of Christ. The Beatitudes describe the actions and attitudes by which one can discover genuine happiness, and they teach us the final end to which God calls us: full communion with him in the Kingdom of Heaven. *(page 104)*

Bible: The collection of Christian sacred writings, or Scriptures, accepted by the Church as inspired by God and composed of the Old and New Testaments. *(page 12)*

biblical exegesis: The critical interpretation and explanation of a biblical text. *(page 40)*

biblical inerrancy: The doctrine that the books of Scripture are free from error regarding the truth God wishes to reveal through Scripture for the sake of our salvation. *(page 11)*

biblical inspiration: The gift of the Holy Spirit, which assisted human beings to write biblical books, so they have God as their author and teach faithfully and without error the saving truth that God willed to give us. *(page 11)*

Body of Christ: A term that when capitalized designates Jesus' Body in the Eucharist, or the entire Church, which is also referred to as the Mystical Body of Christ. *(page 205)*

C

canonical: When referring to Scripture, *canonical* means included in the canon—that is, part of the collection of books the Church recognizes as the inspired Word of God. *(page 64)*

centurion: The commander of a unit of approximately one hundred Roman soldiers. *(page 84)*

Church: The term *Church* has three inseparable meanings: (1) the entire People of God throughout the world; (2) the diocese, which is also known as the local Church; (3) the assembly of believers gathered for the celebration of the liturgy, especially the Eucharist. In the Nicene Creed, the Church is recognized as One, Holy, Catholic, and Apostolic—traits that together are referred to as "marks of the Church." *(page 12)*

civil disobedience: Deliberate refusal to obey an immoral demand from civil authority or an immoral civil law. *(page 221)*

civil law: Law pertaining to the state and its citizens as distinct from the Church. *(page 221)*

codices: Book-like manuscripts that replaced scrolls. *(page 16)*

commission: To commission someone is to send him or her on mission. Jesus commissioned the Apostles to carry out his mission to the world. *(page 98)*

conscience: The "interior voice," guided by human reason and Divine Law, that leads us to understand ourselves as responsible for our actions, and prompts us to do good and avoid evil. To make good judgments, one needs to have a well-formed conscience. *(page 221)*

consecrate, Consecration: To declare or set apart as sacred or to solemnly dedicate to God's service; to make holy. At Mass the Consecration occurs during the Eucharistic Prayer when the priest recites Jesus' words of institution, changing the bread and wine into the Body and Blood of Christ. *(page 55)*

covenant: A solemn agreement between human beings or between God and a human being in which mutual commitments are made. *(page 15)*

D

Deposit of Faith: The heritage of faith contained in Sacred Scripture and Sacred Tradition. It has been passed on from the time of the Apostles. The Magisterium takes from it all that it teaches as revealed truth. *(page 12)*

didache: A Greek word meaning "teaching," referring to the preaching and instruction offered to all who have already accepted Jesus. *(page 63)*

Dispersion (Diaspora): Refers to the Israelites' living outside of Palestine after the Babylonian Exile; *Diaspora* means "dispersion" or "the scattered ones." *(page 270)*

Divine Revelation: God's self-communication through which he makes known the mystery of his divine plan. Divine Revelation is a gift accomplished by the Father, Son, and Holy Spirit through the words and deeds of salvation history. It is most fully realized in the Passion, death, Resurrection, and Ascension of Jesus Christ. *(page 11)*

E

elder: A person appointed to have authority in governing a local church. *(page 143)*

eschatological meal: The Eucharist, which anticipates the heavenly banquet that Jesus will share with the faithful when the Kingdom of God is fully realized at the end of time. The word *eschatological* derives from *eschaton*, meaning "the end of time." *(page 122)*

Eucharist, the: The celebration of the entire Mass. The term sometimes refers specifically to the consecrated bread and wine that have become the Body and Blood of Christ. *(page 52)*

eunuch: An emasculated man. Such men were excluded from the assembly of the Lord (see Deuteronomy 23:1). *(page 138)*

exegete: A biblical scholar attempting to interpret the meaning of biblical texts. *(page 40)*

expiation: The act of atoning for sin or wrongdoing. *(page 278)*

F

fiat: Latin for "let it be done," words Mary spoke to the angel at the Annunciation. *(page 115)*

firstborn: In relation to Christ, *firstborn* is a reference to Jesus' divinity. Jesus is firstborn of creation and firstborn of the dead, that is, the first to be raised from the dead. *(page 248)*

G

Gentile: A non-Jewish person. In Scripture the Gentiles were those outside the covenant, those who did not know how to fulfill God's will. Without this knowledge, they could not be in right relationship with God, and so were considered "unholy" or "unclean." In the New Testament, Saint Paul and other evangelists reached out to the Gentiles, baptizing them into the family of God. *(page 19)*

Gospels: Translated from a Greek word meaning "good news," referring to the four books attributed to Matthew, Mark, Luke, and John, the "principal source for the life and teaching of the Incarnate Word"[1] (*Catechism of the Catholic Church [CCC]*, 125), Jesus Christ. *(page 18)*

H

Hebrews: In some New Testament writings, Hebrew-speaking Jewish Christians. *(page 134)*

Hellenists: Greek-speaking Jewish Christians. *(page 134)*

Holy of Holies: The most holy place in the Tabernacle, which at one time contained the Ark of the Covenant. Only the High Priest could enter, and he only once a year. *(page 263)*

household code: Instructions as to how members of a Christian household should treat one another, similar to but improving upon pagan Greco-Roman codes of conduct for families. *(page 245)*

I

I AM: God's name as revealed to Moses at the burning bush; repeated by Jesus in John's Gospel. John uses the I AM statements to teach the divinity of Jesus. *(page 161)*

incarnate: From the Latin, meaning "to become flesh," referring to the mystery of Jesus Christ, the Divine Son of God, becoming man. In the Incarnation, Jesus Christ became truly man while remaining truly God. *(page 44)*

infancy narratives: The accounts of Jesus' birth and early life. *(page 92)*

J

Jerusalem collection: The collection for the poor in Jerusalem that Paul thought was extremely important and agreed to support. *(page 208)*

justification: God's action of bringing a sinful human being into right relationship with him. It involves removal of sin and the gift of God's sanctifying grace to renew holiness. *(page 215)*

K

kerygma: A Greek word meaning "proclamation" or "preaching," referring to the announcement of the Gospel or the Good News of divine salvation offered to all through Jesus Christ. *Kerygma* has two senses. It is both an event of proclamation and a message proclaimed. *(page 63)*

Koine Greek: The dialect of the Greek language most commonly used from around 300 BC to AD 300, and the language in which the New Testament books were originally written. *(page 124)*

L

lawless one: A symbol of evil, comparable to 666 in the Book of Revelation and to the antichrist in the First Letter of John. *(page 252)*

Lectionary: The official liturgical book containing the readings of the Mass, the Gospels, the Responsorial Psalms, and the Gospel Acclamations. *(page 46)*

libation: The pouring out of a precious liquid as an offering to the Lord. *(page 232)*

literary convention: A defining feature of a particular literary form. An example would be beginning a letter with the greeting "Dear." *(page 27)*

literary forms (genres): Different kinds of writing determined by their literary technique, content, tone, and purpose (how the author wants the reader to be affected). *(page 25)*

liturgical year: The Church's annual cycle of religious feasts and seasons that celebrate the events and mysteries of Christ's birth, life, death, Resurrection, and Ascension, and forms the context for the Church's worship. *(page 47)*

M

Magisterium: The Church's living teaching office, which consists of all bishops, in communion with the Pope. *(page 14)*

martyr: A person who suffers death because of his or her beliefs. The Church has canonized many martyrs as saints. *(page 176)*

Messiah: Hebrew word for "anointed one." The equivalent Greek term is *Christos.* Jesus is the Christ and the Messiah because he is the Anointed One. *(page 75)*

metaphor: A figure of speech in which a word or phrase that ordinarily designates one thing is used to designate another, making an implied comparison. *(page 152)*

ministry: Based on a word for "service," a way of caring for and serving others and helping the Church fulfill her mission. *Ministry* refers to the work of sanctification performed by those in Holy Orders through the preaching of God's Word and the celebration of the Sacraments. It also refers to the work of the laity in living out their baptismal call to mission through lay ministries, such as that of lector or catechist. *(page 209)*

moral truth: A truth dealing with the goodness or evil of human acts, attitudes, and values. *(page 30)*

N

New Eve: A reference to Mary, "mother of all the living," emphasizing her role in the new creation brought about by Christ. It is because Mary is the New Eve that in statues she is often portrayed standing on a snake, which represents the Devil in the Book of Genesis. *(page 158)*

New Jerusalem: In the Book of Revelation, a symbol of a renewed society in which God dwells; a symbol of the Church, the "holy city," the assembly of the People of God called together from "the ends of the earth"; also, in other settings, a symbol of Heaven. *(page 177)*

O

oral tradition: The handing on of the message of God's saving plan through words and deeds. *(page 62)*

P

parable: A story intended to call a particular audience to self-knowledge and conversion through an implicit comparison of the audience to someone or something in the story; the use of parables as invitations to choose the Kingdom of God was a central feature of Jesus' teaching ministry. *(page 77)*

Passover: The night the Lord passed over the house of the Israelites marked by the blood of the lamb, and spared the firstborn sons from death. It also is the feast that celebrates the deliverance of the Chosen People from bondage in Egypt and the Exodus from Egypt to the Promised Land. *(page 129)*

praetorium: The palace of the governor of a Roman province. *(page 233)*

presbyter: A synonym to *elder* in the Acts of the Apostles and an alternative word for *priest* today. *(page 143)*

prophet: A person God chooses to speak his message of salvation. In the Bible, primarily a communicator of a divine message of repentance to the Chosen People, not necessarily a person who predicted the future. *(page 169)*

pseudonymous: Written by one person but attributed to another as a way of honoring an esteemed predecessor. *(page 186)*

Q

Q Source: A hypothetical written collection of the teachings of Jesus shared among the early followers of Christianity surmised by Scripture scholars to be a source for both Matthew and Luke. *(page 66)*

S

salvation: From the Latin *salvare*, meaning "to save," referring to the forgiveness of sins and the restoration of friendship with God, attained for us through the Paschal Mystery—Christ's work of redemption accomplished through his Passion, death, Resurrection, and Ascension. Only at the time of judgment can a person be certain of salvation, which is a gift of God. *(page 178)*

Samaritan: An inhabitant of Samaria. The Samaritans, an interreligious and interracial people (Jewish and Assyrian), rejected the Jerusalem Temple and worshipped instead at Mount Gerizim. The hostility between Jews and Samaritans is often recounted in the New Testament. *(page 110)*

Sanhedrin: An assembly of Jewish religious leaders—chief priests, scribes, and elders—who functioned as the supreme council and tribunal during the time of Jesus. *(page 83)*

scribes: People associated with the Pharisees or Sadducees who were skilled copyists, professional letter writers, and interpreters and teachers of the Law. *(page 75)*

senses of Scripture: The senses of Scripture are the literal and spiritual senses; the spiritual senses are the allegorical, the moral, and the anagogical. *(page 37)*

Septuagint: A Greek translation of the Old Testament begun about 250 BC. The Septuagint included the forty-six books of the Old Testament. It is often referred to by the Roman number LXX, which means seventy, in honor of the legendary seventy rabbis who translated the Hebrew text into Greek in supposedly seventy days. *(page 270)*

Solomon: David's son, a king of Israel renowned for his wisdom. *(page 117)*

Son of Man: A messianic title from the Book of Daniel, used to describe a figure who receives authority over other nations from God; the only messianic title in the Gospels used by Jesus to describe himself. *(page 76)*

symbol: An object or action that points to another reality and leads us to look beyond our senses to consider a deeper mystery. *(page 164)*

synonymous parallelism: A device used in Hebrew poetry in which the same idea is expressed in two adjacent lines but in different words, thus expanding and emphasizing the idea in a balanced composition. *(page 97)*

synoptic Gospels: From the Greek for "seeing the whole together," the name given to the Gospels of Matthew, Mark, and Luke because they are similar in style and content. *(page 55)*

T

Torah: A Hebrew word meaning "law," referring to the first five books of the Old Testament. *(page 216)*

Tradition: From the Latin *tradere*, meaning "to hand on," referring to the process of passing on the Gospel message. Tradition, which began with the oral communication of the Gospel by the Apostles, was written down in Scripture, is handed down and lived out in the life of the Church, and is interpreted by the Magisterium under the guidance of the Holy Spirit. *(page 12)*

typology: The discernment of God's work in the Old Testament as a prefiguration of what he accomplished through Jesus Christ in the fullness of time. Typology illuminates the unity of God's plan in the two Testaments, but does not devalue the Old Covenant. *(page 38)*

W

Word of God: The entire deposit of truth revealed by God throughout history and transmitted through Scripture and Tradition, under the guidance of the Holy Spirit. Through all the words of Sacred Scripture, God speaks of the Word, Jesus Christ, the fullness of Revelation and the Eternal Son of God. Jesus Christ became man (the Word incarnate) for the sake of our salvation. *(page 44)*

Index

Page numbers in italics refer to illustrations.

bishops, 13, 14, 16, 36, 103, 142, 253. *see also* Apostolic Succession; Holy Orders, Sacrament of; United States Conference of Catholic Bishops

Blood, 154. *see also* Body and Blood

bodies, 201, 204–207. *see also* sexual morality

Body and Blood. *see also* Body of Christ; bread and wine; Eucharist
Corinthians and, 204
Crucifixion and, 162–163
Eucharist and, 52, 53, 54, 156
Liturgy of the Eucharist and, 55
Luke's Gospel and, 122
Paul on, 56

Body of Christ, 161, 205, 206, 248. *see also* Body and Blood

Book of Glory, 156, 160

bread and wine, 52, 55, 261. *see also* Body and Blood; Eucharist

Bread of Life, 117, 129, 161, 162

bride of the lamb, 177

brother **(meaning of term),** 187

burning bush, 161

C

canon, 12, 16, 17, 32, 64

canonization, 177

Capernaum, 74, *138*

Catechesi Tradendae **(John Paul II, Pope and Saint),** 123

Catechism of the Catholic Church, 129

catholic, 20, 242. *see also* universality

catholic letters (epistles), 19, 20, 184, 187, 269, 275. *see also specific letters*

centurion, 55, 84

Cephas. *see* Peter

Cephas (Apollos), 188, 190, 199

chastity, 201

children, 95, 202, 225

choices, 48. *see also* free will; works

chores, 160

Christ, 136. *see also* Body of Christ; Holy Trinity; Jesus Christ

Christian Initiation, Sacraments of, 156. *see also specific Sacraments*

Christian life
anagogical sense and, 38
Bible and, 50
Church and, 13
communal life and, 137
criteria for, 17

early Christians and, 49
Jesus and, 278
Matthew's Gospel and, 97, 99
Risen Christ and, 127, 155
Scripture and, 40–41
works and, 271

Christmas, 46, 47, 154, 255

Christos, 75

Church. *see also* Body of Christ; early Church; Eastern Churches; Magisterium (teaching authority); *individual officers; specific offices*
Apostles and, 243–244
apostolic, *133*
Body of Christ and, 163
holiness and, 244
Holy Spirit and, 144
Kingdom of God and, 101
leadership and, 253–254
Mary and, 157, 161
Matrimony, Sacrament of, and, 202
Matthew's Gospel and, 91
meanings of, 12
ministries and, 142
mission of, 137, *189*
New Testament and, 43–57
Paul on, 241, 242–246
Peter and, 105, 140
Revelation, Book of, and, 177
Scripture/Tradition and, 36
spiritual senses and, 38
teaching authority of, 13
unity and, 139, 205, 206, 244–246
universality and, 242–243
women and, 254

circumcision, 140, 143–144, 189, 194, 215, 219

civil laws, 218–221, 275–276

codices, 16–17

college of bishops, 103, 142

Colossae, *232,* 246

Colossians, Letter to the (Paul), 20, 186, 241, 246–249

communal worship *(liturgia),* 63

communication, 11, 12, 17, 24, 25, 41, 229. *see also* prayers

communities, 16, 137, 198–203, 279

compassion, 69, 125

Confirmation, Sacrament of, 136, 137, 156

conscience, 10, 220, 221–222, 224. *see also* morality; reason

Constitution on the Sacred Liturgy **(Vatican II),** 54

Acknowledgments

The quotations in this book labeled *Catechism of the Catholic Church, Catechism,* or *CCC* are from the English translation of the *Catechism of the Catholic Church* for use in the United States of America, second edition. Copyright © 1994 by the United States Catholic Conference, Inc.—Libreria Editrice Vaticana (LEV). English translation of the *Catechism of the Catholic Church: Modifications from the Editio Typica* copyright © 1997 by the United States Catholic Conference, Inc.—LEV.

The excerpts in this book labeled *Roman Missal* are from the English translation of *The Roman Missal,* © 1973, 2010, International Commission on English in the Liturgy Corporation (ICEL). All rights reserved. Used with permission of the ICEL.

The quotation on page 7, © 1981 ICEL, and the passage on page 255 are from *Lectionary for [Sunday] Mass for Use in the Dioceses of the United States of America,* second typical edition, by the United States Conference of Catholic Bishops (USCCB) (New Jersey: Catholic Book Publishing Company, 1998), pages 14 and 109. Copyright © 2001, 1998, 1992, 1986 Confraternity of Christian Doctrine (CCD), Washington, D.C. Used with permission of the ICEL and the CCD, Washington, D.C. All rights reserved. No part of this work may be reproduced or transmitted in any form or by any means, electronic or mechanical, including photocopying, recording, or by an information retrieval system, without permission in writing from the copyright holder.

The excerpts on pages 14, 25, 27, 36, 53–54, and 195 are from *Dogmatic Constitution on Divine Revelation* (*Dei Verbum,* 1965), numbers 10, 12, 12, 12, 21, and 12 in *Vatican Council II: Constitutions, Decrees, Declarations,* Austin Flannery, general editor (Northport, NY: Costello Publishing Company, 1996). Copyright © 1996 by Reverend Austin Flannery.

The quotations on pages 37 and 38 are from "The Interpretation of the Bible in the Church," by the Pontifical Biblical Commission, © 1993 LEV, as quoted in *The Scripture Documents: An Anthology of Official Catholic Teachings,* edited and translated by Dean P. Béchard (Collegeville, MN: Liturgical Press, 2002), pages 280 and 281–282. Copyright © 2002 by the Order of Saint Benedict, Collegeville, MN.

The quotation on page 38 and the excerpt on page 238 are from *Verbum Domini,* numbers 38 and 42, at *www.vatican.va/holy_father/benedict_xvi/ apost_exhortations/documents/hf_ben-xvi_exh_20100930_verbum-domini_ en.html.* Copyright © 2010 LEV.

The excerpt from Pope Benedict XVI on page 40 is from "General Audience," at *www.vatican.va/holy_father/benedict_xvi/audiences/2007/ documents/hf_ben-xvi_aud_20071107_en.html.* Copyright © 2007 LEV.

The second quotation on page 54 and the two quotations describing Mary on page 115 are from *Constitution on the Sacred Liturgy* (*Sacrosanctum Concilium*, 1963), numbers 7 and 103, in *Vatican Council II: The Conciliar and Post Conciliar Documents*, Austin Flannery, general editor (Collegeville, MN: Liturgical Press, 1975). Copyright © 1975 by Costello Publishing Company and Reverend Austin Flannery, OP.

The quotation on page 81 is from *God's Mercy Endures Forever: Guidelines on the Presentation of Jews and Judaism in Catholic Preaching*, number 11, by the USCCB, at *www.usccb.org/liturgy/godsmercy.shtml*. Copyright © USCCB. All rights reserved.

The prayer on page 83 is adapted from *The Catholic Youth Bible*®, third edition (Winona, MN: Saint Mary's Press, 2010), near Mark, chapter 15. Copyright © 2010 by Saint Mary's Press. All rights reserved.

The paragraph describing Matthew's Gospel on page 98 is based on *An Introduction to the New Testament*, by Raymond E. Brown (New York: Doubleday, 1997), page 171. Copyright © 1997 by the Associated Sulpicians of the United States.

The quotation on page 103 is from *Dogmatic Constitution on the Church* (*Lumen Gentium*, 1964), number 23, in *Vatican Council II: The Conciliar and Post Conciliar Documents*, Austin Flannery, general editor (Collegeville, MN: Liturgical Press, 1975). Copyright © 1975 by Costello Publishing Company and Reverend Austin Flannery, OP.

The excerpts on pages 110 and 264 from the English translation of *Rite of Baptism for Children* © 1969 ICEL, numbers 97 and 98; and the excerpts on pages 136 and 137 from the English translation of *Rite of Confirmation (Second Edition)* © 1975, ICEL, numbers 25, 22, and 27, respectively, are found in *The Rites of the Catholic Church*, volume one, prepared by the ICEL, a Joint Commission of Catholic Bishops' Conferences (Collegeville, MN: Liturgical Press, 1990]. Copyright © 1990 by the Order of St. Benedict, Collegeville, MN. Used with permission of the ICEL.

The prayer on page 145 is from "Translation of the Pentecost Sequence," by Sr. Irene Nowell, at *www.mountosb.org/music/sequence.html*. Used with permission of the author.

The words on the doomsday prophet's sign described on page 167 appeared in a cartoon by Mick Stevens in *The New Yorker*, October 9, 1995.

The excerpt on page 191 is from "Paul and the Cross," by Donald Senior, at *www.osv.com/tabid/7636/itemid/1436/Paul-and-the-Cross.aspx*. Copyright © 2010 Our Sunday Visitor, Inc.

The quotation on page 201 is from "Paul's Second Letter to the Corinthians," by Jerome Murphy-O'Connor, in *Update Your Faith*, December 2004, at *www.americancatholic.org/Newsletters/SFS/an1204.asp*.

sible for any changes that may have occurred since our verification. If you find an error in, or have a question or concern about, any of the information or sources listed within, please contact Saint Mary's Press.

Endnotes Cited in Quotations from the *Catechism of the Catholic Church,* Second Edition

Section 1
1. *Dei Verbum* 18.
2. Cf. *Dei Verbum* 12 § 1.

Section 2
1. Tertullian, *De orat.* 1: J. P. Migne, ed. Patrologia Latina (Paris: 1841–1855) 1, 1251–1255.
2. *Lumen Gentium* 5.
3. *Gaudium et Spes* 22 § 5; *cf. Lumen Gentium* 16; *Ad Gentes* 7.
4. Tertullian, *Apol.* 50, 13: J. P. Migne, ed. Patrologia Latina (Paris: 1841–1855) 1, 603.

Section 3
1. Council of Nicaea II: Denzinger-Schönmetzer, *Enchiridion Symbolorum, definitionum et declarationum de rebus fidei et morum* (1965) 601.
2. St. John of the Cross, *Dichos* 64.

Section 5
1. Tertullian, *De Pænit.* 4, 2: J. P. Migne, ed. Patrologia Latina (Paris: 1841–1855) 1, 1343; cf. Council of Trent (1547): Denzinger-Schönmetzer, *Enchiridion Symbolorum, definitionum et declarationum de rebus fidei et morum* (1965) 1542.

Glossary
1. *Dei Verbum* 18.